The EVERYTHING®
Speaking Mandarin Chinese Book

Dear Reader,

At some point in their lives most young people begin to contemplate who they are and what they believe. As a young person, I became particularly fascinated by China and its culture, especially Taoism. I found a lot of inspiration in the Taoist texts and the beautiful and mysterious language in which it was originally written. In addition to learning to understand the language, I also find new insights and discern new truths every time I reread it.

I originally went to China to find out why she speaks to me. As with my experience reading the Tao, I found myself with more questions than answers. But I've come to understand that life isn't about finding answers; it's about finding more questions—more ways to encourage growth and contribute to the betterment of our new emerging global society.

Writing this book has been a life-shaping experience for me. Delving more deeply into the mechanics of Chinese culture helped make me more aware of how unique and special my own culture is. Being Italian-American and Latino made me quite unique in mostly homogeneous China. I often found myself explaining to Chinese people that what makes the United States so unique is that all the world's cultures have a place in our national mosaic. The beauty of the U.S. lies in its amalgam of world cultures. We take the best aspects of each and become stronger. Through this writing experience, I've learned many lessons and grown stronger. It is my sincere hope that this body of knowledge may add to your experiences and lessons, and that you, too, may grow as a person.

J. F. Grasso

The EVERYTHING® Series

Editorial

Publisher	Gary M. Krebs
Director of Product Development	Paula Munier
Associate Managing Editor	Laura M. Daly
Associate Copy Chief	Brett Palana-Shanahan
Acquisitions Editor	Lisa Laing
Development Editor	Katie McDonough
Associate Production Editor	Casey Ebert

Production

Director of Manufacturing	Susan Beale
Associate Director of Production	Michelle Roy Kelly
Prepress	Erick DaCosta Matt LeBlanc
Design and Layout	Heather Barrett Brewster Brownville Colleen Cunningham Jennifer Oliveira
Series Cover Artist	Barry Littmann

Visit the entire Everything® Series at *www.everything.com*

THE

EVERYTHING®

SPEAKING
MANDARIN CHINESE
BOOK

Simple techniques to improve your
speaking and writing skills

J.F. Grasso

Adams Media
Avon, Massachusetts

In loving memory of Anthony Scott Mondella, a brother and a best
friend. "To you, my best friend, no good-byes, only 再见 zàijiàn."

Copyright ©2007, F+W Publications, Inc. All rights reserved.
This book, or parts thereof, may not be reproduced
in any form without permission from the publisher; exceptions
are made for brief excerpts used in published reviews.

An Everything® Series Book.
Everything® and everything.com® are registered trademarks of F+W Publications, Inc.

Published by Adams Media, an F+W Publications Company
57 Littlefield Street, Avon, MA 02322 U.S.A.
www.adamsmedia.com

ISBN 10: 1-59337-723-1
ISBN 13: 978-1-59337-723-6

Printed in the United States of America.

J   I   H   G   F   E   D   C   B   A

Library of Congress Cataloging-in-Publication Data
available from publisher

This publication is designed to provide accurate and authoritative information with regard
to the subject matter covered. It is sold with the understanding that the publisher is not
engaged in rendering legal, accounting, or other professional advice. If legal advice or
other expert assistance is required, the services of a competent professional person should
be sought.
—From a *Declaration of Principles* jointly adopted by a Committee of the
American Bar Association and a Committee of Publishers and Associations

Many of the designations used by manufacturers and sellers to distinguish their products
are claimed as trademarks. Where those designations appear in this book and Adams
Media was aware of a trademark claim, the designations have been printed with initial
capital letters.

This book is available at quantity discounts for bulk purchases.
For information, please call 1-800-289-0963.

Contents

Acknowledgments

I'd like to extend my heartfelt thanks to my editors, Lisa Laing and Katie McDonough, for their patience and encouragement. Further thanks and support go to Drs. A. Bodomo and S. Matthews at the Linguistics Department at the University of Hong Kong for their flexibility and support. My heartfelt gratitude goes to all those who aided me in translation and anecdote writing and particular cultural questions. Thank you to Chad Doering and Chen Tong. My special thanks go to Gu Kaikai Rick for being available for my questions at all hours of the day. More special thanks go to Samantha So, whose daily support and insight helped me beyond words. I can't go without extending my solemn thanks and admiration to Molly Hakes, author of *The Everything® Conversational Japanese Book*, whose inspiration gave me a great deal of direction. Finally, none of this would have been possible without the unswerving support of my beloved friends and family, in particular my mother, Andrea Grasso, and grandmother, Mary Grasso, who wished they could have done so much more from so far away.

Top Ten Reasons to Learn Chinese

1. With 1.3 billion Chinese speakers in the world, you'll have lots of people to talk to!

2. Knowledge of Chinese can help you in learning other languages as well, including Japanese, Korean, and Vietnamese.

3. Knowing how to ask for directions when in China will ensure that your taxi driver doesn't get lost.

4. You will be elevated to near celebrity status when native Chinese speakers hear you using their language.

5. You'll make your mom gush with pride as you order food in Chinese, or carry on conversations with your Chinese-speaking neighbors.

6. You'll know what people's tattoos really mean.

7. You'll be light years ahead of your competition in the job market.

8. You'll be able to buy twice as many Chinese souvenirs because you can bargain like a pro!

9. Who couldn't benefit from a deeper understanding of one of the world's oldest and most fascinating cultures?

10. Learning Chinese will give you a better command of English, as you understand how one language differs from the other.

Introduction

▶ CHINA IS AN ancient land—one that seems almost unfathomable to many citizens of the New World. Its people, language, culture, and philosophy have influenced many of its neighbors throughout the ages. Much of East Asia today is referred to as the Chinese Cultural Sphere of Influence. China's culture has been as profound an influence in Asia as Egypt, Greece, and Rome have been in the West.

Learning to understand another culture and another language is a gift you give to yourself. Learning about other cultures, including all their marvelous whos and whys gives us insight into our own culture. Learning another language gives us a unique perspective on the world around us—and even the world that lies within us. The Taoists view life as cyclical, eternal, and constantly renewing. The idea that what goes around comes around is a focal belief in Buddhism. In English we say, "you reap what you sow."

At one time, in the distant past, the Chinese language represented all aspects of culture in East Asia. Chinese was a language of commerce, communication, and expression. But time passed and things changed, and the Chinese language became less widely spoken. Today, however, it seems it's China's time to rise again. The nation has a booming economy and one of the biggest consumer markets in the world; it's clear that now is a good time to know Chinese.

Chinese is quickly becoming the second most demanded second language in the world, and knowledge of Chinese will become nearly indispensable for business professionals in the next twenty years. After nearly three decades of global isolation the Chinese are not meeting the challenge and opportunity imparted by globalization with timidity and reservation. On the contrary, they are eager to reach out and become contributing members of the global community. To that end, the demand for learning English in a proud but pragmatic China is incredible. English is still the international language of commerce; but before long, we may just see Chinese catch up. By learning Chinese, a Westerner is exposed to dimensions of Chinese culture a non-speaker misses out on. Speaking Chinese in China opens countless doors you may not have ever realized are there. You win an immense amount of respect and admiration from the Chinese when you use their language. Whether you're bargaining, congratulating someone, or apologizing for something by using some of the more formal phrases and expressions, you evoke a certain sense of nostalgia from the Chinese for the classical culture, much of which was suppressed by the Communist Revolution.

Chinese is an extremely colorful and expressive language. Speaking it can seem almost as much an art as it is ability. Likewise, the Chinese language sometimes may seem impossible to learn. The tonal aspect as well as the daunting writing system can seem insurmountable. But have faith and don't be shy about making mistakes. After all, as the Chinese say: "One doesn't catch a tiger cub without venturing into the tiger's den."

Chapter 1

An Overview of China

History plays a huge role in the cultural and individual identity of the Chinese people. In every culture, it's helpful to know where you came from in order to know where you're going. Having even a rudimentary understanding of China's history, historical icons, and belief systems may grant you greater understanding of the people. What's more, it will certainly make an excellent impression on those with whom you interact while in China.

The Chinese Creation Myth

There are many variations of the Chinese creation myth, which is a legend that was passed down orally for about 1,000 years before it was ever recorded. Here's how the most popular versions go: The great Chaos bore an egg of cosmic forces. The being Pangu emerged from the egg after ages of growing within it. The lighter masculine Yang components of the egg floated upward and become the heavens, while the heavier feminine Yin components floated downward and become the earth. In an effort to keep the sky from falling down upon the earth, Pangu stood between them and forced them apart. He stood there for 18,000 years to be sure and then died, his remains becoming the nature of all things.

The first gods were the SānHuáng or the Three August Ones: the god Fuxi and the goddess Nuwa of whom all humanity were born, and the god Shennong, the cultivator. From among the progeny of the Three August Ones came the Wǔdì, or the Five Emperors, who are associated with the five directions according to the Song of Chu. Among The Five Emperors is the Yellow Emperor or Huángdì. The Yellow Emperor is considered to be the father of the Han Nationality of China, and he's associated with several inventions of Chinese culture, including the compass, the guqin, and traditional Chinese medicine. Furthermore, legend has it that when Huángdì died, the gods immortalized him as a dragon, which was his personal symbol. Being that Huángdì is regarded as the ancestor of the Han Chinese, the Chinese often refer to themselves as "the descendants of the dragon."

Scholars believe that Huángdì's original emblem may have been a snake, and that as he slew his foes he incorporated their emblems into his own. This would explain why the Chinese dragon is often portrayed with the body of a snake and the features of other animals, such as the tail of a fish, deer antlers, and demon eyes.

Important Figures in Chinese Culture

While figures featured in the Chinese creation myth are still discussed to this day, it is generally acknowledged that their stories are just legends. The Chinese do revere Huángdì as one of the Five Emperors, but it is understood that he is simply a myth. Just as these myths are part of Chinese history, several real figures have also left their marks. You've likely at least heard of the people covered in the following sections.

Qín Shǐ Huáng

One of the most revered figures of Chinese history is Emperor Qin, or Qín Shǐ Huáng. It was the close of the Warring States period circa 221 B.C.E. when the King of the State of Qin dealt his final blow and reigned victorious over his rivaling neighbors. Emperor Qin proclaimed himself Shǐ Huángdì, or "First Emperor," of the territory that came to constitute China as a unified nation for the first time in history. The title that he assumed—Huángdì—was a fusion of the words *huáng*, meaning "august one," and *dì* meaning "sage-king."

Though a tyrant in most respects, Qín Shǐ Huáng is credited with enacting widespread reforms across China and fostering a sense of unity across the territory. Among his most notable political reforms was the abolition of the Zhou dynasty's regional feudal systems and the installation of a Qin-modeled centralized non-nepotistic bureaucratic system. His centralized bureaucracy was fueled by doctrines of Legalism (*Fǎjiā*), which perpetuated a system of "rule by law" so complex, stringent, and repercussive that subjects were terrorized into order and lawfulness. Centralization and standardization of bureaucratic procedure, laws, monetary issuance, writing, and measurements, as well as schools of thought, were achieved by the most ruthless of methods. Several actions were also taken to quell disapproval of Qin methodologies and discourage popular uprisings. Weapons were confiscated, men aged seventeen to sixty were conscripted to serve in the army for one year, and even Confucian scholars were banished or executed—their books were confiscated and burned.

The fortifications dividing the six former independent states were dismantled and reconnected to form a wall. This wall was the foundation of the Great Wall of China. Qín Shǐ Huáng ordered a great number of other public works as well, including the Grand Canal, smaller canals and bridges, and a fantastic tomb including an army of terracotta soldiers to be built near Xianyang in the area of modern day Xi'an.

Confucius

Known in China as Kǒngfūzǐ, or simply Kǒngzǐ, Confucius is reported to have lived during the Spring and Autumn Period toward the end of Zhou dynasty in the sixth and fifth century B.C.E. He was a Chinese thinker and philosopher, whose teachings on social ideology and other topics have deeply influenced not only life in China, but life throughout East Asia. His teachings embraced morality in personal and governmental life. They outlined propriety in social relationships, and advocated justice and honesty. Kǒngzǐ's school of thought overshadowed all other ideologies during the Han dynasty and from thenceforward helped to form an imperial canon. His philosophical system became known simply as Rújiāsīxiǎng or "Confucianism."

FACT

It was the Jesuit priest Matteo Ricci who first Latinized Kǒngzǐ's name as "Confucius." One of his most famous writings is The Analects, a collection of gospel-like discussions with his disciples.

Confucianism is often mistakenly thought of as a religion. In fact, it bears little reference to theological matters like gods, creation, or the afterlife. Instead, it focuses on ideas of social morality and propriety, such as loyalty and duty to one's nation and family. Ideas of benevolence and righteousness were exercised by putting the needs of others before one's own and working to accomplish long-term beneficial goals rather than immediately satisfying goals. Another Confucian notion was filial piety, a doctrine of respect of the elderly and figures of authority, veneration of ancestors, and support and service to one's family. Confucian concepts of morality pervade Asian culture to this very day.

Mao Zedong

"If there were no Mao, there would be no China." These words still linger on the tongues of mainland Chinese today. Few world leaders have ever been so venerated in their nations as Chairman Mao. He was the chairman of the Central Committee of the Communist Party of China from 1945 until his death in 1976. Under his leadership, the Chinese Communist Party (CCP) successfully defeated the Chinese Nationalist Kuomintang during the Chinese civil war. On October 1, 1949, Mao declared the formation of the People's Republic of China at Tiananmen Square. From that point until his death, Mao instituted a wide variety of economic and political campaigns to advance the people of the PRC.

Chairman Mao's ideas have greatly impacted the Chinese people and, in turn, others in the world as well. His supporters in China credit his policies with having raised literacy, extended life expectancies, and furthered the cause of women's rights more than ever before 1949, not to mention reclaiming China for Chinese after suffering the "Century of Humiliation" attributed to Qing rule, and the carving up of China by Western powers.

But Mao's policies have fallen under sharp criticism as well. Movements such as the Great Leap Forward and the Cultural Revolution have been hailed as political disasters both in China and abroad. Mao endeavored to reshape traditional Marxist ideology such that it could be implemented in China's predominantly agrarian economy. He believed that communism could only succeed in China pending vast, all-encompassing socio-economic changes in the rural areas. In the twenty-first century, China and her people are hardly the same nation and people they were when they toppled the Qing dynasty, or even when the People's Republic was founded. Regardless of how he is estimated, Mao's influence on China is undeniable.

The Dynastic Cycle

Historical events and time periods in China that predate the PRC and the Republic era are referenced in terms of the Chinese dynastic timeline. The dynastic timeline spans some 4,000 or so years. Different traditions cite different dates as the beginning of the first dynasty, but archaeological evidence places the beginning of the first dynasty, the Xia dynasty, at around 2200 B.C.E.

Refer to the following table for a breakdown of the dynastic timeline. Follow along with the CD for practice in pronouncing the names of each dynasty.

TRACK 1

The Chinese Dynastic Timeline

Dynasty	Time Period
Xià	2205–1765 B.C.E.
Shāng	1766–1066 B.C.E.
Zhōu	1066–256 B.C.E.
Qín	221–207 B.C.E.
Hàn	206 BCE–220 C.E.
Sān Guó	220–280 C.E.
Jìn	265–420 C.E.
Liù Cháo	420–589 C.E.
Suí	581–618 C.E.
Táng	618–907 C.E.
Wǔ Dài Shí Guó	907–960 C.E.
Sòng	960–1279 C.E.
Yuán	1271–1368 C.E.
Míng	1368–1644 C.E.
Qīng	1644–1911 C.E.

Chinese Belief Systems

Religion was frowned upon in the early days of the People's Republic, as leaders of the time regarded organized religion as feudalistic and representative of foreign colonialism. Nowadays, however, a wide variety of religions are practiced in China including Islam, Christianity, and, to a lesser extent, Judaism. But Chinese culture has been greatly influenced by three religions above all others. You will read about these in the following sections.

Chinese Folk Religion

Chinese folk religion was intermixed liberally with Chinese mythology and the gods and goddesses of folklore. Practices included ancestor worship, astrology, the worship of animal totems, and the erection of shrines. Alongside these traditional beliefs was the veneration of Heaven. Heaven was a conceptual deity that took on the role of the primary divinity during Imperial reign. The practices are centered on the worship of Heaven, with Heaven representing an omnipotent force of nature.

Heaven played a pivotal role in society during Imperial reign. The governmental dimension in which an emperor's right to rule was in validation was when considering the Mandate of Heaven. If a ruler was overthrown it was understood that he had lost the Mandate of Heaven. The greatest existing shrine to Heaven is the Altar of Heaven, or Tiāntán, in Beijing. Though the Altar of Heaven is often considered a Taoist temple, the worship of Heaven predates it.

Taoism

According to tradition and the records of the great historian Sima Qian, around the sixth century B.C.E. there lived a man named Li Er. Li Er was supposedly an archivist in the Zhou Imperial Library and a man of unfathomable wisdom who shared his teachings in discussions with contemporaries. One of his contemporaries was said to be Confucius, who claimed to have learned more from Li Er than from the library itself.

Possibly anticipating the approaching end of Zhou supremacy Li Er resigned his post and ventured westward. Finally, he reached the westernmost guard tower before entering the Western Desert wastes, which is probably modern day Xinjiang Province. It is there that one of the Great Wall guards convinced Li Er to record his wisdom for all posterity to enjoy. Since that time Li Er has been more popularly known as Laozi, or Lao Tzu, the father of Taoism and his Tao Te Ching (Dào Dé Jīng) the central text of the philosophy.

Religious Taoism and Buddhism have become very intertwined. It's not at all unusual for people who consider themselves Buddhists to pray or make offerings at Taoist temples and vice versa. In fact, so many Taoist figures have been incorporated into Buddhism that it's difficult to discern who came from where.

Taoism exists in two major forms in China today. The first is as a religious system composed of mysteries, rituals, and cosmology. In this fashion it is more akin to Chinese folk religion than to its second form, that being a school of philosophy. Taoism as a philosophy is far more familiar to Westerners than religious Taoism. Taoist philosophy embraces concepts such as non-action, emptiness, balance, flexibility, and receptiveness. After Laozi, several Taoist scholars arose and contributed greatly to the development of the philosophy. Zhuangzi and Liezi both contributed Taoist tomes, which are regarded often as constituting portions of the foundation of Taoism.

Buddhism

Buddhism, having originated in India with the teachings of the Buddha Siddhartha Gautama in the fifth century B.C.E., made its way to China as did many other facets of trade and exchange, along the Silk Road. Buddhism is perhaps the most widely practiced religion today not only in China, but throughout Asia. But the relationship between China and Buddhism was not always an amorous one. The idea of a faith system that advocated self-cultivation and enlightenment did not correlate well with Confucian ideologies advocating duty and service to society and emperor. Buddhism had to be modified in order to conform to already established Confucian values. Ancestor worship was incorporated into Buddhist practices and more obscure sutras regarding filial piety were raised to great significance. Commentaries were written treating the benefits that individual salvation and monasticism have on greater society. Thus, monks would be doing service to their society. The main focus of Chinese Buddhism, or Mahayana Buddhism, as it is practiced today promotes the notions of universalism, enlightenment, and compassion.

Why Come to the PRC?

There are myriad reasons to visit the Middle Kingdom. China offers diversions to charm and enchant everyone. Whether it's sumptuous cuisine, tropical beaches, breathtaking mountain views, or ancient history, you'll find it all in China. One could easily spend half a lifetime in China and not see everything it has to offer. So, if you're only going to be there for a short time, there are some things that should not be missed.

Beijing

Besides the fact that Beijing is the capital of the PRC, it is also arguably the historic center of China featuring some of China's most prized historic treasures and cultural sites. The Forbidden City was the Imperial palace of the Ming and Qing Dynasties; a vast maze of picturesque courtyards, ceremonial gates, great gathering halls, and pristine gardens. It is now a museum that is open to the public.

FACT

Beijing is a terminus for most airlines, so it's quite easy to begin your tour of China there. Be sure to pack warmly if you travel during winter, as it gets quite cold and you may occasionally have to disembark your plane outside of the gate.

The southern gate of the city is called Tiānānmén, or "Gate of Heavenly Peace." This is where Chairman Mao proclaimed the founding of the People's Republic in 1949. Tiananmen Square, said to be able to accommodate 500,000 people, is the site of the 1989 massacre of student protesters peacefully demonstrating to urge democratic reform. The Great Hall of the People, which is the seat of the National People's Congress, borders Tiananmen Square to the west. To the southeast of the square is The Altar of Heaven. The pièce de résistance of the region, of course, is Badaling, lying forty miles north of Beijing. It is a favorite site for beholding the awe-inspiring Chángchéng, or Great Wall.

Shanghai

As China's most populous city and one of the most cosmopolitan cities in all of Asia, the city of Shanghai bears a character and presence that has influenced all the communities around it. Shanghai was a foreign enclave and a treaty port in the nineteenth century; this is clearly observed from its architecture, which is a blend of east and west. A stroll along the Bund will clearly demonstrate this. An evening cruise on the Huangpu river will be memorable indeed. The Shanghai Museum, a world class facility, should not be missed. Yuyuan Gardens, belonging to the Yu Family and featuring the famous Zigzag Bridge, is adjacent to Chenghuang Miao, a Taoist temple dedicated to the local gods.

Within three hours of Shanghai, the beautiful cities of Hangzhou and Suzhou should not be missed. There's an old saying in Chinese: *Shàng yǒu tiāntáng, xià yǒu sūháng*. It means "Above there is paradise, and below there is Suzhou and Hangzhou." Suzhou, a UNESCO world heritage site, often regarded as the Venice of Asia, is a canal-filled city with countless stone bridges and classical gardens. Its sheer aesthetic beauty is definitely something to see. The city of Hangzhou has served as a capital of China and is home to the fabled "West Lake" of Chinese romantic literary fame. The silvery mists rolling down off the mountains and across the lake have been inspiration for Chinese romantics for centuries.

Xian

Known as Xianyang to the Qin rulers, and later called Changan during the Tang dynasty, the city of Xian is a cultural heart of ancient Chinese culture. Located in the center of China, its center is still surrounded by the ancient city walls. Xian is most notably known for featuring the Mausoleum of Qin Shihuang, who commissioned the construction of an army of over 8,000 terracotta soldiers. Called Bīngmǎyǒng in Chinese, these figures were to represent Emperor Qin's army in the afterlife. But the history doesn't end there. Xian was the Chinese launch point for the great journeys that took place along the Silk Road for over a thousand years. Travelers still retrace this route today to explore and discover the wonders and mysteries of the ancient path that linked Eurasia's greatest empires of antiquity.

Major Chinese Festivals

Though a modest and somewhat conservative people, the Chinese will find just about any reason to get together and celebrate. Almost every single month of the year includes at least one holiday or festival celebrating something. So no matter what time of year you go, you could very likely be there during a festival. Festival rituals and activities vary widely depending on the particular holiday, although there do exist some consistencies. For example, festivals often include dancing, drumming, the burning of incense, and, of course, eating. Chūnjié, or Spring Festival, is what the Chinese call their New Year. It is the most important festival of the year and falls on the second new moon after the Winter Solstice. Celebrations can last for up to fifteen days and involve spring cleaning, visiting the relatives, and giving small red envelopes with money called *hóngbāo* to children. At the end of the fifteen days of Spring Festival, the celebration winds down with the Lantern Festival, yet another celebration.

Chapter 2

4,702 Years of Chinese

Language is a fascinating human invention that we have fashioned to serve so many different purposes. Though communication is basically an exchange of information, it manifests itself in various ways. In China the Chinese language served as a way to preserve cultural continuity throughout its long and occasionally tumultuous history, as well as a medium for the spread of their culture throughout the East Asia region. Today, the Chinese language continues to influence Asia and the world.

The Chinese-Speaking World

Chinese is the most widely spoken language on Earth. This is primarily because China is the world's most populous nation. But that fact skirts the reality that Modern Standard Chinese is spoken in a number of countries and territories worldwide, and is becoming more widely spoken everyday. As China's socio-economic policies evolve to create a more open market, the opportunities for interpersonal exchanges also grow. China is thought by most in the business world to be the "Dragon of the twenty-first century." As a result, the demand for Chinese speakers grows congruently. You may ask, "Where is Chinese spoken throughout the world?" The next sections will provide a brief overview.

The People's Republic of China—Zhōnghuá rénmín gònghéguó

Located in the easternmost portion of Asia, China is the world's fourth largest nation with a total area of 9,596,960 sqare kilometers. It is home to one of the world's longest enduring civilizations with a history stretching back nearly 5,000 years. Imperial China was one of the most advanced cultures of antiquity, and its culture has had longstanding influence on its neighboring nations. China's writing system has been continuously employed longer than all others, and was employed at one time or another as the writing system of Japan, Korea, and Vietnam. As you read in Chapter 1, China exists today as the People's Republic of China, or PRC. Founded in 1949, it has a controlled free-market economy within a socialist superstructure and is led by the Chinese Communist Party.

FACT

China considers itself a multiethnic country of fifty-six recognized ethnicities, including the Zhuang, Manchu, Hui, Tibetans, Mongols, Cho Sen (Koreans), Uyghur, and Russians. The Han ethnicity constitutes approximately 92 percent of the population and is generally the majority in most areas of the central and eastern coastal regions of the country.

The Republic of China, Taiwan—Taíwăn, Zhōnghuá Mínguó

Imperial Chinese records indicate that Han Chinese had settled the Pescadores islands as early as the 1100s. However, migration to Taiwan island by the Han is traditionally claimed to have peaked by the Ming dynasty. Taiwan's history is one of invasion and occupation, beginning as early as the 1600s with the Dutch who were usurped by the Ming Navy. After the Ming dynasty fell, the Ming naval leader Lord Cheng established a Ming loyalist kingdom there, which was defeated by Qing forces toward the end of the seventeenth century. The Japanese occupied Taiwan during the Second World War. Then in 1949, after their defeat at the hands of Communist Party forces, the Nationalist army forces of the Kuomintang retreated to the island to establish a government in exile.

The state that presently administers the island groups of Taiwan, the Pescadores, Matsu, and Kinmen calls itself the Republic of China, though it is often simply referred to as Taiwan. Founded in 1912, it replaced the Qing dynasty and ended 2,000 years of dynastic rule in China. Taiwan is a multiparty democratic state with a thriving free-market economy.

Taiwan's political status is a highly controversial subject on both sides of the Straits of Taiwan. As a visitor, it's best to avoid discussing the subject at all, much less taking a staunch position in favor of either side. The PRC does not acknowledge the legitimacy of the government of the Republic of China and considers the island of Taiwan and its territories a rogue province of the greater PRC. The government of Taiwan (the Republic of China) maintains that it is a sovereign state in principle, though it no longer lays claim to the territory of mainland China. The two governments maintain an uneasy peace and relations based on a principle of political ambiguity.

The Hong Kong Special Administrative Region of the PRC—Xiānggăng

A former British colony, Hong Kong was returned to Chinese sovereignty on June 30, 1997, and now exists as a Special Administrative Region (SAR) of the greater PRC under China's "one country-two systems" policy. As an SAR, Hong Kong enjoys a great deal of relative autonomy. The territory of Hong Kong occupies a peninsula and cluster of islands on the southern coast of China's Guangdong Province. Hong Kong has one of the most liberal economies in the world, being almost entirely duty-free. Hong Kong is a huge presence in international trade and banking and, as a result, is home to an extensive expatriate community. It is an exciting and fascinating place, and by far one of the most cosmopolitan cities in Asia. It has a unique fusion of old and new, as well as east and west.

FACT

Though Modern Standard Chinese has taken on a more prominent status in Hong Kong, it still stands second to the Cantonese dialect of the Guangdong province as the lingua franca of the region. The Cantonese dialect is as different from Chinese as French is from Italian. University-level education in Hong Kong is largely English Language Medium. As a result, a great many Hong Kong natives speak English quite well.

The Macau Special Administrative Region of the PRC—Aòmén

The Portuguese first arrived in Macau toward the end of the sixteenth century, and it was proclaimed a colony of the Portuguese Crown in 1862. Macau enjoyed relative prosperity for much of its history until the British established Hong Kong and larger ships attracted to Victoria Harbor's very deep waters docked there. Macau was returned to Chinese sovereignty on December 20, 1999 and, like Hong Kong, it enjoys a great deal of autonomy as an SAR under the "one country-two systems" policy.

Macau's economy is predominately tourist-based, though clothing and textiles have gained ground among their primary exports. Macau is famous throughout the region for its unique culture and cuisine. Macanese food is a fusion of Chinese and Portuguese cuisines; it is definitely something visitors to the region should try. Macau's other claim to fame is its casinos. Macau is a very popular weekend get-away destination for both Hong Kong residents and mainland Chinese in Zhuhai and Shenzhen.

Though Modern Standard Chinese has assumed greater importance in Macau, it is still spoken less widely than Cantonese. English and, to a lesser extent, Portuguese, are also spoken there.

Singapore—Xīnjiāpō

Singapore may be the smallest nation in Asia but it has one of the most prosperous economies. Singapore became independent from the UK in 1963 and then from Malaysia in 1965. The island nation is a more a city-state than an actual country; it is only 692.7 sqare kilometers in size. But its shores bear a rich and diverse multiethnic culture in progress.

Singapore's national language is Malay, but English, Tamil, and Modern Standard Chinese are also its official languages. Chinese is spoken as readily as English. Be forewarned, though: The Singaporeans have their own brand of English that is liberally laced with Chinese language aspects. This veritable creole English is affectionately referred to as "Singlish."

Singaporeans come from all walks of life, and their ancestors come from the far corners of the globe. There are Singaporeans of Chinese, Indian, Malay, European, and Middle Eastern descent, to name but a few. Singapore's gross domestic product (GDP) is one of the highest per-capita in the world. They have fairly low domestic demand and export substantially in electronics and other manufactured goods. A trip to Singapore is an adventure in eating, as you will find tastes, smells, and textures representative of the varied cultural backgrounds of her people. Singapore is an international hub of travel and a popular tourist destination in and of itself. No trip to Asia should exclude a stop here.

Thailand, Malaysia, Indonesia, and Elsewhere

There are Chinese communities all throughout the Asia Pacific region, including the nations mentioned in the previous section and Japan, Korea, the Philippines, Vietnam, Cambodia, and Burma. Chinese is quickly becoming a language of commerce and cultural exchange, even among non-Chinese. Each year China's universities accept more and more students from abroad eager to learn the Chinese language and study Chinese culture. Students from South Korea, Japan, the United States, and the European Union are taking seats in Chinese classrooms. Chinese approaches English as the most commonly learned second language in South Korea.

Different Names for the Language

There's only one name for the English language—English. As you travel around the Chinese-speaking world, though, you will undoubtedly find that the same does not hold true for the national language of China. As with most languages spoken in diverse regions, you will certainly come across regionalisms and other small dialectical variations. One of the most curious of these variations is the name of the Chinese language itself. You may refer to Modern Standard Chinese, or Mandarin, as it is often called in the West, with six different expressions: Zhōngwén, Zhōngguóhuà, Pǔtōnghuà, Hànyǔ, Huáyǔ, and Guóyǔ. Some of these six are more common in some regions than others, and they all have slightly different meanings.

Name Variations

Zhōngwén, Zhōngguóhuà, Pǔtōnghuà, and Hànyǔ are all readily used on the mainland but in some slightly different contexts.

Zhōngguóhuà literally means "the language of China": *Zhōngguó* means "China" and *huà* means "language." *Zhōngwén* carries a very similar meaning, as *zhōng* is an abbreviated term for *Zhōngguó* or "China," and the word *wén* is a multilayered word that carries the meaning of culture and literature, implying language in the "letters" connotation. They're used interchangeably and impart a sense of Chinese national identity.

The word *Hànyǔ* includes the word *Hàn*, which is the name of the largest Chinese ethnic group. The Han are the people we traditionally think of as "Chinese." The word *yǔ* is another word for "language." This term leaves one thinking of the Chinese language in the context of it being the language of the Han ethnic group.

The word *Pŭtōnghuà* is used on the mainland, as well as in Hong Kong and Macau. *Pŭtōnghuà* breaks down into *pŭtōng*, meaning "common," and *huà*, meaning "language." The common language is a name assigned by Chinese linguists, and it brings to mind the notion of the language being a unifying feature of the nation. In fact, Modern Standard Chinese, also referred to as Mandarin, is actually an amalgam of all the northern dialects.

The term *Huáyŭ* is composed of the word *Huá*, which is a poetic reference for China that also means magnificence, and *yŭ*, which, again, means language. You'll generally only hear the term *Huáyŭ* in Singapore and Malaysia.

Lastly, there's the word *Guóyŭ*. *Guóyŭ* contains the words *Guó*, meaning "nation," and *yŭ*, again, as mentioned previously. The meaning is obvious—national language—and you'll hear this term used mostly in Taiwan.

Classical and Literary Chinese

Students of Chinese often mistakenly refer to these two styles of Chinese writing by the same term: Wényánwén. But in fact, Wényánwén refers solely to literary Chinese. Literary Chinese represented the written form of Chinese after the Han dynasty and endured until the beginning of the twentieth century. Though it was largely based on classical Chinese, it was indeed different. Classical Chinese is called Gŭwén, and it is the language and writing style of pre-Han China. It is represented by such great works as the Tao Te Ching, the Confucian Analects, and the 300 Great Tang Poems and was employed as the writing form for virtually all forms of correspondence in China, Japan, Korea, and Vietnam. The early writing forms are quite different from the modern vernacular and can constitute a different language.

Modern Standard Chinese

The language spoken on the streets of China today is referred to in terms of style as *Báihuà*, meaning "plain language." This is the style of writing employed in China since the beginning of the twentieth century. Báihuà is based on the modern vernacular and reflects spoken Chinese. It first gained popularity with the onset of the May 4th Movement of 1919, which was an antiwarlord and imperialist cultural movement spawned in response to China's pale political stance in the presence of foreign influences on her soil. Champions of the May 4th Movement were critical of traditional Chinese culture and longed for cultural reforms in all aspects of Chinese culture, even its language and writing.

FACT

Hanyu Pinyin is not in widespread use in Taiwan, Hong Kong, and Macau, where local romanizations are favored. Hong Kong and Macau's system of romanization are based on Cantonese and not on Modern Standard Chinese. Taiwan recently began employing a locally cultivated variation of Hanyu Pinyin, which they call Tongyong Pinyin, but its use in Taiwan is still not universally accepted.

Hanyu Pinyin translates roughly to "joined sounds," and it was adopted in 1979 as the official system of romanization of the Modern Standard Chinese language in the PRC. Henceforth, it was also adopted by the government of Singapore and became the preferred system of transcription of Chinese by many international institutions including the International Organization for Standardization. It is for this reason that Americans ceased referring to the capital of China as Peking, which is based on the Cantonese pronunciation, and began to refer to it as Beijing, as Beijing natives would. Similarly, provinces such as Canton, Fukien, and Szechuan became Guangdong, Fujian, and Sichuan.

Local Languages

When we refer to the Chinese language we refer to the language commonly known in English as Mandarin, or Mandarin Chinese. In the broadest sense of the word, Mandarin refers to a variety of northern Chinese local languages that all very closely resemble each other. The desire for further unification and standardization across many facets of Chinese society was motivation for the standardization of language. Standard Mandarin can be thought of as a quasi-engineered language in that it is based on the several northern

Chinese Mandarin dialects. Where there are substantial lexical and syntactic disparities, the Beijing dialectic is chosen as the official form. It is this Standard Mandarin that is Putonghua, or Chinese. Mandarin is spoken as a native language by more than 800 million Chinese people. Not all Chinese local languages, however, are Mandarin dialects. In fact, China is home to a wide variety of "Chinese languages." In English, we commonly refer to the various regional Chinese languages as "dialects of Chinese;" but that classification is quite contentious, as the differences between the various regional Han languages are quite vast and are often mutually unintelligible. The truth is the Chinese regional languages, though related, are distinct from each other in the same way the Romance languages are. In the following sections, you'll learn about some of the majorly spoken Chinese regional languages.

Wu

The most notable member of the Wu dialect family is Shanghainese. The Wu dialects are spoken throughout the Shanghai, Jiangsu, and Zhejiang provinces, as well as small regions of the Anhui and Jiangxi provinces. The Wu dialects are spoken by some 90 million Chinese and are often thought to be very soft and light. Many in this region consider the dialect of Suzhou to be the fairest. Shanghainese is one of the two most commonly studied Chinese regional dialects. This is due, of course, to Shanghai's position of prominence in modern China as a center of culture and commerce. Though almost all Shanghainese can speak Mandarin, they are still fiercely proud of their language and speak it readily on streets and in homes.

Yue

The Yue dialects are the languages spoken primarily in the Guangdong province, as well as parts of the Guangxi and Fujian provinces. The most notable Yue dialect is that of Guangzhou, the capital city of the Guangdong province, and is known generally in English as Cantonese. Cantonese is also notable for being the primary variant of Chinese spoken in Hong Kong and Macau. Because of this, Cantonese has achieved a position of prestige and notoriety in China. In Hong Kong, music, news, and television are broadcast in Cantonese, and even some literature is expressed in a written form of

Cantonese. Including Hong Kong and Macau, Cantonese is spoken by some 80 million Chinese. Cantonese is also widely spoken by Chinese communities abroad.

Min

The Min dialects are spoken throughout the Fujian province and are divided into two main variants based on degree of mutual intelligibility. The Minbei, or northern Min, are also occasionally referred to as the Mindong, or eastern Min dialects, and are spoken throughout Fuzhou, the capital of the Fujian province, and its outlying counties. Approximately 50 million Chinese speak Minnan, or southern Min, throughout the southern Fujian province, and it is also spoken widely throughout Taiwan, where it is called Taiwanese. The term Taiwanese can be a bit ambiguous, however, as Taiwan is home to an indigenous non-Han culture whose native Austronesian language is also referred to as "Taiwanese."

Other Regional Languages

Xiang is spoken by more than 35 million people in and around the Hunan province and the Sichuan province. Xiang can be generally understood by both speakers of Mandarin and Shanghainese, but it is still quite distinct. Gan dialect is spoken in much of the northern portion of the Jiangxi Province, as well as in remote regions of the Anhui, Hubei, Fujian, and Hunan provinces. Nanchangese is thought of as the official form of Gan dialect.

Chapter 3

The Sounds of Chinese

Language teachers often point out that learning another language begs us to learn another way of thinking. The biggest challenge to the English speaker in learning Chinese is how to handle the tonal aspects of the language. The idea of tonality will require the English speaker to pay closer attention when listening to others speak, but acquiring Chinese is not as daunting a task as some Westerners believe. In fact, Chinese possesses a smaller repertoire of sounds than English.

Chinese Phonetics

Modern Standard Chinese is a monosyllabic language containing over 400 basic syllables composed of either one or two basic phonetic components. These two components are the initial and the final. The initials are always consonants, while the finals may be vowels or vowel-consonant compounds. A Chinese syllable may consist of an initial plus a final, or simply a lone final. All together, Chinese has twenty-one initials and thirty-eight finals. If you have any experience speaking or studying French, you'll find the vowels of Chinese to be quite similar, and uttering them will be fairly easy.

Hanyu Pinyin is expressed as it sounds. So, learning how to read it is as simple as sounding out a word. Sound the word out slowly and you'll have the exact pronunciation including the tone.

Modern Standard Chinese employs a logographic writing system that is composed of thousands of characters endowed with both meaning and sound. Each character represents a word or morpheme. This system is quite unlike English's alphabetic writing system, which came about thanks to some 400 years of Roman occupation of Britain. English employs a twenty-six-letter variation of the Roman alphabet, yet in some ways English is similar to Chinese. Achieving literacy in English is a far greater challenge than in other European languages, as English orthography is quite irregular due to profound pronunciation changes over time, the abundant loan words from other languages, and partial attempts to normalize orthography. Just take a look at some of the different ways you pronounce "ough" in English: enough, though, through, cough. Achieving literacy in Chinese is also a big challenge. It is for this reason that we will be sticking to Hanyu Pinyin, as opposed to Chinese characters, in this book. Hanyu Pinyin is easier for English speakers to relate to, and it also better facilitates an understanding of Chinese phonetics and phonology.

Initials and Finals

The word "initial" is synonymous with the idea of "beginning." On that note, we'll start our exploration with Chinese consonant letters, or initial letters, expressed in Hanyu Pinyin as the letters B, P, M, F, D, T, N, L, J, G, K, H, Y, W, and S. The good news is all of these sounds in Chinese are virtually identical to their English letter counterparts. The only exception lies with the letters D and T. English tends to pronounce these two letters using the blade or tip of the tongue and pressing it against the roof of the mouth just behind the teeth. You'll get a more Chinese sounding D and T by using slightly more of the front of your tongue and pressing it against the roof of your mouth behind the teeth but also touching the back of your teeth a little bit more. This Chinese D and T will sound more familiar to students and speakers of Spanish and Italian. Listen to the track on the accompanying CD and follow along repeating the pronunciation you hear.

Initials D and T Examples

TRACK 2

Chinese	English
dà	big
děng	to wait
dì	earth
dòu	bean
dù	stomach
tā	he, she, it
tè	particular
tǐ	body
tóu	head
tǔ	ground

While the idea of the initial implies beginnings to us, the final similarly brings to mind the notion of endings. As we've learned so far, a Chinese final may consist of a single vowel, a combination of vowels, or a combination of vowels and consonants. There are thirty-eight finals in Chinese, and some of them are quite different from English sounds. We'll go over the regular finals in the list below. Follow along with the CD and repeat the sounds as you go.

Chinese Regular Finals

TRACK 3

Simple Finals

Final	English Approximation
a	as in "far"
o	as in "song"
r	pronounced as English "r"

TRACK 4

Compound Finals

Final	English Approximation
ai	"ie" as in "tie"
ei	"ay" as in "bay"
ao	"ow" as in "cow"
ou	"ow" as in "snow"
ia	"ya" as in "yacht"
ie	""ye" as in "yell"
iao	y + "ow" as in "cow" (yow)
iu	"yo" as in "yodel"
ua	"wa" as in "wander"
uo	"wo" as in "worn"
uai	pronounced like "why"
ui	prounced like "way"
üe	"y" as in "yes," "oo" as in "woo," and "e" as in "wet"

TRACK 5

Nasal Finals	
Final	English Approximation
an	pronounced like "an" as in "panda"
ian	pronounced like "yen"
in	"een" in "green"
uan	"wan" as in "wander"
un	"une" as in "june"
ang	"ong" as in "ping pong"
ong	"ong" as in "song"
iang	y + "ang" (yang)
iong	y + "ong" (yong)
uang	w + "ang" (wang)
ueng	w + "eng" (weng)

You should review the pronunciation tracks a few times, paying close attention to those sounds unique to Chinese. As you can see from this list there are simply no equivalent English words for some of the sounds produced in Chinese. It's important to remember, however, that this does not mean you cannot reproduce them yourself with time and practice. Modern Standard Chinese is not an Indo-European language like French or Spanish, so it will not just roll off the tongue. Don't be discouraged or intimidated by how different it sounds. You'll master it with practice.

The Special Cases

As you've seen so far, the sounds of the Chinese language as represented in Hanyu Pinyin are quite similar to English. But as with all things, there are exceptions and irregularities. Now that you've become familiar with the initials and finals that resemble English sounds, it's time to take a look at these exceptions. Follow along with the CD and repeat the sounds as you go.

TRACK 6

Chinese Irregular Initials

Consonant	Chinese Example	English Approximation
z	zài	"ds" in "woods"
c	cài	"ts" in "its"
zh	zhù	"dg" in "judge"
q	qù	"ch" in "cheese"
ch	chù	"ch" in "chum"
x	xù	"sh" in "sheep"
sh	shù	"sh" in "shun"

The *q* and *ch* sounds, as well as the *x* and *sh* sounds, are quite similar; the difference is in the vowels they precede. As such, you'll see that *q* always precedes *i*, and when it precedes *u*, it is pronounced more like a *ü*. *Ch* may precede *a*, *o*, and *u*, but when *ch* precedes *u*, it is pronounced like a straight *u*. Similarly, you'll see that *x* always precedes *i*, and when it precedes *u*, it is pronounced more like a *ü*. While *sh* is followed by *a*, *o*, and *u*, and when *sh* precedes *u*, it is pronounced like a straight *u*.

FACT

English speakers are especially apt at pronouncing the Chinese *r*; few languages other than Chinese and English possess this phoneme. Modern Standard Chinese pronunciation, including the liberal use of the r sound in finals, is based on the Northern Mandarin standard accent, which was heavily influenced by Manchu pronunciation of the Chinese language.

Follow along with the CD and repeat the sounds as you go.

TRACK 7

Chinese Irregular Finals

Final	Chinese Example	English Approximation
e	chē	"ir" in "bird" but shorter
en	wén	"urn" in "turn"
eng	děng	e + ng
i after z	zǐ	"i" in "sing" but shorter
i after c	cì	"i" in "sing" but shorter
i after s	sì	"i" in "sing" but shorter
i after r	rì	"i" in "sing" but shorter
i after zh	zhǐ	"ur" in "fur"
i after ch	chī	"ur" in "fur"
i after sh	shí	"ur" in "fur"
ü only follows n	nǔ	similar to the German "ü" and French "eu"
ü only follows l	lǚ	similar to the German "ü" and French "eu"

The Four Tones

Knowing how to sing or play an instrument, or any familiarity with the basic features of music may be a huge help to you in learning to speak Chinese. The reason for this is that Chinese is a tonal language. What this means is that variations in the tone and pitch of a given word may actually change its meaning. English also employs a system of tones that impart meaning. A declarative sentence and an interrogative sentence sound quite different, and we use punctuation to illustrate that difference in writing. For example, an exclamation point demonstrates excitement, while a question mark obviously shows that the speaker is asking a question. In Chinese, however, the word ba when said in any one of the four tones may mean "eight," "to pull out," "target," or "dad."

The four tones may be represented in Hanyu Pinyin with four accent marks. First tone is represented by a macron (ˉ); second tone is represented by an acute accent (´); third tone is represented with a caron (ˇ); and finally, the fourth tone is represented by a grave accent (`). The tone diacritics are placed over the main vowel in vocal diphthongs.

"The four tones" are traditionally represented by a tone chart illustrating the pitch movements of each tone.

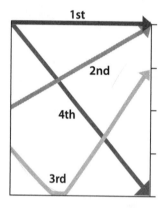

First tone is a flat high-pitched constant tone. It begins at the same high pitch and remains constant and flat from its beginning to its end. It is at a high range in the speaker's voice. Follow along with the CD and repeat the sounds as you go.

TRACK 8

First Tone Phonemes

bā

pā

mā

fā

Second tone most closely resembles the rising in pitch that we hear at the end of a question or interrogative statement in English. It begins at the bottom of the midpoint of the speaker's range of sound. You should say a word in the second tone as if you were asking a question, much the same way we say "huh?" in English. Follow along with the CD and repeat the sounds as you go.

Second Tone Phonemes

TRACK 9

bá

pá

má

fá

Third tone is the most unique and troublesome of all the tones. It is a two-dimensional sound pattern that begins at the mid-low-level point of the speaker's range of sound. Then, it dips down a bit to the bottom of the speaker's range and then sharply ascends to the mid-high-pitch level. It is the only tone that changes direction in its dynamic. Follow along with the CD and repeat the sounds as you go.

Third Tone Phonemes

TRACK 10

bǎ

pǎ

mǎ

fǎ

Fourth tone is a steady, descending tone that most closely resembles the falling pitch that usually comes at the end of a declarative sentence or an exclamation. It begins at the top of the speaker's range of sound and then falls to the bottom of range. Fourth tone and second tone are the easiest for English speakers to manage naturally. Follow along with the CD and repeat the sounds as you go.

TRACK 11

Fourth Tone Phonemes

bà

pà

mà

fà

All together now! Let's listen to the various morphemes rendered in the four tones so you may contrast them and begin to differentiate them. Speaking Chinese requires more than just training your tongue; it requires training your ears, too. Follow along with the CD and repeat the sounds as you go.

TRACK 12

The Four Tones

First Tone	Second Tone	Third Tone	Fourth Tone
bā	*bá*	*bǎ*	*bà*
pā	*pá*	*pǎ*	*pà*
mā	*má*	*mǎ*	*mà*
fā	*fá*	*fǎ*	*fà*
dā	*dá*	*dǎ*	*dà*
tā	*tá*	*tǎ*	*tà*
nā	*ná*	*nǎ*	*nà*
lā	*lá*	*lǎ*	*là*

ALERT!

There is actually a fifth tone in Modern Standard Chinese called the neutral tone. It is regarded as an unofficial tone, as it is not very distinct or profound. You will come across a handful of Chinese syllables that are neutral tone, and this tone is represented in Hanyu Pinyin by a lack of any diacritic mark.

Tonal Nuances and Mistakes

To most Westerners, the idea of tonality is a relatively new and unfamiliar concept in learning a language. As you familiarize yourself with the tones and practice expressing them, however, you will very likely find yourself overenunciating them. In the beginning this is fine and completely to be expected. The student who is new to tonal languages will need to experiment with producing the sounds, and pay close attention in listening to them. As you progress and listen to people speaking Chinese, the better you'll be able to discern how to pronounce words in the correct tones in a more natural sounding way. Remember that the tone chart and tone diacritics are simply guides to follow. They are, at best, rough approximations for a very human thing—language.

Saying a first-tone word followed by a first-, second-, or fourth-tone word will not be much of a challenge for you to say naturally. However, two consecutive second-tone syllables and two fourth-tone syllables will require a bit of practice if you're to sound more natural. Saying two third-tone words is an issue all unto itself. The fact of the matter is that when you say two second-tone and fourth-tone syllables together they don't actually sound like the same two tones. In other words, they do not sound like two distinct ascending or descending utterances of the same notes. In fact, the first syllable sounds as if it starts at a higher note than the second syllable. They simply move in the same direction pitch-wise. Follow along with the CD and repeat the sounds as you go.

Double Second and Fourth Tone Words

TRACK 13

Chinese	English
chángchéng	The Great Wall
móxíng	model
wénxúe	literature
xúexí	study
qíngjíe	plot
shìchǎng	market

Chinese	English
chúfáng	kitchen
húangyóu	butter
píngcháng	normal
yínháng	bank
shùzì	numeral
rìlì	calendar
hùobì	currency
zhuàngtài	condition
hànzì	Chinese character
jiànmiàn	to meet
baòqiàn	sorry
cuòwù	mistake
diànshì	television
jièshaò	to introduce

The matter of the third tone is something all together different. Third tone is distinct from the other three tones in that it contains a change in pitch during the production of the sound. Since it starts in the mid- to low-pitch and descends to the bottom of range and then up again, it would be awkward producing two third-tone words in succession. As a result, when two third-tone words occur one after the other in a complex word, the first third-tone morpheme of the word changes into a second-tone word.

Chapter 4

Upon Arrival

Marco Polo arrived at the court of Kublai Khan in Beijing in 1271. Journeys from Europe to China at that time took several months. Fortunately, a direct flight to China should only take twelve to seventeen hours depending on where you're coming from in North America. It's a marked improvement, but still an arduous journey and a drastic change in time, even by twenty-first century standards. On the day of your flight, eat lightly and avoid carbohydrates. Try to accustom your body to the time you're traveling to a few days before your flight. Stay away from alcohol but drink lots of fluids on the plane. Your adventure is soon to begin!

Visas and Immigration

Zhōngguó huānyíng nǐ! Welcome to China! Customs will be your first destination upon arrival in the Middle Kingdom. Passing through customs need not be an arduous experience. Follow the signs in Chinese and English to the baggage claim area and immigration. You'll have to fill out a yellow Entry Card for Foreign Travelers and a health and quarantine form. Often these forms will be available on your flight prior to landing. Flight crew will usually pass them out upon take off and again on landing. You should fill out these forms in pen and keep them ready and together with your passport to expedite disembarkation.

ALERT!

If you are at all under the weather it might be wise to postpone traveling to China until you're feeling a bit better. This is of particular importance if you're running a temperature of any sort. There are bio temperature sensors in the immigration offices, and if your temp is abnormal you might be quarantined pending a physical.

Initial Questions

All travelers to the PRC require a visa. The most common are the "L" tourist visa, the "F" business visa, and the "Z" employment visa. Though the type of visa you are entering on will give the immigration officer an idea as to your purpose in China, they will still likely ask you what you plan on doing while in China and how long you plan on staying. Here are a couple of sample questions in Chinese and English:

Nǐ zài zhōngguó dǎsuàn zuò shénme shì?

What do you plan on doing in China?

Nǐ zài zhōngguó dāi duōjiǔ?

How long will you be staying in China?

Your responses to the questions, of course, depend entirely on you. Visitors come to China for many reasons. The following are some examples of a few of the main reasons people visit China.

Wǒ lái zuò shēngyì.	**I'm here on business.**
Wǒ lái cānjiā huìyì.	**I'm here to attend a conference.**
Wǒ lái lǚxíng.	**I'm here to travel.**
Wǒ lái dùjià.	**I'm here on vacation.**
Wǒ lái tànqīn.	**I'm here to visit a relative.**

More Questions

The immigration officer will also be able to gauge how long you'll be in China by your visa. Tourists may remain on an L visa for thirty days. Of course, the length of your stay in China may also vary. The following are some examples of how you may indicate the length of your stay.

Wǒ yào zhù …	**I'll be staying…**
Jǐ tiān.	**A few days.**
Jǐge xīng qī.	**A few weeks.**
Yíge yuè.	**A month.**

Let's Talk Luggage

Here's an all-too-common scenario: You get off the plane and unsuspectingly walk down to baggage claim. You watch the conveyor belt move past you over and over again with no sign of your suitcase. Finally, when all the other passengers have retrieved their luggage, you realize what has happened: Your luggage has been lost! If you're an avid traveler, chances are this has happened to you at least once. It's an unfortunate situation, but the problem can be quickly minimized by asking for help. Go right up to the baggage assistant and say:

Láojià, wǒde xínglǐ bú jiàn le.
Excuse me, my luggage is lost.

Finding Lost Luggage

If your baggage is truly lost, the airline staff will do their best to help you locate it and forward it to your hotel. However, it's always helpful to have some pertinent vocabulary on hand. The following are some terms you might need when discussing lost luggage.

Lost Luggage Talk

TRACK 14

Chinese	English
xíngli	luggage
jiàn	to see
qǐng	please
xìng	surname
guì	expensive
míngzi	name
shì	to be; is; are; yes
zuò	to sit
jǐ	which
hào	number
fēijī	airplane
cóng	from
duì	correct, yes
yǒu	to have, exist, there is/are, yes
dēngjī kǎ	boarding pass
fāpiào	receipt
děng	to wait
kuài	fast
chákàn	to look into

Now we'll take a look at a sample dialogue you may use. Repeat the following sentences after the reader as you listen to the CD.

TRACK 15

Visitor:	*Wǒde xínglǐ bújiàn le.* I can't find my luggage.
Baggage Attendant:	*Qǐng wèn, nǐ guì xìng?* May I have your last name?
Visitor:	*Wǒ xìng Smith.* My last name is Smith.
Baggage Attendant:	*Nǐde míngzi shì Mary ma?* Your first name is Mary?
Visitor:	*Shìde.* Yes.
Baggage Attendant:	*Nǐ zuò jǐ hào fēijī?* What flight were you on?
Visitor:	*185 (yī bā wǔ) hào fēijī.* Flight 185.
Baggage Attendant	*Cóng Niǔyuēlaíde ma?* The flight from New York?
Visitor:	*Duì.* Yes.
Baggage Attendant:	*Nǐ yǒu méiyǒu dēngjī kǎ hé xínglǐ fāpiào?* Do you have your boarding pass and luggage receipt?
Visitor:	*Yǒu.* Yes.
Baggage Attendant:	*Hǎo. Qǐng děng yī děng, wǒ hěn kuài chákàn zhè jiàn shì.* Fine. If you'll just wait a moment, I'll look into this matter.

Yes, No, Maybe

Based on the previous conversation exercise you're probably wondering how it can be that there is more than one way to say yes in Chinese. The answer is simple. It's because there is no one Chinese expression for the word "yes" or for the word "no." In Chinese, one properly responds to a question positively by repeating the interrogative verb in the question, much the way we may answer questions in English by saying "it is," "it does," "I am," or "I do." Similarly, to negate a question simply say *bù* followed by the interrogative verb. Often you may be able to skirt the yes-and-no quandary with the catchall words *duì* and *búduì* meaning "correct" or "right" and "incorrect" or "wrong." You must be mindful of context, though. If it is not a yes-or-no question, you should use the verb forms.

Customs

At one time passing through immigration and customs in the PRC was a drawn out and stringent process. Standing in line for over an hour was not at all unusual, and most visitors' baggage was subject to inspection. Nowadays, getting through immigration in mainland China is a relatively (and thankfully) uneventful routine. You'll be able to bring most items into China duty free, though large electronic items like personal computers and televisions are subject to duty. Actually, according to the letter of the law, even your smaller personal effects and items such as watches, cameras, and MP3 players technically should be declared on the customs form upon arrival. If you're found to still have them upon exiting the country, no tax is applied. But according to the spirit of the law, this is rarely done.

To facilitate entry you should have readied any documents you are required to provide. Your travel agent or tour group should be able to take care of that for you. The following list includes the most common forms of documentation. Listen to the track on the CD to hear how each word is pronounced, and then practice saying each word aloud.

TRACK 16

Customs Forms

Chinese	English
rùjìng	to enter a country
chūjìng	to exit a country
dēngjì	to register
kǎ	card
rùjìng dēngjì kǎ	arrival card
chūjìng dēngjì kǎ	departure card
jiànkāng	health
shēnmíng	declaration
jiàn kāng zhèngmíng kǎ	health certification
hǎiguān	customs
shēnbào	declaration
dān	list
hǎiguān shēnbào dān	customs declaration form
hùzhào	passport
jūliú	residence
jiàn or wén jiàn	documentation
zhèng	pass
jūliúzhèng	residence permit
qiānzhèng	visa

Being and Having

The Chinese verb *shì* not only means "to be," "is," and "are," but it can sometimes also be used the way we use the word "yes." *Shì* is what is called an equative verb, meaning that the subject that precedes equals the predicate or object that follows it. You can often think of it as an equal sign whose negator is *bú*. It's a dynamic verb and is used quite often. The verb *yǒu* is also a remarkable bit of language. This little word is burdened with the gargantuan responsibility of communicating various notions of existence. It can mean "to have," "to exist," "there is," "there are," "there was," "there were," "there will be." *Yǒu* is such a special word that it even has its own personal negator: *méi*. We don't say "*búyǒu*"; we say "*méiyǒu*." Note the following examples.

Zhè shì wǒde bàozhǐ.	**This is my newspaper.**
Wǒ búshì yīngguórén.	**I am not British.**
Nǎr yǒu xínglǐ chē?	**Where is there a baggage cart?**
Wǒ méiyǒu rùjìng dēngjì kǎ.	**I don't have an arrival card.**

Word Order

Unlike many of the European languages, English included, Chinese possesses no inflectional endings. These inflections are the elements of speech that communicate such notions as number, state of being, tense, gender, or person. For example, in English, we know that one should say "I want" not "I wants." The reason is that "wants" represents the third person in the singular aspect (he, she, and it). Verb conjugation in the European languages (and most others) is an expression of the various inflectional endings. The "-s" at the end of "wants" serves as an inflectional ending. Similarly, "-ed" and "-ing" are two of many more inflectional endings in English; "-ed" communicates the past tense or past particle in verbs, and "-ing" communicates the gerund, or the notion of the verb in action. In Chinese, however, whether it is *wǒ*, *nǐ*, or *tā*, we still simply say *yào* to mean "want," "wants," "wanted," "wanting," etc. As a result, word order in Chinese is of supreme importance in expressing grammatical relationships between the elements of a sentence.

The big debate among linguists is whether Chinese is a subject-object-verb language (SOV) or a subject-verb-object language (SVO) language. English is generally accepted as being SVO. The reality is that Chinese is a mixture of both. Most simple sentences are SVO, but SOV is used widely in more complex language. As a general rule for simple sentences, you may put the subject first and the predicate second. Take the following three sentences, for example:

Tā lèi le.	**He is tired.**
Wó hěn lèi.	**I am very tired.**
Wǒmén yě hěn lèi.	**We are also tired.**

The subjects of these three sentences are *tā*, *wǒ*, and *wǒmén*, while the focal element of the predicate is the word *lèi*, and is followed by the change implying modal particle *le*. In the first sentence, *lèi* is a stative verb. In the second and third sentences, *lèi* follows *hěn* and *yě*, which are both adverbial modifiers. In Chinese, modifiers such as adverbs always follow the subject, so we can infer that *lèi* in this position is an adjective. Chinese does not have auxiliary words like "to," or verbal inflectional endings like "-s," "-ed," or "-en" to communicate to the speaker that the word is indeed a verb. Nor does it possess adjectival inflectional endings such as "-y," or "-ive," or "-ous" to communicate to the speaker that the word is absolutely an adjective. It is this versatility among Chinese words that make word order so integral.

Coming and Going

Recent years have seen China's airports grow into some of the most impressive facilities in the world. Among them, Hong Kong International Airport, known locally as Chek Lap Kok Airport, and Shanghai's Pudong International Airport have been constructed within the last ten to fifteen years. Beijing Capital International Airport was first opened in 1958 but has undergone extensive renovations, with both terminals only becoming fully operational again in the last five years. These facilities boast excellent services for moving travelers about.

Transport Options

Most cities in China have excellent systems for transporting travelers to and from their major airports and even between the airports and bus and rail stations. Transport options range from taxis to buses to trains. Shanghai Pudong International Airport boasts the first and only commercial magnetic levitation (maglev) train. It moves passengers to the Shanghai city zone. A journey that would normally take forty minutes by car from the airport to Longyang Metrostation takes seven minutes and twenty seconds on the maglev and costs 50 RMB. From there, the Metro can take you to People's Square and the heart of the city.

Hong Kong's airport express train connects travelers to the MTR in under thirty minutes. For 100 HKD, this express train can whisk you away directly to Disneyland or to Kowloon and then Hong Kong Island in half the time it takes to drive.

Beijing Capital International Airport is not connected to the city by a mass transit system, but construction has begun in 2005 to change that. There are, however, several bus lines that provide service between Beijing's city zones and the airport. You can ask for more information about how to get around at the information desk upon entering the main arrival halls. To find that information desk, you can ask the following questions:

Xúnwèn chù zài năr?	**Where is the information desk?**
Lǚguǎn fúwù chù zài năr?	**Where is the hotel desk?**

Transportation Vocabulary

The following list includes some vital transportation vocabulary. Following the list you'll find possible transportation scenarios. Listen to the tracks on the CD and repeat the words as you go.

Airport Transport Vocabulary

TRACK 17

Chinese	English
chūzū qìchē	taxi
zhàn	stand
fùqián	to pay
kéyǐ	possible, able, may, can
yòng	use
xiànjīn	cash
jiāotōng	transportation, communication
bāshì	bus

Chinese	English
dàodá	to arrive, arrival
dōngbù	eastern area
dàtīng	hall
duìmiàn	opposite, opposing
búyòng	there's no need, it's not necessary
kèrén	guest
miǎnfèi	free
wǎng	toward
chéngshì	city
huǒchē	train
gēnsuí	follow
biāozhì	sign
cífú lièchē	maglev train
dānchéng	one-way
piào	ticket

TRACK 18

Visitor: *Nár yǒu chūzū qìchē?*
Where can I get a taxi?

Attendant: *Chūzūqìchē zhàn zài dàodá dàtīng dōngbù.*
The taxi stand is at the east end of the arrivals hall.

Visitor: *Wǒ zěnme fùqián?*
How do I pay?

Attendant: *Nǐ kéyǐ yòng xiànjīn huòzhě jiāotōng kǎ.*
You may use cash or a metro card.

Visitor: *Xièxie.*
Thank you.

Attendant: *Búyòng xiè.*
You're welcome.

TRACK 19

Visitor: *Zài nár děng lǚguǎn de bāshì?*
Where do I wait for the hotel shuttle bus?

Attendant: *Lǚguǎn de bāshìzhàn zài dàodá dàtīng duìmiàn.*
The hotel shuttle buses are opposite the arrivals hall.

Visitor: *Duōshǎo qián ne?*
How much does it cost?

Attendant: *Búyòng fùqián! Wèi kèrén de fúwù shì miǎnfèi de.*
Nothing, the service is free for hotel guests.

Visitor: *Xièxie nǐ!*
Thank you!

Attendant: *Bú kèqì.*
You're welcome.

QUESTION?

Is there more than one way of saying thank you in Chinese?
When showing your gratitude in Chinese you're generally limited to *xièxie*, although you can also attach *nǐ* to it. However to show your appreciation for gratitude you have quite a few more options. *Búxiè*, *bú kèqì*, *búyòng xiè*, and *búyòng kēqì* are all viable options for saying "you're welcome." You can think of these variations as corresponding in English to "my pleasure," "it's nothing," etc.

TRACK 20

Visitor: *Yǒu méiyǒu wǎng chéngli de huǒchē?*
Is there a train that goes to the city?

Attendant: *Yǒu, nǐ kéyǐ gēnsuí biāozhì wǎng cífú lièchēzhàn.*
Yes, you may follow the signs to the maglev train.

Visitor: *Lièchē duōshǎo qián?*
How much does the train cost?

Attendant: *Yì zhāng dānchéng piào shì wǔshí kuài qián.*

A one-way ticket is 50 RMB.

Visitor: *Xièxie!*
Thank you!

Attendant: *Búyòng kèqì.*
You're welcome.

Asking Questions

Asking a question in Chinese can be very simple. We'll discuss the three easiest ways first. Because Chinese is a tonal language, asking a question is not as simple as raising your tone at the end of an interrogative sentence the way we do in English. When a tone is changed in Chinese the very meaning of the word changes. With this in mind you may ask simple questions in Chinese by using an interrogative particle, the affirmative-negative sentence structure, or a question word.

The Question Words

Chinese	English
Shéi	Who
Shénme	What
Nǎr	Where
Shénme shíhòu	When
Zěnme	How
Wèishénme	Why
nǎgè	Which
Duōshǎo	How many/much
Duōjiǔ	How long (time)
Duōdà	How big
Duōzhòng	How heavy
Jídiǎn	At what time

In simple questions the question word usually comes at the end, as seen in the following examples.

Tā shì shéi?	**Who is she?**
Zhè shì shénme?	**What is this?**
Nǐ qù nǎr?	**Where are you going?**

In more complex sentences, where there are transitive verbs, adverbs, and direct objects, the question words become modifiers and precede the verb or object, as seen in the following examples.

Shéi zhīdào dáàn?	**Who knows the answer?**
Nǐ shénme shíhòu huílái?	**When are you coming back?**
Chāojí shìchǎng jídiǎn kāimén?	**What time does the supermarket open?**

It's important to remember that these differences in placement of the question words stems from the fact that they are called interrogative pronouns. As a pronoun it's the job of the question word to replace an element of the sentence. As a result, their placement in a sentence depends on what element they are replacing. In the previous simple sentences the interrogative pronouns are replacing subjects and objects. Since the subject always comes before the object in Chinese, you'll see that when the question word is replacing a subject, it comes at the beginning of the interrogative statement. Conversely, the object always follows the subject in Chinese, and thus when the question word is replacing the object of the sentence it comes at the end. Similarly, as you recall from our review of word order, modifiers such as adverbs and expressions of time immediately follow the subject of a sentence, and therefore fall in the beginning of the sentence.

Interrogative Particle

The second way to ask a question in Chinese is to use an interrogative particle. We'll discuss particles and their functions in more depth later on in the book, but for now you should know that there are two particles, or morphemes, which turn a simple declarative sentence into a question without changing the word order. They are *ma* and *ne*. *Ma* is used universally as an interrogative particle, while *ne* is reserved for alternative or rhetorical questions. So, you're safer to just stick with *ma* for asking questions, as you can see here:

Nǐ xǐhuān tiàowǔ ma?	**Do you like to dance?**
Nǐ déng wǒ ma?	**Are you waiting for me?**
Nǐ qù shìchǎng ma?	**Are you going to the market?**

Affirmative-Negative

The third way to ask a question in Chinese is the affirmative-negative statement construction, which is formed by posing the affirmative and negative elements of the predicate against each other. This sentence structure is classically Chinese and unique to the language. The primary element of the predicate is the verb; so to form a question in this construction you say the verb and then negate the verb immediately afterward, as is done in the following examples.

Tā shì búshì lǎoshī?	**Is he a teacher?**
Nǐ rènshì búrènshì tā?	**Do you know him?**
Nǐ yào búyào qù shìchǎng?	**Do you want to go to the market?**

Exercises

Now it's time to see what you've learned! The following exercises include information covered in various parts of this chapter. Try to answer the questions from memory first, and then refer back to earlier pages if you need to jog your memory or perfect spelling.

1. Do you remember the two initial questions that may be posed to you by the immigration officials upon arrival in China? They are:

Nǐ zài zhōngguó dǎsuàn zuò shénme shì?	**What do you plan on doing in China?**
Nǐ zài zhōngguó dāi duōjiǔ?	**How long will you be staying in China?**

In the following spaces, give one possible answer—in Chinese—to each of these questions:

2. What are two ways of saying "You're welcome" in Chinese?

   ....

   ....

3. Which of the sentences below is a question?

   Tāmen chīfàn ma.
   Tāmen chīfàn le.

4. Reorganize the following words into a sentence and write it in the space provided: *wǒde, zhè, bàozhǐ, shì*.

   ....

5. Fill in the appropriate negator in the following sentences:

   Tā .... *shì Zhōngguó rén.*
   Wǒ .... *yǒu qiānzhèng.*
   Wǒmen .... *xǐhuān tiàowǔ.*

Chapter 5

Finding Lodgings

When you travel anywhere, you need to have a comfortable place to stay. Traveling is tiring, and in a place like China with so much to see and do, you'll definitely need a good night's sleep in comfortable surroundings. Rest assured you'll get fabulous treatment in China. Hotel and hospitality staff will go well out of their way to be friendly and helpful. If you do run into obstacles, though, don't be afraid to voice your concerns. The Chinese care a lot about what foreigners think of their country; they'll want you to leave speaking well of China.

5

Checking In

Checking in at your hotel in China should be fairly stress-free. Just bring your bags over to the fúwùtái, or front desk. Bubbly, impeccably dressed clerks will guide you through the check-in process. Most of the time you or your tour company will have made reservations in your and your party's name. Lone travelers do not always make reservations, as you'll often get a room for a more reasonable rate by simply showing up at the desk and bargaining. This takes a bit of practice, so if this is your first trip, it's probably best to leave these details to your tour agency.

Look over the following vocabulary list and then listen to the conversation that follows on the CD.

Check-In Basics

Chinese	English
wǎnshàng	evening
yǐjīng	already
yùdìng	reserve
zhǎodào	have found
Nín	you (formal)
huì	be able to, would
gèng	more
zhù	live, stay, reside
xiǎng	think
yào	want, will
xiǎngyào	would like
shuāng	double, pair
rén	person
fángjiān	room
rènhé	any

Chinese	English
qítā	other, cursory
qiānshǔ	sign
yòng	use
yīgòng	all together
názhǒng	what kind
tèxuǎn	preference
tuìfáng	checkout
suíshí	whatever time is convenient for you

TRACK 21

Hotel Clerk: *Huānyíng guānglín. Wǎnshàng hǎo!*
Welcome, good evening!

Guest: *Wǎnshàng hǎo. Wó yǐjīng yùdìng le fángjiān.*
Good Evening. I reserved a room.

Hotel Clerk: *Hén hǎo. Nín guì xìng?*
Very good. What is your surname?

Guest: *Wǒ xìng Derrico.*
My surname is Derrico.

Hotel Clerk: *Qíng děng yīděng. À, zhǎodào le. Nímen shì liùwèi yào zhù sān tiān, duì ma?*
One moment, please. Ah, I've found it. A party of six for three nights, correct?

Guest: *Duì le.*
Yes, that's correct.

Hotel Clerk: *Nín huì gèng xiǎngyào sānge shuāng rén fáng háishì tàojiān?*
Would you rather have three double rooms or a suite?

Visitor: *Sānge shuāng rén fáng jiù kéyǐ.*
Three double rooms are fine.

Hotel Clerk:	*Hén hǎo.* Very well.
Visitor:	*Qǐng wèn, shuāng rén fáng yǒu názhǒng chuáng?* *What kind of beds do the double rooms have?*

Hotel Clerk:	*Wǒmen de shuāng rén fáng yǒu shuāng rén chuáng*
	    huòzhě liǎngge dānrén de. Nín yǒu méiyǒu tèxuǎn?
	Our double rooms may have either one double bed,
	    or two single beds. Do you have a preference?

Visitor:	*Wǒmen gèng xiǎngyào shuāng rén chuáng de.* We'd rather have double bed rooms.
Hotel Clerk:	*Hén hǎo.* Very well.
Hotel Clerk:	*Nín yǒu méiyǒu rènhé qítā tèxuǎn?* Do you have any other preferences?
Guest:	*Méiyǒu.* No, none.

Hotel Clerk:	*Hǎo. Qǐng zài zhèr qiānshǔ nínde míngzi. Ránhòu*
	    zài zhèr xiě nínde dìzhǐ.
	Okay. Please, sign your name here, and write your
	    address here.

Guest:	*Wǒ kéyǐ yòng yīngwén xiě ma?* May I write it in English?
Hotel Clerk:	*Kéyǐ. Fángfèi yīgòng shì sānwàn liùqiān rénmínbì.* That's fine. The total is 36,000 RMB.
Guest:	*Hǎo.* Okay.

Hotel Clerk:	*Xièxie nín! Nímen yào zhù yāosìlíngwǔ zhì*
	    yāosìlíngqi hào fáng. Zhù nímen guòde yúkuài.
	Thank you very much. You'll be in rooms 1405
	    to 1407. Enjoy your stay.

Guest: *Xièxie. Qǐng wèn, jǐ diǎn tuìfáng?*
Thank you! May I ask what time is checkout?

Hotel Clerk: *Zhèngshì de tuìfáng shíjiān shì shísāndiǎn. Kěshì nín kéyǐ zǎo yī diǎnr tuìfáng.*
The official checkout time is 13:00, but you may check out at your convenience any time before then.

Guest: *Xièxie.*
Thank you.

Hotel Clerk: *Búyòng kèqì!*
You're welcome!

Making Requests

You were introduced to new grammatical constructions in the check-in conversation in the last section. The Chinese, in general, are a very modest people. It's out of character to give someone an order or use an imperative phrase. To that end, we say *děng yī děng* to soften the request along with the word *qǐng*, meaning "please." The "verb *yī* verb" construction is a way to demonstrate brevity or minimality. Take a look at the following examples:

Qǐng kàn yī kàn.	**Please have a look.**
Qǐng cháng yī cháng.	**Please try some (eat).**
Qǐng cháng yī cháng.	**Please try some (drink).**
Qǐng shì yī shì.	**Please give it a try.**

There is another variation of the "verb *yī* verb" construction. The "verb *yī* modifier" construction is versatile and can be used in different situations to add a degree of minimality to verbs. The minimality often manifests in terms of spans of time. Here are the different words in order of shortest to longest perceived durations of time: *yīdiǎnr*, *yīxiàr*, and *yīhuìr*. *Yīdiǎnr*, which literally means "one point," generally translates simply to "a little" or "some" when used by itself to describe a quantity. But when used in conjunction with adjectives, it conveys the comparative degree in adjectives.

kuài yīdiǎnr	**hurry up (a little faster)**
zǎo yīdiǎnr	**a little earlier**
duō yīdiǎnr	**a little more**

When you want to ask someone to do something for a just a brief moment, the expression of choice is *yīxiàr*. It can be used in a number of different ways.

chǎo yīxiàr	**stir fry it a bit**
tán yīxiàr	**chat for a bit**
xiūxi yīxiàr	**rest a bit**

When you wish to request that someone do something for a while, use *yīhuìr*.

děng yīhuìr	**please wait**
sànbù yīhuìr	**stroll a while**
liú yīhuìr	**stay a while**

In colloquial Chinese speech, *yīxiàr* and *yīhuìr* can often be used interchangeably. Still, it's good to stick with the guidelines to perception mentioned previously.

ALERT!

The Chinese love to haggle. This may take you a bit by surprise at first, but don't be too shy to try your hand at it. Also, don't assume you're being cheated. Haggling is a game for the Chinese; it's a pastime and practically an art form. Don't be afraid to ask to see your hotel room before you settle on it.

This or That

There are two ways of expressing the word "or" in Chinese, but there are tricks to remembering how to know which one to choose. The words you may use are *hái shì* and *huòzhě*, or just huò. Háishì can be regarded as the exclusive "or." It is used in sentences where you must choose between two options. You'll see it in questions and negations. Take a look at the following.

Nǐ shì lǎoshī háishì xuésheng?	**Are you a teacher or a student?**
Wǒ bù zhīdào jīntiānde tiānqì	**I don't know if the weather today**
hén lěng háishì hěn rè?	**is cold or hot.**

The second "or" is the conjunctive, or inclusive, "or." You use *huǒzhě* when two options are considered of equal importance or status.

Wǒ xiàtiān qù Běijīng huòzhě	**I'm going to either Beijing**
Shànghǎi.	**or Shanghai this summer.**

A good trick to use in remembering which "or" to use is to try and plug the sentence into the "either. . . or. . . " construction. If a sentence doesn't fall into the "either. . . or . . ." construction, then it's probably a *háishì* sentence. Look at the previous sentences again. It doesn't make sense to ask "Are you either a teacher or student?"

Wake-Up Calls

Unlike in Japan, only a handful of hotel rooms in China come with alarm clocks these days. So if you need a morning wake-up call, you have to call the front desk. In a growing number of Chinese hotels, however, there is a special number for a switchboard you may call to register your wake-up call. In some hotels, the system is computerized, and you can input your wake-up time by voice menu. If you need to speak with an actual representative, say and indicate what time you need to be woken up.

Don't get too far ahead of yourself, though. You still haven't learned how to talk about time in Chinese! This section will give you all the new vocabulary you need to chat about the hour.

As you learned previously, diǎn means a point or stroke of time. As such, it serves as the Chinese expression for "o'clock." It is attached to the end of a number as "o'clock" is in English, followed by the word zhōng. Minutes are expressed in terms of fēn.

Telling time

Let's start at the very beginning. Among some of the interesting aspects of Chinese mathematics is the fact that 0 is a number. Chinese uses a ten-digit base numeric system. Unlike English, Chinese has no unique equivalent expressions for the numbers "eleven" and "twelve." Chinese numbers are quite regular; that is, until you count too high. Look over the following vocabulary list and then listen to sample sentences that follow. Repeat what you hear aloud for pronunciation practice.

Chinese Numbers

TRACK 22

Chinese	English
yī	one
èr	two
sān	three
sì	four
wǔ	five
liù	six
qī	seven
bā	eight
jiǔ	nine
shí	ten
yībǎi	one hundred
yīqiān	one thousand

Chinese	English
wǔqiān	five thousand
yīwàn	ten thousand
shíwàn	one hundred thousand
bǎiwàn	one million
qiānwàn	ten million
yīyì	one hundred million

TRACK 23

Xiànzài jídiǎn zhōng?	**What time is it?**
Xiànzài xiàwǔ liùdiǎn zhōng.	**It's 6:00 P.M.**
Wǒ zǎoshàng wúdiǎnbàn qǐchuáng.	**I get up at 5:30.**
Wǎng Běijīng de huǒchē wǎnshàng jiúdiǎn sānshíliùfēn chūfā.	**The train to Beijing leaves at 9:36 P.M.**

The easiest aspect of learning to count in Chinese is the knowledge that turning all these cardinal numbers into ordinal numbers is a piece of cake. Simply put the particle *dì* before the cardinal number to make it ordinal. For example, "first" is *dìyī*, and "second" is *dìèr*.

Sample Request

There's no one corresponding Chinese noun for "wake-up call." Instead, you'll ask the service clerk to "call to wake you up" (*jiào qǐchuáng*). Listen to the conversation that follows and repeat it as you go.

TRACK 24

Guest: *Qǐng wèn nǐ kéyǐ ānpái jiào qǐchuáng ma?*
I would like to arrange a wake up call?

Clerk: *Dāngrán kéyǐ. Nín xiǎng jídiǎn qǐchuáng?*
Of course. What time would you like to be woken up?

Guest: *Míngtiān zǎoshàng qǐdiǎnbàn qǐng jiào wǒ.*
Wake me at 7:30 tomorrow morning.

Clerk: *Hǎo, zǎoshàng qīdiǎnbàn. Wǒ lái bàn zhè jiàn shì.*
Very well. 7:30 AM. I'll take care of it.

Wake-Up Call Vocabulary

Chinese	English
ānpái	arrange
dāngrán	of course
bàn	half
bàn(shì)	take care of...
míngtiān	tomorrow

Types of Accommodations

The English language includes lots of different words for places where a weary traveler can get a good night's rest. Some common examples include: hotel, motel, inn, and motor lodge. Chinese also has a number of expressions for such accommodations. Traveling throughout China, you'll see that a wide variety of rest places are available to you. Which one you choose depends on a number of different factors. Criteria for where you decide to stay can include what services you desire, your price range, location, and even who you're traveling with. All these determine the type of lodgings you may wish to seek out.

During your investigation into lodgings, you'll find the Chinese use a star system of rating the quality of their services and locations, just like the United States. Be aware, however, that the scale does not correlate directly with the Western standard. As a rule of thumb, when you count the stars given to a hotel in Chinese ratings, subtract one star and that will be the Western equivalent.

Dàjiǔdiàn (Fàndiàn)

These pristine, elegant, and modern upscale establishments offer a wide variety of services. They are the picture of comfort, particularly the joint Sino-Western ventures. They often boast several restaurants and comprehensive business and travel services. Rooms are quite lovely and come equipped with DDD/IDD (Domestic Direct Dial/International Direct Dial) phones, Internet access, and satellite TV. They offer twenty-four-hour hot water, private bathrooms, air conditioning, and every other amenity of comfort. Many *dàjiǔdiàn* offer such luxuries as spas with massages, salons, and even exercise facilities. Look over the following vocabulary list and then listen to the conversation that follows. Repeat what you hear aloud for extra speaking practice.

Room Service Requests

Chinese	English
kè	visitor
kèfáng	guest's room
cān	meal
bù	department
kèfáng yòngcān fúwùbù	Room Service
wèi	for
yèxiāo	late night snack
diǎncài	to order
sānmíngzhì	sandwich
gēn	with/and
zhá	to deep fry
shǔ	potato
tiáo	sticks
zháshǔtiáo	French fries
dàyuē	about; approximately

TRACK 25

Clerk: *Wéi, zhè shì kèfáng yòngcān fúwùbù. Wǒ kéyǐ wèi nín fúwù ma?*
Hello. This is Room Service, how may I help you?

Guest: *Wéi, Nǐ hǎo. Wǒ xiǎng chī yèxiāo.*
Hi. I'd like a late night snack.

Clerk: *Hén hǎo. Nín zhù jǐ hào fáng?*
Very well. What room are you in?

Guest: *Wǒ zhù yāosìlíngwǔ hào fáng.*
I'm in room 1405.

Clerk: *Hěn hǎo. Nín xiǎng diǎn shénme cài?*
Okay. What would you like to order?

Guest: *Wǒ xiǎng chī sānmíngzhì gēn zháshǔtiáo.*
I'd like a sandwich and a side of fries.

Clerk: *Hǎo, nín xiǎng hē shénme?*
Okay. Would you like something to drink?

Guest: *Búyòngle, xièxie.*
No, thank you.

Clerk: *Dàyuē xūyào shíwǔ fēn zhōng.*
It should be about fifteen minutes.

Guest: *Xièxie.*
Thank you.

ESSENTIAL

These days almost all Chinese hotels use magnetic keycards. But the key cards are more than just keys. As you enter your hotel room you'll find a small slot on the wall at about eye level. This slot is the room's electricity monitor. In an effort to ensure energy is not wasted, these slots were installed so that you may place your key card in them to activate the current. When you leave the room, remove the card and the current will be cut in about five minutes.

Bīnguǎn

A step down in scale from the *dàjiǔdiàn* is the midrange *bīnguǎn*. These types of lodgings are almost everywhere. They lack the glitz of the *dàjiǔdiàn*, but what they lack in luxury they makeup for in savings. Many of these establishments are shabby chic. The facade of the buildings are a bit run down, and the wall paper and carpet may be worn; but the rooms are clean and are quite comfortable. *Bīnguǎn* often offer three types of accommodations: economy (*jīngjì*), standard (*biāozhǔn*), and deluxe (*háohuá*). Amenity-wise, the *bīnguǎn* offers a bit less than the big names, but often you'll find they still offer restaurants, laundry services, and DDD/IDD phone. All rooms have air conditioning and hot water. Review the following vocabulary and then listen to the conversation that follows. Repeat it aloud as you go.

Laundry Language

Chinese	English
xǐ	wash
yīfú	clothes
céng	floor
xǐyījiān	laundry room
jīběn	basic
yòngwán	to use up
suíbiàn	at your convenience
qīngjiéjì	detergent
shòuhuòjī	vending machine

TRACK 26

Guest: *Wǒ xiǎng xǐ yīfú.*
I'd like to wash my clothes.

Clerk: *Hén hǎo. Wǒmen zài dièr céng yǒu xǐyījiān,*
Nín kéyǐ zài zhèr mǎi xǐyī kǎ.
Very well. We have a laundry facility on the second
floor. You may buy a laundry card here.

Guest: *Yi zhāng kǎ duōshǎo qián?*
How much is the card?

Clerk: *Jīběn kǎ shì sānshíwǔ kuài qián. Měicì shuíxǐ shì wǔ kuài qián.*
The basic card costs 35 RMB. Each wash is 5 RMB.

Guest: *Xǐyī kǎ yòngwán de shíhòu, wǒ xūyào zài mǎi xīn de ma?*
When the card is used up, must I buy a new one?

Clerk: *Bú yòng. Nín kéyǐ suíbiàn jiā duō diǎnr qián dào kǎ shàng.*
No. You may add money to the card at your convenience.

Guest: *Zài nár kéyǐ mǎi qīngjiéjì?*
Where can I buy detergent?

Clerk: *Zài xǐyījiān lǐmiàn yǒu yīge shòuhuòjī.*
There's a vending machine in the laundry room.

Guest: *Hǎo! Xièxie.*
Great! Thanks.

Clerk: *Búyòng xiè!*
You're welcome!

Lǚguǎn

Lǚguǎn establishments are bottom rung, so don't expect much in the way of services and amenities. You'll see more stars on a cloudy night in Shanghai than you'll see attributed to these forms of lodging. Many of them offer only a bed to sleep in dormitory style. Showers are communal, and hot water may only be turned on for a few hours a day. The degree of cleanliness may be questionable at best. The experience is more like staying in a hostel rather than a hotel, and the prices are the lowest anywhere in China. If you're thinking this lodging option doesn't sound too appealing, don't worry; most of the low-quality businesses are not even licensed to house foreign nationals. Unbeknownst to many, a guest house must apply for a license issued by the government to house foreigners.

Creature Comforts

In the *dàjiǔdiàn* you'll see that the layout of the room resembles the layouts of Western hotels of the same scale. In fact, many large Western luxury hotel chains have branches in China. The midrange hotels, especially the Chinese-owned establishments, all tend to be laid out similarly. This is uninspiring in that they lack character, and yet, at the same time, it can be reassuring to know how most everything works and where everything is. Travel around China and the all-too-familiar surroundings everywhere you go will be at best comforting and at worst be comical. Though Chinese hotels overall have double rooms with either one large-sized bed or two double beds, double-bed rooms predominate. When you enter the room, bathrooms will be immediately at the doorway and across from a closet. Walk further inside and there is usually a chest, desk, and TV stand. The beds are opposite the furniture and there is the usual control panel and drawer between the beds.

ALERT!

There's an old Chinese saying: *Shuì yìngchuáng bǐ shuì ruǐnchuáng, kéyǐ shuì de gèng xiāng.* It translates as: "Sleep on a firm mattress rather than a soft mattress, and you'll be able to sleep more sweetly." Bear that in mind when you get into bed in China because if you have a bad back, you'll be pleasantly surprised. If you're used to a soft bed, however, prepare for a surprise.

The control panel has on/off switches for just about everything in the room, including all the lights, the TV, and the air conditioning or heat. Another interesting point about Chinese culture is the preference for hot drinking water over cold drinking water. If you were to ask a Chinese person why he prefers hot water over cold you'd get a host of different reasons. Some say hot water is better for your *qi*, and some say the body absorbs hot water more easily. Another common theory, which is one of the more plausible and tangible reasons, is that the tap water in most of the country is not drinkable. As a result, most everyone boils water before using it. You'll notice either an electric kettle in your room or an actual metal thermos. Housekeeping will be sure to change your thermos daily.

Money Matters

China's currency is called the *rénmínbì*—commonly abbreviated as RMB—which means "the people's currency." Currently, the exchange rate is 8.1 RMB to 1 U.S. dollar. The RMB is a fixed unit of currency. It is not traded internationally; therefore, it can only be obtained in China. Among the various services your hotel will provide, there's one service that all travelers smile about. You'll be glad to take advantage of currency exchange services in most hotels. You can change both cash and travelers checks at your service desk. China has a standardized fee of exchange of 7.75 percent, so regardless of where you go to exchange money, no other commission is permitted.

Review the following vocabulary and then listen to the conversation that follows. Repeat what you hear aloud for extra practice.

Money Talk

Chinese	English
měiyuán	U.S. dollars
huànchéng	exchange (verb)
tián	fill out
shōu	receive
duìhuàn	exchange (noun)
dān	slip
wàihuìquàn	foreign exchange certificate

Guest: *Ní hǎo. Wǒ xiǎng bǎměiyuán huànchéng rénmínbì.*
Hi. I'd like to exchange U.S. dollars for Renminbi.

Clerk: *Nín xiǎng huàn duōshǎo?*
How much would you like to change?

Guest: *Wǒ xiǎng huàn sānbǎi měiyuán.*
I'd like to change 300 U.S. dollars.

Clerk: *Hěn hǎo. Qǐng nín tián duìhàndān.*
Very well. Please fill out the exchange slip.

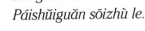

TRACK 27

Clerk: *Hǎo. Sānbǎi měiyuán gòng huànchéng rénmínbì liǎngqiān liǎngbǎi sìshíyī yuán liùmáo bāfēn.*
Okay. That's 2,241.68 RMB in exchange for 300 U.S. dollars.

Guest: *Xièxie.*
Thanks.

Clerk: *Qǐng shōu hǎo nín duìhuàn de wàihuì hé fāpiào.*
Please take your foreign exchange certificate and receipt.

Guest: *Xièxie nǐde bāngzhù!*
Thank you for your help!

Dealing with Problems

Your stay in the upscale hotels will generally be completely without incident. As the old adage goes, you get what you pay for. That holds very true when it comes to Chinese accommodations. However, the reality is that you're occasionally going to encounter problems and snags. When something doesn't meet your approval, or if something doesn't work correctly, you should feel free to speak up. Here are some examples:

Wǒde fángjiān méiyǒu lěngqì.	**My room has no air conditioning.**
Wǒde fángjiōn méiyoǔ nuǎnqì.	**My room has no heat.**
Diànshì, huài le.	**The TV is broken.**
Kōngtiáo huài le.	**The air conditioning is broken.**
Páishǔiguǎn sōizhǔ le.	**The drain is clogged.**

Remember, the Chinese place a lot of importance on what others think of them, as individuals and as a nation. They want to know if you're dissatisfied with something so they can correct the situation.

Exercises

You've learned a lot about the various kinds of accommodations in China, as well as the specific amenities and services you can expect—or not expect. The following exercises include information covered in various parts of this chapter. Try to answer the questions from memory first, and then refer back to earlier pages if you need to jog your memory or perfect spelling.

1. Fill in the blanks with either *háishì* or *huòzhě*.

   Wǒ xiǎng zhù dàjiǔdiàn .... *bīnguǎn.*

   Wǒ bù zhīdào zhètái diànshì shì zhōngguóde ....
   měiguóde.

2. Write the following times in Chinese.

   7:30 ....

   9:45 ....

   10:28 ....

3. Translate: I'm staying on the fourth floor.

   ....

Chapter 6

Getting Around

Urban planning is being realized more and more in cities all over China. In most Chinese cities all the streets are clearly marked in both Chinese characters and Hanyu Pinyin. Bus systems are becoming more expansive, and mass transit systems are popping up throughout the nation. With a good map, you should be able to make your way around just about everywhere. If you need help, the Chinese will be only too happy to lend a hand.

Grammar Lesson: Verbs

In a chapter about getting around China, it seems appropriate to start out with the action words of language: verbs. Chinese verbs are quite different from English verbs. They have a great deal more flexibility and function and adapt themselves to serve many purposes. Understanding Chinese verbs can be a bit difficult, but don't be discouraged. Remember that learning another language begs one to learn another way of thinking. One widespread trend in Chinese that is worth mentioning is that Chinese likes syllabic harmony. This means that even though each syllable of the Chinese language may constitute a sound and idea—and, in turn, a word—Chinese likes its vocabulary paired up. Many Chinese verbs come in complements of two syllables. The following sections briefly outline five basic applications for Chinese verbs.

Stative Verbs

Simply put, a Chinese verb is called stative when it can also be described as an adjectival predicate. This is tricky because, in Chinese, though all verbs can be predicates, not all predicates are verbs. The following are some stative verb sentences in English:

I am happy.
He is tall.
She is pretty.

Stative verbs express basic states of being. Notice the role played by the verb "to be" in all those sentences. Though the Chinese verb *shì* functions very similarly to "to be" in English, they are not direct translations. *Shì* is the equative verb in Chinese, and it functions in a sentence just like an equal sign. *Shì* equates the items that precede it and follow it, but doesn't necessarily describe its state. As a result, in order to communicate simple states, Chinese simply uses the subject, some kind of adverb, and then the adjective. Here's how the previous sentences translate into Chinese:

I am happy.	*Wǒ hěn kāixīn.*
He is tall.	*Tā hěn gāo.*
She is pretty.	*Tā hěn měi.*

Coverbs

Coverbs are fairly numerous in Chinese. They are verbs whose complements are their very own objects. Some examples of coverbs in English are "to read" and "to eat." "To read" in Chinese is *kànshū*, which is composed of *kàn*, meaning "to look at," and *shū*, meaning "book." "To eat" in Chinese is *chīfàn*, which is composed of *chī*, meaning "to eat," and *fàn*, meaning "food."

Optative Verbs

Optative verbs are those that are used somewhat like auxiliary verbs in English. They serve to help other verbs by communicating ability, possibility, or intention. Some optative verbs are *yào* (to want) and *xiǎng* (to think or wish). *Yào* and *xiǎng* indicate intention or volition, though *yào* emphasizes a person's will and is often used to communicate the future tense. The verb *huì* means "to be able to," as in a skill acquired by study. *Huì* is often used to communicate the future conditional tense. The verbs *néng* and *kéyǐ* are used to express ability to do something or general possibility. Generally, *Néng* more closely corresponds with "can," while *kéyǐ* corresponds with "may." The verb *yīnggāi* is usually translated as "should," but it is used just as often to mean "must."

Resultative Complement Verbs

Resultative complement verbs combine words whose first component introduces the action and whose second component features the result of that action producing a more illustrative verb. Examples of resultative complement verbs include "to comprehend/understand," "to rain," and "to finish reading." "To understand" in Chinese is *tīngdǒng*, composed of *tīng*, meaning "to listen," and *dǒng*, meaning "to understand." "To rain" in Chinese is *xiàyǔ*, which is composed *of xià*, meaning "to fall" or "come down," and *yǔ*, meaning "rain." "To finish reading" in Chinese is *kànwán*, which is composed of *kàn*, meaning "to look at," and *wán* meaning "completion."

Combined Directional Verbs

These types of verbs communicate aspects of motion and direction based on the position of the speaker. These verbs make ample use of directional verbs such as *lái* and *qù* to further illustrate direction in verbs of motion. Verbs such as "to come in" and "to go out" are combined directionals. *Jìnlái*, which is composed of *jìn* (to enter) and *lái* (to come), means "to enter," while *chūqù is* composed of *chū* (to exit) and *qù* (to go) and means "to go out."

Grammar Lesson: Particles

Particles are functional parts of speech that can't stand alone by themselves. They require other elements of speech to augment. Chinese makes liberal use of these particles, as it lacks inflection and verbal expressive tones like the Western non-tonal languages. The particles you've met up with most frequently thus far are *de* and *ma*. Make friends with *de*. You and *de* will be working together very closely in your exploration of Chinese. *Ma*, the question particle, is also a great ally to have on your side, but *ma* will only show up when asking a question. You'll generally find *de* in three basic situations. First and foremost, *de* likes to follow adjectives:

měilì de fēngguāng	**beautiful scenery**
yǒumíng de gēxīng	**famous star (singer)**
yǒuyòng de zhōnggào	**useful advice**
zhēngshì de tuìfáng shíjiān	**official checkout time**

The second place you'll find *de* is after nominal expressions. A nominal expression is an adjective-like clause that plays the role of a relative clause. Chinese does not have words for "that," "which," "who," etc. Check out the following examples; the "that" in the Chinese serves to clarify the subject.

English	Explained Translation	Chinese
These are the clothes that I wear.	These are the \<I wear\> *de* clothes.	*Zhè shì wǒ chuān de yīfú.*
The man who came yesterday	The \<yesterday came\> *de* that man	*Zuótiān lái de nèige rén*

Lastly, *de* shows that the phrase that precedes it is attributive. As a result, to say the words "my," "his/her," or "our," you simply add *de* to the corresponding simple pronouns. Thus, *Wǒ + de* = "my," and *Tā + de* = "his," etc. For example:

shèhuǐde wèntí	**society's problems**
wǒde shū	**my book**
Āmín de kāfēi	**Amin's coffee**

Subways and Buses

In China, cars are generally less expensive than they are in the West. However, they are very expensive to license. This is due in part to government initiatives to encourage use of public transportation and reduce traffic congestion, gas emissions, and noise pollution. As a result, public transportation is very popular.

Buses are the most common form of public transportation in China second only to bicycles. The bus system in most Chinese cities is extensive. Next in line after buses in terms of popular use are mass transit train systems. Several of China's large cities have metros, including Beijing, Shanghai, Guangzhou, Shenzhen, Chongqing, and Hong Kong, among others.

Unfortunately, due to its popularity, regardless of the time of day, all forms of public transport are crowded. After all, China is the world's most populous nation. In the past, travelers to China generally did not take the bus. Few stops were indicated in Hanyu Pinyin, and fewer drivers and conductors spoke English. But that is slowly changing. In Shanghai, for example, the new public buses and the Metro are equipped with displays that indicate the stops and information in Chinese and English. They are also equipped with automated public announcement systems that tell riders where they are on the route and what the next stop is in both Chinese and English. If, however, you are on a bus or train that is not equipped with such features, just go ahead and ask someone "[Destination] *zài nǎr?*"

Where is the airport?	*Jīchǎng zài nǎr?*
Where is the bus stop?	*Gōnggòng qìchē zhàn zài nǎr?*
Where is the taxi stand?	*Chūzū qìchē zhàn zài nǎr?*

Subway Speech

Chinese	English
lù	street
zhèr	here
nàr	there
jìn	close
yuǎn	far
dìtiězhàn	subway station
pángbiānr	side
huǒchēzhàn	train station
zuì	most
hào	number
cóng	from
wǎng	to; toward
dōng	east
nán	south
xī	west
běi	north
dìxiàlièchē	subway train
chē	colloquial abbreviation for vehicle
shǒuxiān	firstly

Chinese	English
yīnggāi	should, ought to, must
ránhòu	then, afterwards
huànchéng	transfer
qiánwǎng	bound for, toward
míngbái	understand
xīwàng	hope, wish, expect
mílù	get lost, lose one's way
qiáng	wall

Here are some sample conversations for asking directions:

TRACK 28

Tourist: *Láojià, zuì jìn de dìtiězhàn zài nǎr?*
Excuse me, where is the nearest subway station?

Local: *Yī hào xiàn de Héngshān lù dìtiězhàn cóng zhèr wǎng xī zǒu liǎng lù kǒu.*
Hengshan Lu station on the Number 1 Line is two streets west of here.

Tourist: *Yī hào xiàn chē qù Lùjiāzuì jīnróng màoyìqū ma?*
Does the Number 1 Line go to Lujiazui Financial District?

Local: *Búqù. Nǐ shōuxiān yīnggāi zuò yī hào xiàn qù rénmín guángchǎng. Ránhòu huàn-chéng èr hào xiàn. Qiánwǎng Zhangjiang de lièchē qù Lùjiāzuǐ.*

No, you have to take the Number 1 Line to People's Square and then transfer to the Number 2 Line. The Zhangjiang bound train stops at Lujiazui.

Tourist: *À, wǒ míngbái. Wǒ xīwàng bú huì mílù le.*
Oh I see! I hope I won't get lost.

Local: *Búyàojǐn, zài suóyǒu de dìtiězhàn dōuyǒu dìtú guàzài qiáng shàng. Hěn fāngbiàn a!*

Don't worry, there are maps on the walls in all the subway stations. It's very convenient!

Tourist: *Xièxie!*

Thank you very much!

China's immense population has led to great overcrowding in all the urban areas. Because of this, you'll almost never see people waiting patiently in an orderly line. Boarding buses and trains is a free-for-all, so don't be surprised if you find yourself pushed or bumped into. Just keep your head down, brace yourself, and push forward yourself.

Bus Banter

Chinese	English
dàxué	university
dàyuē	approximately
cónglái meí / cónglái bù	never
tōngzhī	notify, inform

TRACK 29

Tourist: *Láojià, zhè lù chē qù Xiānggāng dàxué ma?*
Excuse me, does this bus go to the University of Hong Kong?

Local: *Shì.*
Yes, it does.

Tourist: *Dào nàr xūyào duōcháng shíjiān?*
How long does it take to get there?

Local: *Dàyuē xūyào sìshí fēnzhōng.*
It takes about 40 minutes.

Tourist: *Wǒ cónglái dōu méi qù guò, wǒ zěnme huì zhīdào zài nǎr xiàchē?*
I have never been there before, how will I know where to get off?

Local: *Dào zhàn de shíhòu wǒ huì tōngzhī nǐ.*
I will tell you when we arrive at the stop.

Tourist: *Xièxie.*
Thank you.

Maps

There are many travel agencies and tour associations in both the Americas and Europe that offer package sightseeing tours to China. Seasoned travelers generally prefer to go it alone and explore independently. Tour groups for China, however, are a good way to avoid some of the headaches involved in Chinese bureaucracy that make traveling around China occasionally troublesome for the lone Westerner. That said, there's still satisfaction in striking out on your own.

Tour groups focus on the most popular of sites, as they are catered to groups. But everyone has their own individual tastes and interests. Being able to get around on your own will enable you to see sights you might not have otherwise gotten to see. For example, few organized tours include visits to China's public parks and gardens. Somewhat unlike parks in the United States where nature simply takes its course, Chinese parks are often elaborately landscaped. In fact, the word for park in Chinese is *gōngyuán*, which translates literally as "public garden." This is what Chinese parks more closely resemble. Get a map with Hanyu Pinyin on it and feel free to wander off on your own. Knowing how to ask the way to various sites will help you.

Tour Talk

Chinese	English
qián	straight
biān	side
zuǒ	left
zuǒbian	left side
yòu	right
yòubiān	rightside
guǎi	to turn
gōngyuán	park
lùkǒu	corner

TRACK 30

Tourist: *Láojià, qǐng wèn dào Béihǎi gōngyuán zěnme zǒu?*
Excuse me, can you tell me how to get
to Beihai Park?

Local: *Wǎngqián zǒu, dào lùkǒu xiàng yòu guǎi.*
Go straight ahead down this road and then turn
right at the street corner.

Tourist: *Lí zhèr yuǎn bùyuǎn?*
Is it far from here?

Local: *Bú tài yuǎn. Cóng nàr zài zǒu shí tiáo lù, na nǐ
jiùdào le. Dàyuē zǒu shíwǔ fēnzhōng.*
No, not at all; from there walk about another
ten streets. It's about a fifteen-minute walk.

Taxis

Taxis abound in China in numbers about as great as buses. The taxis are all
mostly privatized, and several companies compete with each other for riders. You'll find taxis roaming free in most developed areas of the cities. Inside

the taxis, the driver is separated by a plastic partition from the front passenger seat and the back of the car. Drivers are usually formally dressed with a button-down shirt, dress pants, and even white gloves. Depending on the city you're in, the base fare can be anywhere from 5 RMB to 10 RMB. Taxi drivers can be hit or miss. They will rarely if ever be able to speak English; in areas of the country where there is a local dialect that is distinct from Mandarin, they may only speak that language. Don't lose heart! Just use your Chinese!

Just as in the United States, China has both legitimate taxis and illegal taxis. In China the illegal ones are called "black taxis," and you should be wary of them. Sometimes the black taxi drivers will try to negotiate a deal to chauffer you about for the day, and not just to and from your destination. As appealing as this may sound, you should be aware that they have no insurance and will bear no liability if you happen to get into an accident or another sticky situation. The overwhelming majority of legitimate taxis in China bear the logos of their companies. Look for those.

Chinese Addresses

Chinese addresses basically run to the reverse of U.S. addresses. The format looks something like this: country, province/municipality, city, district, street, block, building number or name, flat number/suite/office room number. So, if you had an appointment with Mr. Gao in suite 14 on the seventh floor of the Shēnfāzhàn building, number 1303, on East Shēnnán road in Luóhú district in Shenzhen, it might sound something like this:

Driver:	*Nín yào chūzūchē ma?* Do you need a cab?
Passenger:	*Shìde. Wǒ yào.* Yes, I do.
Driver:	*Qǐng shàng chē.* Please get in.

Driver:	*Qù nǎlǐ a?*
	Where to?

Passenger:	*Wǒ xiǎng qù Luóhúqū, Shēnnán dōng lù yāo*
	sān líng sān hào, Shēnfāzhàn dàshà.
	I'm going to the Shenfazhàn building, number 1303,
	on East Shennán road in Luóhúdistrict.

Driver:	*Zěnme zǒu?*
	Any particular route?

Passenger:	*Zuì kuài de zǒufā jiù kéyǐ.*
	No, however is fastest is fine.

Driver:	*Hǎo.*
	Okay.

Passenger:	*Xūyào dàyuē duōcháng shíjiān?*
	About how long should it take?

Driver:	*Rúguǒ jiāotōng bú tài jǐ, zhǐ xūyào búdào shíwǔ*
	fēnzhōng de shíjiān.
	If traffic is light, it should take no more than
	fifteen minutes.

Being Taken for a Ride

You chose your hotel not only because it offered some delightful services and amenities, but also because of its location. You chose a hotel that is strategically located very close by to all the great sites. You hopped into a cab early so you could beat the crowds at your most anticipated attraction. The concierge said it was only about ten minutes from the hotel, so why have you been driving around for twenty?

Passenger:	*Nǐ huì qù Xīhú ma?*
	Do you know how to get to the West Lake?

Driver: *Huì a. Wǒmén chàbùduō dàole.*
Sure, we're almost there.

Passenger: *Wǒ fàndiànde kān ménrén shuō zhǐ xūyào
búdào shí fēnzhōng de shíjiān.*
The concierge at my hotel said it takes no more than
ten minutes to get there.

Driver: *Shì a, Wǒmén chàbùduō dàole.*
Yes, we're almost there.

Passenger: *Wǒmén zǒule èrshífēnzhōng. Wǒ hái méiyǒu
kàndào shuǐ.*
We've been driving for twenty minutes. I still haven't
seen water.

Driver: *Hǎo, hǎo, Wǒmén kuài dàole.*
It's okay, it's okay, we'll arrive soon.

Driver: *Hǎo, dàole. Qǐng fù wǔshí kuài qián.*
Okay, we're here. That will be 50 RMB.

Passenger: *Wà! Nǐ fēng le ma? Wǒ jùjué fù zhème duō! Nǐ ràole
tài duō wānlù. Wǒ géi nǐ shíwǔ kuài qián.*
Are you nuts? I refuse to pay so much. You drove
completely out of the way. I'll give you 15 RMB.

Driver: *Hǎo, Hǎo, wǒ géi nǐ zhékòu. Sìshí kuài qián.*
Okay, okay, 40 RMB, I'll give you a discount.

Passenger: *Nǐ búyào piàn wǒ. Wǒ gěi nǐ shíwǔ kuài qián, ér wǒ
búyào xiàng dāngjútóusù nǐ.*
Don't cheat me, I'll give you 15 RMB and I won't
report you to the authorities.

Domestic Travel

In the past, residents of expansive cities and remote provinces of China were limited to their immediate vicinity for obtaining goods and services or traveling. However, the Chinese infrastructure is becoming more developed every year. Moving people to and fro between regions and provinces and within cities becomes easier and more convenient every year.

Intercity Buses

The intercity long-distance bus system in China is by far the most convenient method for traveling around the country. The convenience is marked by the fact that the tickets are easier to secure than train tickets, not to mention cheaper. Furthermore, buses go practically everywhere. Of course, buses also tend to be less comfortable than trains. Buses can be in horrendous states of repair and comfort, and the competency of the drivers is questionable at best. If the buses themselves aren't a deterrent enough, sometimes the road conditions can really frighten travelers. Luckily, newer buses pop up more and more, though you still have no way of knowing if you'll get one.

Intercity Trains

A big step up from the bus system, trains are only slightly less popular for long-distance travel in China. The quality of service is a step up from the buses, too. You have your choice of four classes of comfort: hard seat, soft seat, hard sleeper, and soft sleeper. Naturally, they all increase in price from hard seat up. Hard seat is exactly what it says: a hard, upright chair you sit on for the whole trip. Next up from that is soft seat, which is much more comfortable and less crowded. Then there is hard sleeper, which is your choice of three beds: bottom, middle, and top bunk. Hard sleeper beds come with sheets and a pillow. Soft sleeper is the most comfortable way to travel on a train, as well as the most expensive. Tickets can be hard to get, especially near holidays, as so many people travel then. Often, you cannot buy your ticket too far in advance, as the schedules are only published several times a year. It's very possible you won't be able to buy your ticket round trip from your point of origin; you may have to buy a return from your destination. It's best to be specific.

Train Talk

Chinese	English
piào	ticket
fā	set off, launch
chē	vehicle
fāchē	to depart
xiàwǔ	afternoon
chēcì	train number
tè	special; especially
kuài	fast
tèkuài	express
dìng	reserve
děng	wait; class/type
cāng	cabin/compartment
yìng	hard
ruǎn	soft
zuò	sit; seat
wò	recline; sleep
pù	berth
dānchéng	one way
láihuí	round trip

TRACK 31

Passenger: *Wǒ xiáng mǎi yìzhāng dào Guìlín de piào.*
I'd like to buy a ticket to Guilin.

Ticket Clerk:	*Jǐ hào chūfā?*
	On what day would you like to depart?
Passenger:	*Míngtiān xiàwǔ kéyǐ ma?*
	Would tomorrow afternoon be possible?
Ticket Clerk:	*Kéyǐ. Míngtiān xiàwǔ wǔshíbā cì tèkuài chē, kéyǐ ma?*
	Yes. The Number 58 express train is available.
Passenger:	*Hǎo, qǐng dìng piào.*
	Good, please reserve the ticket.
Ticket Clerk:	*Nín xiǎng zuò jíděng cāng?*
	What class would you like?
Passenger:	*Wǒ yào ruǎnwòpù.*
	I want soft sleeper.
Ticket Clerk:	*Hǎo, dānchéng, háishì láihuí?*
	Okay. One way or round trip?
Passenger:	*Láihuí.*
	Round trip.
Ticket Clerk:	*Hǎo, Sān bǎi kuài qián*
	Okay, that will be 300 RMB.

Exercises

Now it's time to see what you've learned about getting around China. The following exercises include information covered in various parts of this chapter. Try to answer the questions from memory first, and then refer back to earlier pages if you need to jog your memory or perfect spelling.

1. Translate the following sentences into English:

   Èr hào xiàn Jiāngsū lù dìtiězhàn wǎng dōng zǒu sāntiáo lù.

   ....

Wăngqián zŏu, dào lùkŏu xiàng zuŏ guăi.

....

2. Put the particle de in the proper place in the following sentences.

   Zhè shì wŏ qìchē.

   ....

   Wŏ măi qìchē hĕn guì.

   ....

   Hóngsè qìchē shì wŏ.

   ....

3. Read the following English sentences and choose whether the verb to be is stative (*hĕn*) or equative (*shì*).

   This coat is quite lovely.   ....

   I'm worried.   ....

   My wife is a banker.   ....

4. Ask for two one-way train tickets to Beijing in Chinese.

   ....

5. Render the following address into Chinese and in Chinese format:
   100 Guilin Road, Xuhui District, Shanghai, China.

   ....

Chapter 7

Beginning Conversation

More and more people are going to China for business as well as pleasure. Your stay could be anywhere from two weeks to two months. Seeing the same faces day after day is simply an invitation to just say hi. Getting to know the people around you will make you feel more at home. The Chinese will take it as an immense compliment if you try to greet them in Chinese. Give it a try and see how many doors it opens for you.

Salutations and Greetings

Be brave. You never know what opportunities may arise from building the bridges of communication between people. Travelers are the type of people who wish to learn about life, the world around them, and themselves. They are idealists, adventurers, and romantics. A "hello," or *níhǎo*, is an invitation to a whole new dimension of your visit to China. So don't hold back. Greetings are the beginning of language mastery.

Taking the First Step

Níhǎo is by far the most common simple greeting in Chinese. It translates to "hello" but is usually taken to mean "are you well?" As you can see *níhǎo* is lacking the question particle *ma*, so you might ask how it can be translated to "are you well?" Well, put simply, it is for that reason and the fact that *níhǎo* is used much like "hello" (the response would simply be another congenial *níhǎo*) that "hello" seems to be a more satisfactory translation. This greeting can also be modified for more specificity by replacing the initial subject with another as seen here:

Lǎoshī hǎo.	**Hello teacher.**
Jīnglǐ hǎo.	**Hello manager.**
Gāo xiáojiě hǎo.	**Hello Ms. Gao.**

If you were to add the question particle to the end of *níhǎo*, making it *níhǎo ma*, you would then be asking "how are you?" The typical and polite way to respond to *níhǎo ma* is by saying *hén hǎo* (I'm fine). But you are by no means restricted to this. In fact, there are a number of more colloquial ways to respond to this question, including the following.

Responses to Níhǎo ma

búcuò	not bad
hái kéyǐ	not bad
méiyǒu shénme kěbàoyuànde	I can't complain.
mámǎ hūhū	so-so

More Choices

While *nǐhǎo ma* is the textbook traditional way of greeting someone and asking how they are, it is not the only way to ask. Perhaps this is because "hello" and "how are you" are so similar in Chinese that there are more colloquial ways to inquire after someone. In some regions of China they are more widely used than *nǐhǎo ma*.

Perhaps influenced by the English way of asking "how" someone is, another common way of saying "how are you" is *Nǐ zěnmeyàng?* or *Zěnmeyàng a?* Literally, this means "How are you?"

A very traditional and very Chinese greeting still used commonly literally translates as "Have you eaten?" Here are three ways to say this in Chinese:

Chī le ma?

Chī le méiyǒu?

Nǐ chīfàn le ma?

The correct response to this question is *chīle* if you have eaten and *méichī* if you have not eaten. The important thing to remember here is that this is just a traditional, simple greeting. The person is not truly asking out of a desire to know if you've eaten or not.

If it's been a while since you've seen your friend, and you're catching up, you can say something like:

Hǎo cháng shíjiān bújiàn!   **Long time no see!**

Another very popular though very colloquial expression has manifested likely as a result of China's economic boom. In a day-to-day life when most Chinese are working long hours in a growing white collar economy, the expression *Nǐ zài nǎr gāojiù a?* has emerged. It can be taken to mean "What have you been up to?" but literally means "Where have you been advancing work-wise?" Either way, you can presume to answer the question honestly with something like *Wǒ zuìjìn hěn máng* (I've been quite busy recently), *wǒ gānggāng kāishǐ xīn de gōngzuò* (I just recently started a new job), or *wǒ háishì gànhuí wǒde láoběnháng* (I've gone back to my original line of work).

Special Occasions

Who doesn't love a good party? And what are get-togethers for if not to mix, mingle, and make friends? Even if your Chinese is less than perfect, take advantage of the opportunity and find new friends for language exchange. The Chinese have tons of their own holidays and have also begun celebrating some Western secular holidays such as Halloween, Christmas, and European New Year.

Happy Birthday

Birthday celebrations are more of a Western tradition, but like many other Western traditions, birthday celebrations are catching on in China. The Chinese enjoy any form of celebration, so the idea of cake, candles, singing, and presents is a very easy tradition to pick up. The usual expression for happy birthday is:

Zhù nín shēngrì kuàilè.	**May your birthday be happy.**

There are three ways of asking someone his or her age in Chinese. The most common of these is:

Nín jǐ suì le?	**Literally: How much is your age?**

Other ways include:

Nín duōdà le?	**Literally: How great are you?**
Nín duōdà niánjì le?	**Literally: How great is your age?**

Asking this question with *nín* softens the blow. It is still out of the question for you to ask a woman her age, regardless of how young she may appear. Also, regardless of how you may ask this question, there is still only one way to answer it. You must use the format of the first question.

Wǒ sānshí sān suì le.	**I'm thirty-three.**

The word *suì* is both a noun and a measure word. As a measure word, you can use *suì* in a sentence like, *wǒde háizǐ sān sì suì le.* My children are three and four. You can use it as a noun when saying *qùsuì* (last year) or *fùsuì* (good year) if you'd like to sound a bit more poetic in place of using the word *nián*. Unlike many other countries, China does not have a specific age at which you come of age. In Latin America it is fifteen and sixteen, the sweet sixteen party is well known in the United States, and in Japan it is the age of twenty. In China, eighteen is the age at which you become a legal adult, but it is not widely celebrated. Considering how fast trends catch on in China, that may change sooner rather than later.

Congratulations!

Life is a cause for celebration. With luck, during your stay in China you will have myriad reasons and occasions to celebrate. The more intertwined your life becomes with the locals and natives you see daily, the more you will learn about them. Whose son just graduated from middle school? Whose daughter just got married? Who just had a baby? You may be in a number of situations where offering congratulations may be in order. The basic component for wishing someone a hearty congratulations is the word *gōngxǐ*. The occasion for which you're offering the congratulatory wishes will follow it, as shown here:

TRACK 32

Gōngxǐ ní mǎifáng le.	**Congratulations on the new home.**
Gōngxǐ nǐ shēng zhí le.	**Congratulations on the promotion.**
Gōngxǐ nǐ mén shēng le ge háizǐ.	**Congratulations on your new baby.**
Gōngxǐ nǐ bìyè le.	**Congratulations on your graduation.**

If you're not exactly sure what the occasion is or how to say it, a hearty *gōngxǐ gōngxǐ*, will definitely suffice. Sometimes you don't have to worry about specificity.

Sympathies

Life brings change—sometimes for the worse. Hopefully, you will never need to express your sympathies to someone on the passing of a loved one. But you never know; you should be prepared. Nothing would be more touching than offering your condolences in the native language of the bereaved. You can be sensitive, eloquent, and show your concern all at the same time. A very formal way to express your sympathy on someone's passing would be:

[Name of deceased] *qùshì, wǒ jǐnzhì āidào zhī chén.*

Allow me to convey my most profound condolences on the passing of (name of deceased).

QUESTION?

Do mourners in China dress in black as they do in other countries?
When someone is in mourning in China, it is traditional for the family members to don a piece of black cloth on their arm. The black cloth can be any size or design, and in the past it was traditionally worn for forty-nine days. China has many elaborate mourning rituals. Today, however, they have been adapted for urban living in the modern age. The hēibù (black cloth) is worn only for a week or so now.

Qùshì is a polite way of saying "to pass away." Literally, it means, "to leave this world." *Qùshì* is an eloquent way of saying "to pass on, or communicate formally." *Chén* is a powerful word meaning sincerity, warmth of heart, and cordiality. There are other options for expressing your sympathies:

*Qǐng jiēshòu wǒ chéngzhì   **Please accept my sincerest
    de āidào.*   condolences.**

Or you can simply say:

Wǒ shēngǎn bēitòng.   **Literally: I deeply feel great sadness
                                for you.**

All the Long Day

The Chinese people can be an interesting dichotomy. Though they are often shy around new people, they are quite jovial with friends and rather easy to befriend. A smile and a greeting once will earn you another each time you cross paths with someone. Walking around the streets of China you'll see friends standing together laughing and joking at all hours of the day. There are greetings for each time of the day, and they're all fairly easy to remember.

To Start Off

Ride a bicycle, take a cab, ride the Metro, or hop in your company's shuttle. The day starts off with an enthusiastic good morning to your friends and neighbors. In Chinese, one way of saying that is *zǎoshànghǎo*. But this is not the only way of saying it. You can also say *zǎoān*, or simply *zǎo*. Your choice of expression may be directly proportional to how awake and alert you are at the time. For those who don't rise and shine so swiftly, a short and sweet *zǎo* is the preferred morning greeting. But as you've no doubt already found, Chinese are rich in overlapping meaning. *Zǎo* is not only the noun for "morning," it can be an adjective as well meaning early or soon. The word for breakfast is *zǎofàn* or *zǎocān* meaning morning rice or morning meal. Along with all the different ways of saying good morning, there are also a handful of different ways of waking up. Some examples of them are as follows:

TRACK 33

Wǒ jīntiān zǎoshàng wǔ diǎn bàn qǐchuáng.

I woke up this morning at 5:30.

Měitiān zǎoshàng yángguāng huànxǐng wǒ.

The sunshine wakes me up every morning.

Wǒ dìdī bí wǒ zǎo yīdiǎnr qǐchuáng.

My brother wakes up earlier than I do.

Midday

The notion of noon being 12:00 P.M. is a Western idea. From this word noon, we get the English word afternoon, which is generally thought of as the time between noon and around 5:00 P.M. In China, however, the word for midday is *zhōngwǔ*, but it does not specifically correspond to 12:00 P.M. Traditionally, *wǔ* is regarded as the hours between 11:00 A.M. and 1:00 P.M. and not a specific time. Lunch in Chinese is *wǔfàn*, or *wǔcān*. The Chinese translation for afternoon is *xiàwǔ*, or "after *wǔ*," and is usually regarded as the hours between 2:00 P.M. and 6:00 P.M.

FACT

Like many Latin American and European nations, China has a midday "siesta" called the *wǔshuì*. It is usually from 12:00 P.M. to 2:00 P.M. and runs only during the warm months (May through October). During this time, most schools and businesses close temporarily.

As you've seen in previous chapters the directional adverb *shàng* means "on top of," "prior to," or "previous," while *xià* means "beneath," "afterwards," or "next." Knowing that *xiàwǔ* is "after *wǔ*," and *zhōngwǔ* is "mid-*wǔ*," it would stand to reason that *shàngwǔ* would mean the period of time prior to midday. This is true but also somewhat problematic, as it begs the following question: "Well, if *zǎoshàng* is morning, when is *shàngwǔ*?" If you feel the conversation is coming to a lull, and wish to elicit a major debate, ask a group of Chinese what the difference between *shàngwǔ* and *zǎoshàng* is. The most common expression for good afternoon is *xiàwǔ hǎo*. But, of course, like most other time expressions in Chinese, it is also an adverbial modifier to help clarify when an event is taking place, as in: *Wǒ xiàwǔ sāndiǎnzhōng shàngkè.* (I have a lecture at 3 P.M.)

Nightfall

In Chinese there is no difference between evening and night,; the traditional word is *yèwǎn*, but it is a literary expression. The more common expression for "evening" or "night" is *wǎnshàng*. Many Chinese dictionaries and phrase books translate "good evening" and "good night" using the same Chinese expression *wǎnān*, similar to *zǎoān* (good morning). But this is inaccurate, as *wǎnān* more closely corresponds to "good night" alone. You say *wǎnān* to someone before going to bed. The nighttime greeting that more closely resembles the English "good evening" would be *wǎnshàng hǎo*.

Time References

Chinese does not have a past or future tense in the same way that English does. Instead, Chinese communicates variations in time using aspect, time referents, and other adverbial modifiers. As a result, it is always important to specify at what point in time an event took place. Below is a table of various time referents.

Time Referents

jīntiān	today
zuótiān	yesterday
míngtiān	tomorrow
jīntiān zǎoshàng	this morning
jīntiān xiàwǔ	this afternoon
jīntiān wǎnshàng	this evening/tonight
zuótiān zǎoshàng	yesterday morning
míngtiān xiàwǔ	tomorrow afternoon
qiántiān	the day before yesterday
hòutiān	the day after tomorrow
sāntiān hòu	three days from now
sāntiān qián	three days ago
jīnnián	this year
qùnián	last year
míngnián	next year
liǎngge yuè hòu	two months from now

Paying a Visit

Most cities in China are giving birth to new modern housing projects all over the place. These housing communities may differ somewhat in architecture, but they all share a certain number of commonalities. Most of the communities are gated in some way with a security guard kiosk at the entrance, and most buildings have some sort of concierge or manager. The concierge or building manager either sits at a desk or in a modest office affording him a view of the entrance and lobby.

FACT

There is no colloquial way of saying "to visit" in Chinese. When you go to pay a visit to a friend, you'd simply say *qù kàn péngyǒu* (go to see a friend). The closest equivalent to visiting is *fǎngwèn*, and it sounds more like "paying someone a visit" than simply dropping by for tea. It also means "to interview."

Even though China is a huge nation with an unfathomable population, sometimes it will feel very much like a small town. The concierge of the building where your friends live will undoubtedly possess every secret and snippet of information regarding every resident of the building. Passing through the lobby may be slightly harder than passing through customs. Be prepared for a greeting:

Huānyíng! Nín guòlái kàn péngyǒu ma?	**Welcome! Have you come to visit friends?**
Nín zhǎo shéi?	**Who are you looking for?**
Qǐng jìnlái!	**Please come in!**

Thank You for Having Me

You won't have to spend much time in China to discover that the Chinese are superb hosts and supremely hospitable. A visit to a Chinese friend's home will wow you with the comfortable atmosphere and attentive nature of the family. Chinese extend blanket invitations to their friends and family to visit. So, if you simply stop by you'll be most welcomed. In general, Chinese are also aware that dropping in uninvited is a faux pas among Westerners, and Americans in particular, and will likely wait for you to extend an invitation to them. When you arrive at a Chinese friend's home you'll be immediately ushered in:

Qǐng jìn, qǐng jìn!   **Please come in!**

Similarly, if you are entertaining friends or colleagues be sure to welcome them into your home enthusiastically:

Qǐng jìnlái zuò!   **Please come in and have a seat!**

You'll also no doubt take note of how great a virtue humility is deemed in Chinese culture; displaying humility yourself will be regarded as exceedingly polite and welcoming. Once you have been invited in to the house, pour on the charm. One of the most polite expressions you can use is *bùhǎoyìsī, dárǎo nǐ le*. This phrase is laden with humility, as you're apologizing for being an inconvenient disturbance. The expression *bùhǎoyìsī* literally means "to be embarrassed," and it is used alone to mean "I'm sorry." The verb *dárǎo* means to disturb or trouble. Naturally, your Chinese host will never allow you to feel that way and will quickly dismiss your apology by saying *nálǐ nálǐ. Nálǐ* literally means "where" and is often used to humbly skirt a compliment or other such homage. By apologizing for disturbing your host, you will certainly be paying her a compliment.

When to Depart

As surely as you arrived, so you should not be in a rush to leave. It's true you shouldn't wear out your welcome, but at the same time, if you seem too anxious to leave your hosts will no doubt take it that you are dissatisfied with their hospitality. Chinese love to chat, debate, and generally entertain, so sit tight and enjoy the night. Even if it's getting late, you'll likely get a *shíjiān hái hén zǎo, zài duō zuò yīhuìr* (It's early yet, stay a little longer). You should stay a bit longer so as not to disappoint your hosts, but it's completely appropriate to decide on a time that you finally will leave. You can say it like this:

Hǎo, wǒ jiù duō zuò yīhuìr, dànshì zuìwǎn liú dào shíyī diǎn zhōng.

Okay, I'll stay a little longer, but I can stay no later than 11 P.M.

Then just sit back, relax, and have another cup of tea. When 11:00 starts rolling around and it's time to go you can begin saying your goodbyes with:

Nà wǒ yǐjīng hěn dárǎo nínmén le!

Literally: Well, I've already troubled you enough.

Follow this up with:

Hěn gǎnxiè nínmén de shèngqíng kuǎndài.

Thank you so much for the lavish hospitality.

Don't be afraid to extend an invitation to your hosts to allow you the opportunity to repay them for their kindness.

Xīwàng wǒmén xiàcì zài yǒu jīhuì chīfàn. Xiàcì wǒ qǐng kè.

Hopefully we can do this again. I'll treat you next time.

If you were the host, you can say:

Qǐng zàilái wánr ba!

Please do come back!

The word *wánr* literally means "to play," but figuratively it means "to have fun" or "to spend time," or even more colloquially, "to hang out." Thus, the sentence, *wǒ shàngge zhōumò hé péngyǒu zài yìqǐ wánr*, should be read as "Last weekend, I spent time with my friends."

I've Heard So Much about You!

Chinese is a remarkable and quite poetic language. What requires a full sentence of English can often be rendered in half the words in Chinese. Many terse Chinese expressions come from literary Chinese, whose style of expression was more stylized. Words and characters as used in literary Chinese embody a great deal of meaning. An example of such an expression in modern use is *jiŭyăng dàmíng*. This expression translates roughly as "I've been so hoping we'd meet," "I've been so looking forward to seeing you," or "I've heard so much about you." The appropriate response is *bĭcĭ, bĭcĭ,* which means "likewise."

An exchange between friends who may have recently met or been introduced by others may go something like this:

TRACK 34

Friend 1:	*Jiŭyăng dàmíng.*	
	I've heard so much about you.	
Friend 2:	*Bĭcĭ, bĭcĭ, zhēn shì xìnghuì.*	
	Likewise, what a fortunate coincidence that we meet.	
Friend 1:	*Lín xiáojiĕ tánle hăo duō guānyúnĭde shìqíng.*	
	Ms. Lin has spoken a great deal about you.	
Friend 2:	*Xīwàng nà guānyú wŏde shìqíng dōu bú shì huài de.*	
	I hope it was all good.	
Friend 1:	*Wánquán bú shì huài de.*	
	Absolutely, it was all good.	

Exercises

Now you know how to greet people on your travels in China. But do you remember everything you just read? The following exercises include information covered in various parts of this chapter. Try to answer the questions from memory first, and then refer back to earlier pages if you need to jog your memory or perfect spelling.

1. What does *mámǎ hūhū* mean?

   ....

2. Match the Chinese greeting with its corresponding English greeting.

xiàwǔ hǎo	have you eaten
zěnmeyàng a	good night
jiǔyǎng dàmíng	good evening
chīle ma	how are you
wǎnān	I've heard so much about you
wǎnshàng hǎo	good afternoon

3. Fill in the missing expression:

   .... *dárǎo nín le.*

4. Rearrange the words to make a sentence: *zài xiàcì xīwàng, jīhuì chīfàn, yǒu, wǒmen.*

   ....

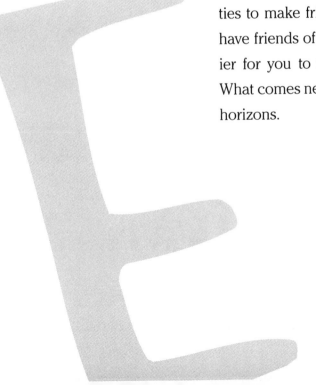

Chapter 8

Making Friends

Walking the streets of Chinese cities, particularly areas apart from the tourist zones, you may find you attract a lot of attention. Curious stares and inquisitive smiles just might accompany the whispers. If you're lucky someone will attempt to chat with you. Use these opportunities to make friends. These new friends have friends of their own, making it easier for you to meet more new people. What comes next will only broaden your horizons.

Grammar Lesson: Complement of Degree

It's a well known fact that English is the most commonly spoken second language in the world. It's regarded as the language of commerce. With China currently invested in one of the most profound economic booms of the twentieth and twenty-first centuries, it is no small wonder that the demand to learn English in China would also boom. English schools abound and most universities are stepping up English requirements across the board. CDs and software are all well and good, but in terms of practice nothing beats a native speaker. If you happen to be in a tourist or shopping area, don't be at all surprised if Chinese people, especially young people, eye you eagerly in the hopes of practicing some of their English. The Chinese are generally a shy people, so they may not approach you. Many Chinese are embarrassed to make mistakes, and so they will stay away. Break the ice yourself by showing them that the only way to improve is with practice:

Nǐ huì shuō yīngyǔ ma?	**Do you speak English?**

Chinese humility may force the young person to deny any English ability, even if he has it. Although he may have passed CET 7 (English aptitude test) with flying colors, he may still say:

Duìbùqǐ, wǒ bú huì shuō yīngyǔ.	**I'm sorry, I don't speak English.**
Wǒ tīngbùdǒng yīngyǔ.	**I don't understand English.**

If he feels somewhat adventurous you might get:

Wǒ tīngdedǒng yīngyǔ,
     kěshì wǒ shuōde bútài hǎo.
	I understand English, but I can't
	     speak it well.

Wǒ huì shuō yīdiǎnr yīngyǔ.	**I speak a little English.**
Wǒ huì shuō yīngyǔ, kěshì *shuōde bù liúlì.*	**I can speak English, but not fluently.**

Complement of Degree

Having learned the phrases in the previous section, you're probably wondering why there are adjectives following the verb + *de* constructions instead of nouns. The reason for that is because the particle *de* used in the previous sentences is not the same particle *de* used to form adjectives or nominal phrases. Though they are rendered the same way in Hanyu Pinyin and articulated identically, they are different characters in written Chinese.

The *de* used in the sentences is part of a very commonly used phrase construction in Chinese called the complement of degree (COD). A verb or adjective may take on this particle and another verb or adjective in order to communicate the degree, extent, or quality of the action denoted by the verb or the characteristic denoted by the adjective. The simplest complements of degree consist of a verb, the complement particle *de* (COD *de*), and an adjective. However, an adjective functioning as a stative verb in Chinese can also take on the complement of degree construction. That is what distinguishes this construction from simply being an adverbial phrase.

Using the Complement of Degree

Often we can use a complement of degree to indicate an action that has already been realized or that occurs with frequency. In the sentences in the last section, the complement of degree construction is being used in three ways. In the sentence *Wǒ tīngdedǒng yīngyǔ, kěshì wǒ shuōde bútài hǎo,* the COD *de* appears in the first portion of the sentence, between *tīng* and *dǒng. Tīngdǒng* is a resultative complement verb, which means that *dǒng* (understand) is the result of the initial *tīng* (listen). When the COD *de* is placed between the components of a resultative complement verb, it communicates capacity. So, the first part of the sentence means "I can understand." In the second portion of the sentence the COD *de* follows the verb *shuō* (speak), and precedes *bútài hǎo* (not too well), an adjectival phrase. In this position, the COD *de* functions to convey the meaning that the adjectival phrase is the degree to which the verb is expressed. Thus, it means "don't speak it so well."

Finally, the complement of degree construction manifests in the sentence *wǒ tīngbùdǒng yīngyǔ.* In this case, the COD *de* is not used; it is instead negated. In order to negate a sentence with a verbal predicate and the complement of degree, you simply replace the particle *de* with the negator *bù*. So, the previous sentence means "I cannot understand English."

Twenty Questions

As much as China has opened up in the last few decades, the reality is that foreigners, particularly non-Asians, are still quite a novelty in her cities and streets. Whether you like being the center of attention or not, you most certainly will get attention. Don't be put off if young people approach you to practice their English. See it as an opportunity for you to also get some Chinese practice. In many universities in China, it is very common for international students to take part in school-organized language exchange activities with the Chinese students. In this format you'll no doubt be confronted with dozens of questions. You should know how to ask them in return if this is going to be a true language exchange:

TRACK 35

Nǐ cóng nǎr lái?	**Where do you come from?**
Nǐ shì nǎguórén?	**What country are you from?**
Nǐ shì měiguó nǎzhōu rén?	**What state in the United States are you from?**
Nǐ cóng měiguó shénme dìfāng lái?	**What part of the United States do you come from?**
Nǐ xǐhuān zhōngguó ma?	**Do you like China?**
Nǐ lái zhōngguó dùjià ma?	**Are you in China on vacation?**
Nǐ lái zhōngguó duōjiǔ le?	**How long have you been in China?**
Nǐ qùguò zhōngguó bié de dìfāng ma?	**Have you been to other parts of China?**
Nǐ qùguò duōshǎo guójiā?	**How many countries have you been to?**

Twenty Answers

No, you're not passing through customs again, though it may feel like it. All the undo attention may seem unsettling at first, but remember you're a guest in a distant nation whose contact with everyday Westerners is still relatively novel. Take a deep breath, and take comfort in knowing that these people are genuinely interested in you. That can be a genuinely nice feeling. So, once you've got a handle on what's been asked of you thus far, try to answer as best you can. In turn try to ask your own questions:

TRACK 36

Wǒ cóng niǔyuēshì lái.	**I'm from New York City.**
Niǔyuēshì shì niǔyuēzhōu de yíbùfèn.	**New York City is in New York State.**
Fóluólǐdá zhōu zài měiguó nánbù.	**Florida is in the southern United States.**
Jiùjīnshān zài měiguó xīàn.	**San Francisco is on the west coast of the United States.**
Xīyàtú zài měiguó xīběibù.	**Seattle is in the northwest region of the United States.**
Zhījiāgē zài měiguó zhōngbù.	**Chicago is in the central United States.**

Favorites

Do you have any favorite things? If you've never considered this question, it's best to start sooner rather than later. One of the Chinese English student's favorite things to ask is what *your* favorite things are. Here are some questions you may be asked:

TRACK 37

Nǐ zuì xǐhuān de yánsè shì shénme?	**What's your favorite color?**
Nǐ xǐhuān chǒngwù ma?	**Do you like pets?**
Nǐ xǐhuān zhōngguócài ma?	**Do you like Chinese food?**

Nǐ zuì xǐhuān de jìjié shì shénme?	**What's your favorite season of the year?**
Nǐ zuì xǐhuān de yīnyuè shì názhǒng?	**What is your favorite kind of music?**
Nǐ zuì xǐhuān de měiguó zuòjiā shì shéi?	**Who is your favorite American author?**
Nǐ xǐhuān zúqiú ma?	**Do you like soccer?**

As you can see there's no one single word for "favorite." In Chinese you express your like for something by calling it your "most liked" or what you "like the most."

Favorite Responses

You should, of course, answer as honestly as possible; but diplomacy always calls for a little tact. Don't be hesitant to express a dislike for something, but just remember you attract more flies with honey than with vinegar. There are certain questions they may ask that will hit a nerve and possibly arouse a negative memory or experience. Just bear in mind that it's usually better to express a negative attitude gently:

Xǐhuān, qíshí, wó yǒu liǎng zhī māo.	**Yes, I like pets, in fact, I have two cats.**
Wǒ méiyǒu tèbié xǐhuān dex zuòjiā shì shéi?	**I don't have a particularly favorite American author.**
Wǒ zuì xǐhuān chūntiān.	**I like the spring most.**
Wǒ zhēn xǐhuān zhōngguó cài.	**I really like Chinese food.**
Wǒ cónglái méi tīngshuōguò Michael Learns to Rock.	**I've never heard of Michael Learns to Rock.**
Bù, wǒ bú tài xǐhuān zúqiú.	**No, I don't really care for soccer.**

As you can see, the format for expressing your likes and dislikes is very simple. The verb *xǐhuān* can be augmented with the superlative modifier *zuì* (most) giving you "most liked" meaning "favorite." You can augment feeling and mood with other select adverbial modifiers like *zhěn* (true) and *tèbié* (especially). Using these modifiers and the negator word *bù*, you can tactfully soften any negative comment.

Shall We Get Personal?

Well, the fact is whether you like it or not you more than likely will get more personal with your language partners. Remember that China is a different land. Every nation on Earth has not only its own laws and customs but its own standards of propriety. On of the most distinct cultural differences between China and the West is the standard of propriety regarding personal information. Often, what your average American considers private or personal information is not regarded as terribly private by the average Chinese person. So you should prepare yourself to face questions such as:

Ní jǐ suì le?	**How old are you?**
Nǐ jiéhūn le méiyǒu?	**Are you married?**
Nǐ yǒu méiyǒu nán/nǚ péngyǒu?	**Do you have a boy/girlfriend?**
Nǐ yǒu duōzhòng?	**How much do you weigh?**
Nǐ yuè/niánxīn duōshǎo?	**How much do you earn a month/ year?**
Nǐ zūfèi duōshǎo?	**How much is your rent?**

No, you haven't misread any of this. An enduring stay in China will show you that the Chinese have very different ideas regarding privacy and personal space. In terms of privacy, the Chinese attitude can be gathered from a popular saying: "Why lock your door unless you're doing something bad?" These particular kinds of questions would be regarded by the Chinese as simply factual information as commonplace as your birthday or e-mail address.

FACT

This question-and-answer format is something that would be quite familiar to many Chinese English students. In an effort to get English practitioners to meet and learn from each other, many schools engage in a language practice activity very much like this called *Yīngyǔ jiǎo* (English Corner). Many schools of varied levels employ foreign teachers who often take part in these gatherings.

The Art of Evasion

As more and more Chinese are learning English, they learn about Western culture. Along with this knowledge, naturally, comes Western ideas of propriety. Quite often, the more well read English students will be aware of the difference in norms between the two cultures. But, many an unknowing but well-meaning novice English student will casually ask these questions. Now, simply being asked these questions does not mean that you should feel compelled to answer them. As much as it may feel like you're being interrogated, you are quite free to refuse to answer any question you don't feel comfortable answering. Not to worry, though; you can refuse to answer these questions politely:

Bùhǎo yìsī, bù fāngbiàn huídá.

Literally: I'm sorry, it would be inconvenient to respond.

Figuratively: If it's all the same to you, I'd rather not answer that.

If you don't want to outright refuse to answer a question this way, you can parry, block, and otherwise evade such questions tactfully, as shown here:

Wǒ bú quèdìng wǒquèqiè de zhòngliàng.	I'm not sure what my exact weight is.
Wǒ rèn wéi shōurù píngjūn.	I think my income is average.
Zūfèi bútài gāo.	The rent is not too high.

A Matter of Family

Since the 1970s, China has engaged in a form of family planning to curb their enormous population crisis. This system, known in China as *jìhuà shēngyù*, is known in the West as the "One Child Policy." This system is the focus of a great deal of examination and inspection both in China and abroad. Contrary to reports that it is illegal for Chinese families to have more than one child, according to the terms of the One Child Policy, Chinese families are simply encouraged to have no more than one child. The government maintains the policy through incentives to one child families and fees to multichild households.

FACT

China is the most populous nation on Earth, with a population of over 1.3 billion inhabitants. China's population is the source of countless social obstacles facing her as a nation. Therefore, population control is taken very seriously by the average Chinese person and is viewed as a necessary evil.

Because of the One Child Policy, most Chinese under the age of thirty do not have siblings. So, they will likely ask you a lot of questions about your family. Talking about family is a bit more complicated in Chinese than it is in English, as almost every relation has its own particular term. Here are some examples:

Your Immediate Family

me	*wǒ*
husband	*lǎogōng*
wife	*lǎopó*
elder sister	*jiějie*
younger sister	*mèimei*

elder brother	*gēge*
younger brother	*dìdi*
daughter	*nǚér*
son	*érzi*

Now that you know what to call your family, you're prepared to answer questions about them. For example:

Nǐ yǒuméiyǒu zǐnǚ?	**Do you have children?**
Nǐ yǒuméiyǒu xiōngdìjiěmèi?	**Do you have siblings?**
Nǐ lǎopó/gōng jiālǐ rén duō ma?	**Does your wife/husband also have a big family?**
Nǐ zhùzài nǐ xiōngdìjiěmèi fùjìnma?	**Do you live near your siblings?**
Nǐ zǔfùwàizǔfù zhùzài nǎr?	**Where do your grandparents live?**

Before answering these questions, you may need to know about a few more relationships. The extended family forms of address will probably seem confusing at first, but with some practice you'll get a handle of who is who and who you are in all of it. In-law forms of address tend to be the most confusing. In English, regardless of whether you are referring to your spouse's siblings, or your own siblings' spouses, in-laws are in-laws. Your husband's brother is your brother-in-law, just as your sister's husband is also your brother-in-law. Likewise, for the gentlemen, your wife's brother is your brother-in-law as much as your sister's husband is your brother-in-law. In Chinese, however, a distinction is made between your spouse's siblings and your sibling's spouses. As a husband, you will refer to your wife's siblings using the same forms of address for your own siblings. Similarly, a wife will refer to her husband's siblings as if they were her own, using the familiar address of the immediate family. In contrast, however, when referring to the spouses of your siblings, you'll use the forms of address in the following table.

The Spouses of Your Siblings

your elder sister's husband	*jiěfū*
your younger sister's husband	*mèifū*
your elder brother's wife	*săosao*
your younger brother's wife	*dìmèi*

But it doesn't end there. There are a large number of forms of address for the entire family. The following list includes the closest members of the extended family.

The Extended Family

your wife's mother	*yuèmŭ*
your wife's father	*yuèfù*
your husband's mother	*pópo*
your husband's father	*gōnggong*
maternal grandmother	*lăolao*
maternal grandfather	*lăoyé*
paternal grandmother	*năinai*
paternal grandfather	*yéye*
father	*bàba*
mother	*māma*
son	*érzi*
daughter	*nŭér*
son-in-law	*nŭxù*
daughter-in-law	*érxí*
grandson (son's child)	*sūnzi*
granddaughter (son's child)	*sūnnŭr*
grandson (daughter's child)	*wàisūn*
granddaughter (daughter's child)	*wàisūnnŭr*

Now that that is all crystal clear, you may go ahead and answer your questions:

Wó yŏu liăngge nǚér hé yíge érzi.	**I have two daughters and a son.**
Wó yŏu yíge jiĕjie.	**I have an older sister.**
Wó lăopó yŏu liăngge gēge, yíge jiĕjie, hé yíge dìdi.	**My wife has two older brothers, an older sister and a younger brother.**
Wó jiĕjie hé jiĕfū zhùzài wŏmen fùjìn, dànshì wó lăopó jiālĭrén zhùzài bōshìdùn.	**My sister and her husband live near us, but my wife's family live in Boston.**
Wó zŭfùwàizŭfù dōu zhùzài fóluólĭdá zhōu.	**My grandparents all live in Florida.**

Compare and Contrast

As relatively few Chinese get the opportunity to travel outside of China, much of what the Chinese know about the United States, or any country for that matter, is based on movies, television, music, and other fragments of Western popular culture and media. As a result, you might find some of their questions a little skewed, as they are based on their perceptions of the media. Of course, the determining factors to the nature of the questions they will ask are based on the level of the individual's English. You won't too often come across university English majors who are fluent in English and eagerly hoping to engage you, but you can still be prepared:

Zài nĭmen guójiā, fànzuì shìbúshì yíge dà wèntí?	**Is crime a big problem in your country?**
Nĭmen guójiāde shīyèlǜ zĕnmeyàng?	**How is the unemployment rate in your country?**
Zài mĕiguó wūrăn de qíngkuàng hĕn yánzhòng ma?	**Is the pollution situation very severe in the United States?**

Xīfāngrén rènwéi zhōngguórén zěnmeyàng?	**What do Westerners think of Chinese?**
Nǐ shǔyú nǎge zhèngdǎng?	**What political party do you belong to?**
Zài měiguó dàjiā dōu kāichē ma?	**Does everyone in the United States drive a car?**

It won't be every Chinese English speaker who will be able to ask you these kinds of questions. But, you may be sincerely surprised at how many will try to. The Chinese are congenially argumentative amongst their friends. They like to debate and discuss. You can increase your vocabulary on your own. Don't be afraid to try and get into discussions on this level—you learn by doing. Furthermore, the Chinese will be ecstatic that you're trying to speak their language; they take it as a huge compliment. Don't be surprised if they know more about current events in your own country than you do, though. The Chinese are avid readers and like to keep up on what's going on. The fact that they can and do discuss international politics as much as they do is steeped in profound irony, as it is largely because they cannot discuss much of their own domestic politics.

Exercises

Now you're all ready to make friends in China, right? Test your skills with the following exercises. Try to answer the questions from memory first, and then refer back to earlier pages if you need to jog your memory or perfect spelling.

1. How do you express the potential form of the verb *kāichē* using the complement of degree?

   ....

2. How do you negate the potential form of *kāichē* using the complement of degree?

   ....

3. Translate the following sentence into Chinese: "I have two elder sisters."

    ....

4. Organize the following words into a question: *cài zhēn zhōngguó xǐhuān wǒ.*

    ....

Chapter 9
Be Our Guest

At some point in your sojourn in China, it is very likely that a Chinese colleague will invite you to his home. This will likely happen whether you are there to vacation or work, or whether you are there for a short or long period of time. This is an exciting and fascinating opportunity to get a glimpse into the social life of average Chinese people. If you are planning on being in China for longer than a vacation, bringing a few tokens from home would be wise. You should never pay a visit without a gift or two to offer.

Visiting a Chinese Home

The Chinese are very hospitable. They truly go out of their way to make their guests feel welcome. As a result, you should try to do your best to show your appreciation. This is how long lasting relationships are built. There's a saying in Chinese, *Qièjì liángshŏu kōngkōng*, which means "never have two empty hands." It's said regarding paying a visit to someone's home. Gift giving is a big practice in Chinese social interaction, and it's not out of as much social obligation as it is simple pleasure. The Chinese sincerely do enjoy *sòng lǐwù* (giving gifts). As Westerners are often taught growing up that "the gift is in the giving," the Chinese seem to take this to heart.

ALERT!

In your search for gifts, steer clear of clocks and umbrellas. The term for giving a clock as a gift would be *sòngzhōng*, which sounds identical to *sòngzhōng*, meaning to send someone to their final rest. The term for giving an umbrella as a gift would be *sòngsǎn*, which sounds identical to *sòngsǎn*, meaning to separate or disperse. Neither are associations to share with a good friend.

Gifts for the Host

When you go to visit someone's home in China you should bring some tokens of appreciation. Do not take "tokens of appreciation" to mean that you should appear at someone's door as if coming down a chimney with a bag full of gifts; there is such a thing as overkill. In China it is traditional to offer gifts in pairs, as even numbers are considered lucky. Tokens of appreciation can be anything! They can be a couple of nice bottles of wine, a box of pastries from a bakery, or a bag or box of seasonal fruits. In most supermarkets some fruits will be sold in a decorative netting or boxes. These are specifically meant to be used as gifts.

Presenting Gifts

When you present your gifts, regardless of how far or wide you may have traveled to obtain them or how expensive they may actually be, you must be humble. In general, the Chinese are not very concerned with how much something costs or how rare or prized a gift is so much as the sincerity of the act. For example, a truly unique gift that was chosen carefully will impress more profoundly on your hosts than any price tag ever could. So if your intention is to wow your hosts, consider a token that is unique, perhaps something from your homeland that is not so easy to obtain in China. Exchanging gifts with the Chinese is not a simple task, though, because regardless of what you've brought, modesty demands that the gift recipient refuse the gift at least twice, and traditionally a full three times before accepting it. When you offer your gift you may do so by saying something like:

Qǐng jiēshòu wǒ zhèfèn lǐwù, zhù nǐ wànshì rúyì.	**Please accept this small token of my appreciation.**

Now, prepare for your first refusal. Your host will say something like:

Búyào kèqì, qǐng nǐ shōuhuí nǐde lвwù à.	**Don't be so polite, please take the gift back.**

Your second attempt to offer the gift can be even more polite:

Xiǎoxiǎo yìsī, bùchéng jìngyì.	**It's absolutely nothing, hardly even respectful.**

Your hosts second attempt to refuse the gift may sound something like this:

Wǒmen yǐjīng bú shì wàirén le, nǐ búyòng kèqì le!	**We're not strangers anymore, you don't have to be so polite!**

Your third and probably final attempt to offer your gift will be both polite and reassuring:

Zhè diǎn xiǎo lǐwù yídìng yào shōuxià.	**It's hardly even a gift at all, please take it.**

The final refusal will likely be the refusal where they actually accept your gift:

Nǐ búyòng tài kèqì le, wǒmen yǐjīng shì yìjiārén le.	**You really mustn't be so modest, we're family.**

Inside a Chinese Home

The Chinese home and home decorating in China have changed dramatically over the last century. Chinese homes in the past were often single-family or extended-family dwellings. Among the upper classes, many houses were very luxurious. They were often comprised of several rooms, generally situated in a U shape. The center of the building was a courtyard with a shrine. On the sides of the shrine were the senior bedrooms. The junior bedrooms and other household rooms were distributed throughout. There were serious legal constraints on the style of the house depending on the class of its inhabitants.

The overall layout of the average Chinese urban apartments is not too dissimilar to those of U.S. cities. Kitchens are quite small so families usually eat in the dining room much as Western families. There are bedrooms, a living room, and quite often, either a wash room or balcony where clothes are hung to dry. Few Chinese people have clothes dryers.

Nowadays, China's daunting population crisis has crowded living areas and forced large families into smaller spaces. Single-family structures more closely resembling the old style homes do still exist in China, but they are more common in the rural areas. They are not by any means lavish, but they retain elements of the old style dwellings. Single-family homes in the cities are very expensive and more closely resemble Western one-family homes. Residential life in the cities is centered in high-rise complexes, and they clog skylines throughout China. High rises range anywhere from fifteen to fifty-five stories or higher. Apartments in these high rises are the picture of space efficiency.

A few differences between Chinese and Western style homes lie in the arrangement of the furniture. Many Chinese employ the principles of Feng Shui in decorating their home. *Fēngshuǐ*, meaning "wind and water," is a traditional metaphysical practice for arranging the home to maximize the house's flow of *qì*. It is also popular with Chinese businessmen, who design their offices according to *Fēngshuǐ* principles. Many Chinese people have altars in their homes that contain pictures of ancestors (*zǔtán*) or images of the various Buddhist arhats (*fótán*) who are special to the family. You can ask questions about it like this:

Zhè shì shénme luóhàn?	**What arhat is this?**
Zhèxiē rén shì búshì nǐ zǔfùmǔ?	**Are these your grandparents?**
Zhèxiē rén shì shéi?	**Who are they?**

Admiring the Décor

A sure-fire way to ingratiate yourself with your hosts is by paying compliments to the house. If you read up a bit on *Fēngshuǐ*, you may take notice of some strategic *Fēngshuǐ*-related placements of objects. This will certainly impress your host. Apart from simply referring to someone's home, belongings, or company with the pronoun *nǐde* or *nínde*, you can attach the word *guì* (precious) to the subject noun as a form of polite respect. See the following examples:

Guì jiā hēn piàoliàng!	**Your home is lovely!**
Guì jiā hēn qīngliáng!	**Your home is cool and fresh!**
Guì jiā hēn módĕng!	**Your home is quite fashionable!**

Shoes

The Chinese, especially in urban centers, are notoriously obsessive about cleanliness, almost to a fault. This is even more evident since the advent of Severe Acute Respiratory Syndrome (SARS). Many cities have public hand-washing units with antibacterial hand gel. Most apartment buildings have disinfectant mats outside to wipe your feet on before entering. Building management staff are constantly wiping down surfaces, especially in elevators and during the winter. Naturally, when you go into someone's house, it is required that you remove your shoes.

FACT

The Chinese words for both "slippers" and "to take off your shoes" are homophones: *tuōxié*. The difference is in the first word *tuō*. The verb "to take off" or "to remove" with regard to clothing is *tuō*. In the word for slippers, however, *tuō* is a different character meaning "to drag," as in the way flip flops drag on the floor.

When you enter a Chinese home, often directly to the side of the apartment entrance you will find the *xiéjià* or shoe shelf. The *xiéjià* is not always a shelf, though; sometimes it's more like a rack upon which you may place your shoes while visiting someone's home. Or sometimes it can be a small closet-like cupboard called a *xiéguì*. In some homes the *xiéjià* is outside the apartment in the vestibule, in which case, it may come with a key. Shoe shelves can be elaborate pieces of furniture or simply modest metallic racks. Families often leave guest slippers hanging in the shoe shelf, so you should feel free to take a pair and replace them in the shelf with your shoes. Your host will invite you to make yourself at home by taking off your shoes.

Qǐng tuōxié.	**Please take off your shoes.**
Zhèr shì tuōxié, bǎ zhè dāng zìjǐ de jiā yíyàng.	**Here are some slippers, make yourself at home.**

Usually if there is no shoe shelf, it's acceptable to lay your shoes on the floor near the door, where everyone else's shoes will likely be. Line them neatly with the toes facing the door so they are easy to put back on when it's time to leave. Don't worry if you forget to line up your shoes; if you don't do it, your hosts will probably do it for you. If there is a shoe shelf but it is full, you may place your shoes underneath it or in front of it, remembering to point the toes toward the door.

Stay for Dinner

In terms of etiquette, dining in a Chinese home isn't all that different from a *yànhuì*, or traditional Chinese banquet, which is held to celebrate a wide array of festivals, holidays, and occasions. (You'll learn more about the *yànhuì* in Chapter 12.) There are some basic rules of dining etiquette that you should know before sitting at the table in a Chinese home.

Table Manners

The contrast between East and West can be seen at the dinner table. Some Western dining habits would be considered rude by the Chinese, and Westerners might view Chinese table manners as a complete lack thereof. For example, you may remember your mom scolding you for propping your elbows up on the dinner table as you ate. In China, few are concerned with your posture while eating. As long as you're not slouching all the way down in your chair, you're fine. Have you almost finished your soup? Is there just a bit left in the bowl? Lift the bowl to your mouth. When drinking soup, you may of course use a spoon, but sipping from the bowl, particularly to finish it is not considered rude by Chinese standards. In fact, when eating, it is quite common to hold your rice bowl with one hand, and your chopsticks with the other. If your host sees you adhering to Western table manners, and trying to be as polite as possible, he may ask you to relax:

Wŏmen shì yì jiā rén le! *Fàngsōng yíxià.*	**We're family! Just relax.**
Qĭng suíyì.	**Make yourself comfortable.**

Unlike at a Western dinner table where everyone spoons individual portions into their main plates, Chinese eat in *jiācháng* fashion. The closest and most accurate English rendering of this term is "home style," or "family style." By eating family style, it means that all the dishes are brought out and placed in the center of the table, while everyone is provided with an individual rice bowl. Everyone serves himself by simply taking from the dinner dishes with chopsticks and bringing the food to their rice bowls. Again, if your hosts think you're holding back, they will simply tell you not to:

Búyào bùhǎo yìsī.	**Don't be embarrassed.**
Qǐng zì biàn.	**Please help yourself.**

Grammar Lesson: Being Polite

If you have discerned anything about Chinese culture by now it should be that politeness and modesty are highly prized virtues. Without any inflection in Chinese, you can simply render a verb into the affirmative imperative in two basic ways. The first and most common way is by placing the adverb *qǐng* (please) before the verb. Omitting *qǐng* would only be appropriate in the case of parents talking to children. The second most common way is a bit more colloquial and best reserved for friends. The particle *ba* may be placed at the end of a phrase to give it a suggestive tone. This is comparable to "shall we" or "let's" in English. For example:

Wǒmen chīfàn ba.	**Shall we eat lunch?**
Wǒmen zǒu ba.	**Shall we go?/Let's go.**

There are a handful of ways of expressing the negative imperative in Chinese. The adverb *wù* is often seen written on signs where it is understood to mean "do not" or "it is prohibited." This word is more of a literary expression. It was probably used in everyday speech at one time but has since been replaced by two other expressions. The expressions *bié* and *búyào* are both used to mean "do not," though the latter is more common. *Bié* is also an old expression rich with many meanings and usages, but its sense of "do not" is still in use today. By far, *búyào* (do not want) is the most commonly spoken way of expressing the "do not." When you are communicating "need not + verb," it is colloquially acceptable to leave out the *qǐng*. However, as with all imperatives in Chinese, don't forget the *qǐng* before a verb if you are trying to outwardly say "do not." For example:

Qǐng bié wàng le.	**Please don't forget.**
Qǐng búyào wàng le.	**Please don't forget.**
Qǐng búyào gàosù tā.	**Please don't tell him.**

I'm Stuffed!

Even when you have tried every dish on the table (and there will probably be quite a few), your hosts may continue to try to feed you. As hosts, the Chinese try to be as accommodating as possible. Not knowing what your favorite dishes are, your host will very likely just make everything. The spread may include a chicken dish, beef dish, tofu, fish, vegetables, noodles, etc. You should at least try everything that's served to show your gratitude. But when you truly feel full, go ahead and say so:

Xièxie, wǒ chībǎole.	**Thank you, I'm full.**
Wǒ bù néng zài chī le.	**I couldn't eat another bite.**

The cook(s) probably went through a great deal of trouble preparing this feast. Now would be a good time to rave about the cooking:

Yīqiè dōu hěn kěkǒu!	**Everything was delicious!**

The Chinese are not big on very sweet desserts, so the meal is usually rounded off with some seasonal fresh fruit. If there was a dish or two that you particularly enjoyed during the dinner, chances are that your hosts noticed. Don't be surprised if you're given the *shèngfàn* (leftovers) in a little plastic container as you leave. Naturally, it is the dish you took considerable notice of. It's at this point that you should thank your hosts, and don't forget to apologize for being a terrible bother to them: *Bùhǎo yìsī, dárǎo nǐ le!*

Exercises

Now you should be fully prepared to be a guest in a Chinese home. Do you remember all the new Chinese you learned in this chapter? Test yourself with the following questions to find out. Try from memory first, and then refer back to earlier pages if you need to jog your memory or perfect spelling.

1. How do you politely let your host know that you are full?

   ....

2. Rearrange the following words to form a sentence: *yíyàng tuōxié zhèr shì jiā, bǎ dāng zhè de zìjǐ*.

   ....

3. What word should you fix to a subject noun to make it more polite.

   ....

Chapter 10

Shopping

As big fans of malls, outlets, and shopping centers, Americans do their fair share of shopping. But no one shops quite like the Chinese; they take shopping to an entirely new level. Asians and travelers come from all over to China's major cities for high-quality products and low prices. It's a bargain hunter's paradise. So, if shopping to you is not simply an activity but a challenge, get ready for the ride of your life.

Currency

The Renminbi, the official currency of China, has been in use since December of 1948. The most commonly used unit is the yuan. One *yuán* consists of ten *jiao*, and one *jiao* consists of ten *fen*. There have been several series editions of the Renminbi since 1948. The latest edition includes *yuán* banknotes in denominations of ¥1, ¥5, ¥10, ¥20, ¥50, and ¥100; jiao banknotes come in 1 and 5. Coins include: ¥1, 5 *jiao*, 1 *jiao*, and 1 *fen*.

China's economy has evolved a great deal since the founding of the People's Republic. What began as a Socialist economy with "Chinese characteristics," in the last thirty years has slowly privatized nearly half of its enterprises. Most of China's cities now are SEZs or "special economic zones," and the nation as a whole has become largely a free-market economy. However, the Renminbi, as it is issued by the Chinese monetary authority known as the People's Bank of China, has not kept up entirely with that evolution. The cost of living varies greatly throughout China. For example, products and services that you may purchase in Lanzhou will likely be considerably more expensive in, say, Shanghai. Personal checks are also a relative novelty in Chinese banking. Most monetary exchange involves bank cards, credit cards, and to an even greater extent, cash. It is not at all uncommon for business transactions to involve an exchange of large numbers of banknotes.

FACT

Renminbi banknotes are decorated with Mao Zedong on the obverse side. On the reverse side are various Chinese images, including Taishan, Three Gorges, Guilin, Potala Palace, and Tiantan. The numbers appear in financial Chinese numbers along with Arabic numbers. The words "China People's Bank" appear in Mongol, Uyghur, Zhuang, and Tibetan.

In recent years, the Renminbi has been used to a great extent among local residents of Mongolia. This is supposedly due to the relative instability of the Mongolian Tug rug. This is a clear reflection of China's growing economic prosperity.

Other Currencies

If your travels to China take you to Hong Kong, Macau, or Taiwan you'll find other currencies in use besides the Renminbi. Hong Kong's currency is the HKD, or Hong Kong dollar, and it has been in official circulation in Hong Kong since 1937. The Hong Kong dollar is accepted not only within the territory of Hong Kong, but also in Macau, many areas of southern China, especially in Guangdong province, and in some shopping malls in Singapore. Hong Kong dollar banknotes come in denominations of $1000, $500, $100, $50, $20, and $10. There are HKD coins in the values of 10, 5, 2, and 1, and 50-, 20-, and 10-cent coins. One U.S. dollar comes to about 7.8 Hong Kong dollars.

The currency of Macau is called the pataca. One U.S. dollar is worth 7.9 Macau patacas. Although the pataca is in fact, the local currency for Macau, it's estimated that at least half of all money transactions occurring in Macau are in Hong Kong dollars. The reason for this is the externality associated with the HKD that the pataca does not share. While the Hong Kong dollar can be readily exchanged in Macau and mainland China, the pataca is confined only to Macau for exchange.

If your journey should take you to Taiwan, the currency you'll be using is also called the *yuán* in Chinese by the locals. But, actually, the Taiwan *yuán* is not the Renminbi. It is, instead, the New Taiwan dollar. The New Taiwan dollar runs in banknotes of denominations of $100, $200, $500, $1000, and $2000. NTD coins come in denominations of $0.50, $1, $5, $10, $20 and $50. One U.S. dollars comes to about 32.4 NTD, and unlike the Hong Kong dollar, NTD can only be exchanged in Taiwan.

Expressing Money

Whether you're spending RMB, Hong Kong dollars, patacas or New Taiwan dollars, there is one basic format for expressing monetary units in Chinese. The main standard unit is referred to most often as *kuài*, but occasionally as *yuán*. Given the choice, most Chinese go with *kuài*. These expressions would correspond to dollars in U.S. currency. *Máo* is the term used for the subunits, which would equate to "cents" in U.S. currency. Many people also say the word *qián* (money) at the end. The reason for this is that *kuài* is

THE EVERYTHING SPEAKING MANDARIN CHINESE BOOK

actually a counting word for money. Check out the following list and listen to the track on the CD.

TRACK 38

Expressing Yuan and Mao

Chinese	English
shí kuài	10 RMB
èrshí wǔ kuài	25 RMB
sìbǎi èrshí wǔ kuài	425 RMB
yīqiān qībǎi liùshí sān kuài	1,763 RMB
shí kuài sān máo	10.3 RMB
shí'èr kuài wǔ máo wǔ	12.55 RMB
èrshí wǔ kuài sān máo wǔ	25.35 RMB
yībǎi èrshí bā kuài yī máo liù	128.16 RMB
liángbǎi bāshí wǔ kuài jiǔ máo jiǔ	285.99 RMB

Measurement Systems

Pioneered by the French some two centuries ago, the metric system was intended to universalize measurement systems worldwide. Come the twenty-first century, we find that the metric system has spread far and wide across the globe and is now used popularly by roughly 95 percent of the earth's population. In fact, all but four nations of the world popularly use the metric system in all sectors of society. What this means is that if you come from the United States or Great Britain, it's time to search for your grammar school math books and brush up on your conversions.

But the lesson doesn't end there. China has moved to the forefront in mass production. Chinese factories produce textiles to be sold domestically as well as in New York, London, Tokyo, and Rome. As a result, as you browse Chinese markets, boutiques, and department stores, you'll be confronted with the great measurement quandary. The nature of this quandary is the fact that you will often find clothing marked with not only Chinese measurements in the stores, but U.S. and European measurements as well.

If you were to go through the typical urban Chinese closet, you'd likely find several articles of clothing of comparable dimensions, but with several different size tags. As a result, if you're going to do some serious shopping, as most everyone who comes to China does, you'll need to familiarize yourself with U.S. and European measurements in addition to Chinese.

The Tall and the Short of It

Given the choice between meters and centimeters, the Chinese tend to use centimeters to measure height. What's more, if you consider yourself to be of average height or weight in the United States, it may surprise you how tall or big you may feel in certain regions of China. If a Chinese person asks you any of the following questions, you should assume that he or she is speaking in terms of centimeters and kilograms.

How tall are you?	*Ní yǒu duōgāo?*
How much do you weigh?	*Ní yǒu duōzhòng?*

Here are some example responses:

I am .... centimeters tall.	*Wǒ yǒu .... límǐ gāo.*
I weigh .... kilograms.	*Wǒ yǒu .... gōngjīn zhòng.*

Be sure to express the numbers in Chinese in proper decimal places. You should say "I am one hundred seventy five centimeters tall and weigh fifty seven kilograms," as opposed to "I am one seven five centimeters tall and weigh five seven kilograms."

Chinese Women's Measurements

For women shopping in China, it is absolutely vital to know your measurements in centimeters. This fact cannot be stressed enough. You should know your *xiōngwéi* (bust), *yāowéi* (waist), *túnwéi* (hips), *nèicháng* (inseam), and *shēngāo* (height). You should pay particular attention to your height and bust size in centimeters. Dresses, blouses and other such items of clothing are often measured in terms of height/bust ratio.

Women's Blouses and Dresses

Letter Size	Labels	Approximate Dimensions
Small	155/80A	bust: 80–83cm; waist: 60–63cm; hips: 80–85cm
Medium	160/84A	bust: 84–87cm; waist: 64–67cm; hips: 84–89cm
Large	165/88A	bust: 88–91cm; waist: 68–71cm; hips: 90–95cm
X-Large	170/92A	bust: 92–95cm; waist: 72–75cm; hips: 96–101cm

ALERT!

Measurements for domestic products are by no means universal in China. Often, different factories go by their own particular size charts. Thus, it is truly vital that you know your metric measurements. Letter sizes such as S, M, and L are purely subjective. Always try things on before purchasing.

Women's trousers often run in U.S. measurements, so waist size is measured in *yīngcùn* or "inches." A distinct number system is also employed on occasion.

Women's Trousers

Chinese Size	Waist in Centimeters	Waist in Inches
2	63cm	24
4	67cm	26
6	71cm	27
8	74cm	28
10	78cm	30

Chinese Men's Measurements

Just as with women's clothing, the most important dimensions to consider for men's shirts are height and chest size. Men's clothes are somewhat similar to women's. As such, you'll see that men's clothes sizes simply run a few centimeters larger. One distinction you should be aware of is that men's shirts, like women's trousers, sometimes run in distinct number sizes.

Men's Shirts

Chinese Size	Letter Size	Height/Chest in Centimeters
37	S	165/88
38, 39	M	170/92
40, 41	L	175/96
42, 43	XL	180/100
44, 45	2X	185/104

When buying trousers, once again the sizes that seem to be considered are primarily your height and chest. Why would your chest be considered, you might ask? Well, clothing is often designed with the notion that waist size and chest size are not too divergent. In most Chinese online clothing stores, the average waist dimensions for men are often only two to three centimeters smaller than chest dimensions. As a result, you'll often find the same size labels on trousers that you'll find on shirts.

Men's Trousers

Size	Letter Size	Heights	Waist
160/68	S	160–165cm	66cm
165/72	M	165–170cm	70cm
170/76	L	170–175cm	74cm
175/80	XL	175–180cm	78cm
180/84	2X	180–185cm	82cm

Footwear

Socks and shoes are generally in a class all their own. Socks come in small, medium, and large generally, but the exact range in centimeters of those sizes is often a mystery. It's usually best to tell the sales person what your shoe size is and he'll help you find appropriate socks. As far as your shoes are concerned, this is where there is the least mystery in your shopping. The Chinese use the European shoe measurement system, and it's used fairly universally. Also, more often than not, if you indicate the U.S. shoe size, that will be recognized as well.

A Brief Overview of European Measurements

There are two major classes of clothing available for retail in China. They are *zhōngguó fúzhuāng* (Chinese textiles) and *wàimào fúzhuāng* (export textiles). Chinese textiles are those clothes that are labeled in Chinese measurements; the export textiles, however, are often labeled with mostly European, but also U.S. measurements. As a result, it's helpful to be familiar with some of the European non-metric measurements:

Western Women's Dresses

U.S. Size	European Size
8	38
10	40
12	42
14	44
16	46
18	48
20	50

Men's Shirts

U.S. Size	European Size
14	36
15	38
15.5	39.5
16	40
16.5	42
17	43
17.5	44

Men's Suits

U.S. Size	European Size
32	42
34	44
36	46
38	48
40	50
42	52
44	54

Shoes

U.S. Women	European Women	U.S. Men	European Men
4	35	6	38
5	36	7	40
6	37	8	41
7	38	9	43

U.S. Women	European Women	U.S. Men	European Men
8	39	10	44
9	40	11	45
10	41	12	46

Traditional Chinese Measures

Like many nations, China had its own system of measurements that has been in use throughout its long history. China officially employs the metric system, but some of the traditional measurements also continue to be used. The most common of these measurements are included in the following list. Look over the vocabulary list and then listen to the track that follows and repeat it as you go.

Chinese Measurements

Chinese Name	English Name
cùn	inch
chǐ	foot
lǐ	mile
jīn	pound
shēng	quart

TRACK 39

Clerk: *Nín xiǎng mǎi shénme?*
May I help you?

Customer: *Taór hé píngguǒ duǒshao qián yì jīn?*
How much per jin are peaches and apples

Clerk: *Píngguǒ wǔ kuài wǔ máo yì jīn, taór liù kuài yì jīn.*

Apples are 5.5 yuan per jin and peaches are 6 yuan per jin.

Customer: *Hǎo, wǒ yào mǎi yì jīn píngguǒ hé liǎng jīn taór.*
Fine, I'll take one jin of apples and two jin of peaches.

Clerk: *Hái yào biéde ma?*
Anything else?

Customer: *Bú yào biéde.*
No, nothing else.

Clerk: *Yígòng shíyī kuài wǔ máo.*
That will be 11.5 yuan all together

Customer: *Gěi nín qián.*
Here you are.

Clerk: *Zhè shì èrshí kuài, zhǎo nín bā kuài wǔ máo.*
From 20 yuan, that's 8.5 yuan change

Measure Words

Measure words are special words attached to numbers. The type of object you're counting determines the specific measure word you use. English has measure words, too. You really only see English measure words when counting animals; for example, a pack of wolves, a flock of sheep, a pride of lions, a school of fish, etc. The good news is that though there are indeed many measure words to learn, a great deal of them have fallen out of common usage. The following list includes some of the more commonly used ones. Even more good news is that the measure word *gè* is a fairly universal catchall measure word. Even if *gè* is not a normally accepted measure word for an item, you will be understood if you use it. Don't worry if you've forgotten the correct measure word—just express yourself.

Common Measure Words

Measure Word	Description	Example	English
kē	trees	*yìkē shù*	a/one tree
duǒ	flora	*yìduǒ huār*	a/one flower
zhī	animals	*yìzhī māo*	a/one cat
běn	volumes; bound items	*yìběn shū*	a/one book
zhāng	flat things	*yìzhāng zhàopiàn*	a/one picture
xiàng	events, projects	*zhèxiàng huódòng*	this activity

Measure Word	Description	Example	English
tiáo	long narrow things	*yìtiáo lù*	a/one street
zuò	structures, buildings	*zhèzuò dàlóu*	this building
tái	bulky objects	*yìtái diànshì*	a/one television
kuài	chunks, blocks, money	*yíkuài qián*	1 RMB
jiàn	matters; clothing	*zhèjiàn shì*	this matter
fēng	letters, mail	*yìfēng xìn*	a/one letter
liàng	vehicles	*yíliàng chē*	a/one car

Trying on Clothes

This is an absolutely essential step when shopping in China. Because measurements are not universal, you can never be too sure if an article of clothing will fit. In department stores, the service staff will be amiable and happy to be of whatever assistance they can. Outside of department stores, such as out in the open markets, it's not unheard of that a vendor will remove a label and place the label of the size you need on the item. Never buy something unless you've tried it on! Ask questions. Look over the following vocabulary list and then listen to the conversation that follows. Repeat what you hear aloud for extra practice.

TRACK 40

Shopping Vocabulary

Chinese	English
pídài	belt
nǚchènshān	blouse
yǐ tiáo qún zi	dress
màozi	hat
wàitào	jacket
dàyī	coat
kùzi	pants
páozi	robe
wéijīn	scarf
chènshān	shirt
qúnzi	skirt
xīzhuāng	Western suit
lǐngdài	tie
gēngyīshì	changing room

Is there a changing room?	*Yǒu méiyǒu gēngyīshì?*
May I try this on?	*Wǒ kéyǐ shì yí shì ma?*
Could I trouble you to take my measurements?	*Máfán nín kéyǐ liáng wǒde chǐ cùn ma?*

Colors

Expressing colors in Chinese is as simple as adding the word *sè* (color) to the noun and affixing the particle *de* at the end. Just as in English, colors can be both nouns and adjectives.

Colors

English	Chinese Noun Root	Chinese Adjectival Form
red	*hóng*	*hóngsè de*
orange	*júhóng*	*júhóngsè de*
yellow	*huáng*	*huángsè de*
green	*lǜ*	*lǜsè de*
blue	*lán*	*lánsè de*
purple	*zǐ*	*zǐsè de*
brown	*kāfēi*	*kāfēisè de*
grey	*huī*	*huīsè de*

English	Chinese Noun Root	Chinese Adjectival Form
black	*hēi*	*hēisè de*
pink	*fěnhóng*	*fěnhóngsè de*
white	*bái*	*báisè de*

FACT

One color deserves special mention. It is the color qīng (*qīngsè de*). You may hear reference to this color, and when you do you should request specificity. The reason is that *qīngsè* can often be used to mean either green or blue. It also communicates the concepts of youth, health, and life. It's often used in idiomatic expressions.

Materials

Some people are allergic to some materials. Perhaps you want to launder your purchase. Knowing what an item of clothing is made of can be vital. Below, find the most common cloths available:

Chinese	English
kāishìmǐ	cashmere
miánbù	cotton
xiéwénbù	denim
pígé	leather
huàxiān	polyester
duànzi	satin
sīchóu	silk
yángmáo	wool

Beyond Clothing

Clothing is far from the only thing you can buy in China. China has a wide variety of goods and souvenirs to enjoy. In addition to large department stores, you'll find everything from fine jewelers, arts and crafts shops, stationery shops, shoe stores, music and video stores, thrift shops, photography shops, and a host of electronic shops. In the tourist areas you'll be able to buy folkloric items such as calligraphy sets including brushes and ink stones. You'll find Buddhist and Taoist scrolls, name seals, *xiàngmù* (Chinese fragrant wood), lacquer ware, porcelain ware, fabrics, embroidery, carpets, incenses, paper crafts, bamboo crafts, and all manner of fine teas.

Antiques are a special case. Antiques abound in an ancient land like China, but be forewarned that there are some very strict restrictions on the exportation of antiques. All antiques, regardless of where you purchase them, must bear the red wax seal of the Chinese State Relics Bureau. This seal may be obtained from the local cultural artifacts bureau. A good antique dealer will secure this for you, and it is vital. Generally, across the board, objets d'art, particularly porcelain ware dating back to early Qing dynasty or over 200 years old may not be exported. In the case of wooden items, some items fashioned from three particular rare woods may not be exported.

The Art of Negotiation

As China races to catch up with the West, most markets in major cities nowadays have been converted into upscale department stores and pricey boutiques. As a general rule, bargaining is accepted and expected in most places with the exception of department stores and restaurants. Even if there are fixed price signs, goods and services are still negotiable in most cases. When in doubt, there is no harm in asking the vendor for a cheaper price.

When you're preparing to bargain ahead of time, the first step is to research the market price. Usually, market price can be discounted 10 to 50 percent of the asking price. In some cases, the price given by the vendor can be as outrageous as 500 percent above market price. Before making any purchases, compare the prices of the items you would like to purchase at various shops in your vicinity.

Do not hesitate to ask for selling prices due to the language barrier. Point to an item with a questioning look and most vendors will whip out the calculator faster than you can blink to show you a price. Once you ask for the initial price of the item, the vendor will most likely tell you that they can offer you a cheaper price if you are genuinely interested in making a purchase.

Follow these steps once you think you want to bargain for an item:

1. **Make sure you really want the item.** If you are sincerely interested in acquiring the item, continue on to the next step. Unless both parties are unable to compromise on the final price, it is considered very rude to commence with the bargaining process if you have no intention of or change your mind about buying the item midway through the process.
2. **Begin the bargaining process.** Think of this as a roleplay. If too much interest is shown in the item, the vendor will believe the upper-hand is theirs and will be more reluctant on coming down on the price. Haggling for a bargain can take awhile. Be friendly, have a sense of humor, be patient, and keep smiling.
3. **Reduce the asking price.** At this point, you will most likely be asked how much you are willing to pay for the item. In response, ask what the lowest possible price is. Then provide your opening negotiation price.
4. **Provide a counteroffer.** Depending on the vendor and where in China the bargaining is taking place, the asking price can generally be cut down

by half. Look for imperfections on the item to depreciate the value of the item as a negotiation tactic. Start with an approximately 50 percent discount from the last price given by the vendor.

5. **Have patience and a sense of humor.** Do not be discouraged if the vendor repeatedly says no. Be persistent and keep smiling as the vendor explains why the price cannot be lowered. Increase your offer at the same increment as the vendor decreases the offer. If the vendor cuts the price by 20 RMB, increase your offer by 20 RMB. Continue until a compromising amount can be reached.

6. **Try bluffing, and then move on.** If the final price given by the vendor is still unacceptable, give your final price and pretend to leave reluctantly. The vendor may call out their lowest final price as you walk away. If not, approach another vendor with a slightly higher price.

The following is a sample conversation you can use as a model for your own bargaining experiences:

Shopper:	*Zhè jiàn yīfu dūo shǎo qián?* How much does this outfit cost?
Vendor:	*Liǎng bǎi sìshí kuài, nǐ yào shì zhēn xiǎng mǎi de huà, wǒ kéyǐ gěi nǐ piányì yī diǎn.* 240 RMB, if you're really interested in buying it, I could give you a little discount.
Shopper:	*Pián yì duō shǎo?* How much of a discount?
Vendor:	*Èr bǎi sān shíwǔ kuài zěn me yàng?* How is 235 RMB?
Shopper:	*Tài gùi le, gěi wǒ hǎo yidiǎn de jià gé ma?* That's too expensive, can you give me a better price?
Vendor:	*Èr bǎi sān shí kuài zùi dī le.* 230 RMB is the lowest I can go.
Shopper:	*Yībǎi èr shí kuài kéyǐ ma?* Will 120 RMB do?

Vendor:	*Bù xíng, tài shǎo le, wǒ lián mǎihuò dōu mǎi bù lái. Nǐ yàoshì chéngxīn xiǎng mǎi jiù jiā duō yìdiǎn yībǎiliùshí kuài zhēnde zùi dī le.*
	No, can't do it. That's too little. I couldn't even buy my merchandise for that price. If you're sincerely interested in buying it, bring it up to 160 RMB, that's really the lowest I can go.
Shopper:	*Děng wǒ xiǎng yī xiǎng ba.* Okay, wait while I think about it.
Vendor:	*Xíng!, Yībǎièrshí, wǒ mài le.* Okay! 120 RMB it is.

Exercises

Now it's time to see what you've learned about shopping and bargaining in China. The following exercises include information covered in various parts of this chapter. Try to answer the questions from memory first, and then refer back to earlier pages if you need to jog your memory or perfect spelling.

1. Match these words with their correct meanings:

xiōngwéi	waist
yāowéi	height
túnwéi	hips
nèicháng	bust
shēngāo	inseam

2. How do you say "domestic textiles" and "export textiles" in Chinese?

   ....

   ....

3. What English color does *qīng* correspond to?

   ....

Chapter 11

Epicurean Delights

Whether you are a fan of seafood, beef, or vegetables, China has tastes and smells that will delight and perhaps even sometimes baffle you. The term "Chinese food" makes many Americans think of greasy takeout in little white containers. Leave those notions behind. Dining in China is as important as any other aspect of its culture, and many visitors to China come to greatly enjoy the native cuisine. Go in with an open mind and try as many new dishes as you can.

The Spectrum of Chinese Cuisine

Chinese cuisine is a broad category, including many different types of cooking traditions. Topographically China is a very diverse country. The North is very dry, and many of the northern provinces border desert regions. The eastern and southern coastal regions are very lush, green, and humid. In the same way that the spoken Chinese language varies from province to province, the cuisine differs from place to place. Each province boasts its own specialties due to the fact that each region has its own particular crops and spices. There's much debate as to what the different schools of Chinese cuisine are. Generally they can be broken down into four basic categories reflecting the four regions: the North, South, East, and West. You should definitely ask about trying local specialties in every place you visit in China.

Northern Cuisine

The cuisine of northern China is also called Mandarin cuisine. The North is usually thought to consist of the provinces that lie north of the Yangtze River. Northerners tends to consume more meat, such as beef, lamb and duck. Like the southerners, they also enjoy grain products. Unlike the southerners, though, rice is not as common. Instead, northerners consume more wheat products, including noodles and buns. Their cooking is also generally blander in taste. Signature dishes of the North include Beijing duck and all manner of dumplings.

Eastern Cuisine

Under this umbrella term you'll find the cuisines of the central eastern coast, and the Yangtze River delta, the cuisines of Shanghai, Hangzhou, and greater Zhejiang, and Jiangsu provincial cuisines. The schools of the East avail themselves of their proximity to the ocean and an abundance of lakes and rivers. The food of this region is known to be very sweet, particularly Shanghai's cuisine. Shanghainese cooking uses a lot of sugar. Signature dishes of the East include Xiaolongbao, Shengjian, and of course, Shanghai Hairy Crab.

Southern Cuisine

Better known as Cantonese cuisine, this school of cooking is the most recognizable Chinese cuisine among Westerners. The majority of the Chinese immigrant communities of the last century in the United States, Canada, and the UK are predominantly from the South, and particularly Canton (*Guǎngdōng*) Province. Southern cooking utilizes a great deal of seafood, fresh fruits, and vegetables. Strong seasonings are generally avoided, and often foreign ingredients are incorporated into the local cuisine. This is due in part mostly to the fact that this area of China has had the most contact with the Western world. In fact, popular egg tart pastries known in Portugal as *pasteis de nata* are popular in south China and known there as *po tat*.

QUESTION?

I've heard of Macanese cuisine, but what does it include?
One of the least well known but most deserving of honorable mention is Macanese cuisine. The cuisine of Macao is a fusion of Asian and Portuguese, and it's an experience that should not be missed.

Sichuan and Hunan Cuisine

Though often lumped together into one category due to their mutual liberal use of chili peppers, Sichuan and Hunan cooking traditions are quite distinct. What these two provinces have in common is their hot and humid climate. This climate is conducive to the growth of hot peppers. Hot chili peppers, which were brought to China from the West, grow in abundance and are used liberally in cooking in this region. Cooking practices of this region also include pickling, salting, drying, and smoking. Shallots, garlic, and honey are also widely used ingredients. Due to the widespread use of oxen in the region, beef is also a common choice of ingredients in the cooking here.

Menu Mayhem

Going to a restaurant in China can often be a harrowing experience. Making heads or tales of the menu can be challenging. Also, the menus in Chinese restaurants are often not in English. Occasionally, when they are in English, the names of the dishes that they use will not be familiar to you. Chinese dishes often have catchy names. If you've ever looked at a menu from a Chinese restaurant in the U.S. you've probably noticed how some of the chef's specialties have unique names. Sometimes the names are very descriptive. It's quite a similar experience in China. You'll find that many of the traditional Chinese dishes go by the same very descriptive or illustrative names. On the upside, though, the popular dishes tend to be on all menus. So, you'll likely find certain dishes in all the restaurants no matter where you go. Just don't let this stop you from trying the unique regional specialties. The following list contains some simple but popular Chinese dishes:

Popular Chinese Dishes

Chinese	English
yúxiāng ròusī	spicy shredded pork
háoyóu niúròu	beef with oyster sauce
hóngshāo páigǔ	sweet-and-sour spareribs
gānbiǎn niúròu sī	stir fried shredded beef
qīngjiāo niúròu sī	shredded beef with green peppers
gōngbǎo jīdīng	diced chicken with hot peppers (kung pao)
gālí jīdīng	diced curry chicken
níngméng jī	lemon chicken
gělì	clams
pángxiè	crab
xiārén	shrimp

Chinese	English
lóngxiā	lobster
fúróng xiārén	shrimp with eggwhites
xiārén dòufǔ	shrimp with beancurd
shāguō dòufǔ	bean curd casserole
mápór dòufǔ	bean curd with minced pork in pepper sauce
sù shíjǐn	sautéed mixed vegetables

Conversations in a Restaurant

In this section you'll find new vocabulary lists and sample conversations that may take place in a Chinese restaurant. The first conversation is about being seated, and the second is about being served. Follow along with the tracks on the CD and repeat what you hear out loud.

Seating Speech

Chinese	English
wèi	measure word for people
xī	to smoke
chù	area
fēi	prohibit, no, not
xīyānqū	smoking area
fēixīyānchù	non-smoking area
gēnzài	follow
mǎshàng	immediately; right away
guòlái	come by
zhù	wish, blessing
wèikǒu	appetite

TRACK 41

Host: *Wǎnshàng hǎo, jǐ wèi?*
Good evening, how many in your party?

Guest: *Wǒmén yǒu sì wèi?*
We're a party of four.

Host: *Nín xǐhuān xīyānqū háishì fēixīyānqū?*
Would you prefer smoking or non-smoking?

Guest: *Fēixīyānqū.*
Non-smoking.

Host: *Qǐng gēnzhe wǒ.*
Right this way.

Host: *Nínmén de fúwùyuán mǎshàng guòlái. Zhù nínmén yòng cān yú kuài.*
Your server will be along shortly. Enjoy your meal.

Server: *Wǎnshàng hǎo, wǒ shì nínmén de fúwùyuán. Zhè shì Nínmén de càidānr.*
Good Evening. I'm your server. Here are your menus.

TRACK 42

Patron: *Nǐ yǒu méiyǒu yīngyǔ càidānr?*
Do you have an English menu?

Server: *Wǒmén de càidānr shì shuāngyǔ de.*
Our menu is bilingual.

Patron: *Tài hǎo le! Wǒmén lái kàn yīxiàr.*
Great! We'll look it over.

Dining Dialogue

diǎncài	to order food
háiyǒu	and; furthermore
tuījiàn	suggest
dàchúshī	chef
sìchuānrén	Sichuanese

Chinese	English
náshŏucài	specialty dish
zhīyī	one of
hăochī	delicious, tasty; good
là	spicy; hot
yìbān	general; in general
kuàngquánshuĭ	mineral water
píng	bottle

TRACK 43

Server: *Nínmén xiànzài kéyĭ diăncài le ma?*
Are you ready to order?

Patron: *Kéyĭ ā.Wŏmén xiăng diăn tiébănniúròu, háiyŏu dòumiáo.*
Yes. We'd like to order the beef on a sizzling platter and the bean sprouts.

Server: *Háiyŏu ne?*
Anything else?

Patron: *Hái yŏu shénme cài kéyĭ tuījiàn yīxiàr ma?*
Is there anything else you could recommend?

Server: *Èn, wŏmén de dàchúshī shì sìchuānrén. Tāde náshŏucài zhīyī shi Mápórdòufū. Hén hăochī à.*
Hmm, our chef is Sichuanese. One of his specialties is Mapo Tofu. It's quite delicious.

Patron: *Là bú là?*
Is it spicy?

Server: *Yìbān de Sīchuāncài dōu hĕn là? Kéyĭ ma?*
Sichuanese food in general is quite spicy. Is that okay?

Patron: *Kéyĭ. Wŏmén dōu xĭhuān là.*
That's fine. We like spicy.

Server: *Hái yào diǎn shénme cài?*
Would you like to order anything else?

Patron: *Nǐ yǒu méiyǒu kuàngquánshuǐ?*
Do you have mineral water?

Server: *Yǒu, sān píng ma?*
Yes, three bottles?

Patron: *Kěyǐ.*
Please.

Beverages

In just about any Chinese restaurant that is not westernerized or serving Western food, you will be served complementary tea when seated for dinner. Don't worry if tea is not your cup of tea; establishments all over China will offer an assortment of other beverages. You'll find everything from soft drinks and juices to coconut milk and Chinese spirits.

Be careful when ordering Chinese wine. The Western and Chinese ideas of wine are two very different things. Often the Chinese word *jiǔ* is translated as "wine," but that is not entirely accurate. *Jiǔ* should be better rendered as "spirit" or "liqueur." *Jiǔ* is often much higher in alcohol content than traditional Italian, French, or Californian wines made from grapes. If it is grape wine that you wish to order then you should ask for *pútáojiǔ* or "grape wine." You can then specify whether you'd like *hóngpútáojiǔ* or *báipútáojiǔ*. When asking for a particular kind of beverage it should be mentioned that the measure words for beverages depend on their containers. For example:

yī bēi chá	**a cup of tea**
yī píng píjiǔ	**a bottle of beer**
yīguàn	**a can of soda**

ALERT!

It is absolutely vital that you be sure to say *báipútáojiǔ* instead of simply *báijiǔ* when asking for white wine. *Báijiǔ* is a traditional Chinese spirit that can be brewed from wheat, corn, or sorghum. Most of it is brewed from wheat, and it is extremely potent.

You'll be able to find most of your favorite carbonated beverages in China. You'll likely recognize them by sight, as the packaging will be nearly identical; but you probably won't recognize their names in Chinese. Here are some examples:

Coca Cola	*Kékǒu kělè*
Pepsi Cola	*Běishì kělè*
Sprite	*Xuěbì*
7-Up	*Qī-xǐ*

Vegetarians

For as great a land area as China occupies its relative amount of arable land is quite small. China simply doesn't have sufficient grasslands to support large livestock. Historically, as a result, meat—and beef, in particular—has been quite expensive, and thus, a symbol of prosperity. Chinese cuisine is usually thought to make little use of meat, but meat and fish are actually used quite often to give food flavor.

Meat and fish are very common ingredients in broths and stocks, which makes maintaining a vegetarian diet challenging to say the least. To add insult to injury, if you request a meal to be made without meat or ask for meals on the menu designated as vegetarian, the meal you get may still have fish bones in it. The Chinese word *ròu* means "meat" in the sense of any kind of animal flesh. If you ask a server if the vegetarian dish was made with any meat they will probably say no, despite the fact that there is oyster sauce in it. It won't even occur to the server that this will be a problem. To the server, fish is not thought to be meat, or *ròu*. Therefore, a vegetarian must be especially clear. The following are ways to make yourself understood as a vegetarian. Follow along with the track and repeat what you hear aloud.

Meat Mutterings

English	Chinese
beef	*niúròu*
pork	*zhūròu*
lamb	*yángròu*
ham	*huótuǐ*
lunchmeat	wǔcānròu
bacon	*yānròu*
fish	*yú*
meat foods	*hūn*
broth	*tāng*

TRACK 44

Wǒ bù chī hūn.	**I don't eat meat. / I'm a vegetarian.**
Nǐ huì zuò sù cài ma?	**Can you make it without meat?**
Tāng shì shénme yàng de?	**What kind of broth is it?**
Sù de cài yǒu méiyǒu?	**Do you have any items without meat?**

Taking It To Go

Most Chinese people work nine to ten hours a day. Longer working hours mean less time to cook. This is as much a problem for native Chinese as it is for visiting foreign business people. Perhaps you've had a long day of touring. In a country like China with so much to see and probably very little time to see it you may want to invest as much time in touring as possible. In which case, you'll put less emphasis on sit-down meals. Perhaps you'd simply like to eat with a little privacy. Sometimes we are simply not in the mood to sit in a crowded restaurant, especially after a long day of meetings. So take it to go! Take your meals to your apartment or hotel. "Set" or prearranged meals are a nice and convenient alternative to TV dinners. You don't have to prepare them yourself, and they do not come frozen. Many people think of set meals as an equitable alternative to cooking. This is mostly because set meals tend to be traditional dishes and they're home cooked. Set meals are not very exotic; they are what people would consider home cooking. Similarly, they are not considered by the Chinese to be fast food in the same way McDonald's is. Below you'll find tips on how to order one.

Take-Away Talk

Chinese	English
wài mài	take away
tàocān	set meal
hē	drink
dàizǒu	to take something with you; carry something
sònghuò	delivery (general items)

TRACK 45

Customer:	*Wài mài kéyǐ ma?* May I place an order to take away?
Clerk:	*Kéyǐ, qǐng kàn yīxiàr wǒmén de wài mài càidānr.* Sure, please have a look at our take away menu.

Clerk:	*Jīntiān wǎnshàng de tàocān shì yúxiāngròusī.*
	    Měi kuǎn bāokuò qīngcài hé báifàn.
	Today's evening set meal is spicy sliced pork. Each
	    set includes baby green bok choy and rice.

Customer:	*Hǎo, wǒ diǎn zhèige.* Great, I'll have this.
Clerk:	*Nǐ xiǎng hē shénme?* Would you like anything to drink?

Customer: *Yī píng kělè kéyǐ ma?*
May I have a can of soda?

Clerk: *Kéyǐ.*
Absolutely.

Clerk: *Nǐ xiǎngyào dàizǒu háishì wàisòng?*
Would you prefer to take it to go or have it delivered?

Customer: *Dàizǒu jiù hǎo le.*
I can take it to go.

Clerk: *Hǎo, yào shíwǔ fēnzhōng.*
Very well, it will be fifteen minutes.

Ordering In

Chinese	English
sòngcān	delivery (food)
xīcān	Western food
yìdàlì	Italy
shì	style
miàntiáo	noodle
pèicài	side dish
jiā	add
máimǎn	purchase up to/at least
yǐshàng	upwards of; and above

TRACK 46

Guest: *Wéi, sòngcān kéyǐ ma?*
Hello, may I place an order for delivery?

Clerk: *Kéyǐ, nǐde dìzhǐ shì shénme?*
Sure, what's your address?

Guest: *Wǒ zhù Běishān dàjiǔdiàn. Dìzhǐ shì Yángzhōu lù, wǔshíbā hào, shísān lóu, èryāobā shì.*

I'm staying at the Beishan Hotel. The address is 58
Yangzhou Road, 13th floor, room 218.

Clerk: *Hǎo, diǎn shénme?*
Okay, what would you like?

Guest: *Xīcān yǒu méiyǒu?*
Do you have Western food?

Clerk: *Yǒu. Wǒmén yǒu hànbǎobāo tàocān hé yìdàlìshì
miàntiáo tàocān.*
Yes. We have a hamburger set meal and a spaghetti
set meal.

Guest: *Tàocān bāokuò shénme pèicài?*
What side dish comes with the set meal.

Clerk: *Hànbǎobāo de bāokuò zhá shūtiáo. Miàntiáo de
bāokuò shūcài shālā.*
The burger meal comes with fries. The spaghetti
meal comes with a garden salad.

Guest: *Hǎo, wǒ yào hànbǎobāode, dànshì qǐng wèn,
jiā shālā duōshǎo qián?*
Okay, I'll take the burger meal, but, may I ask, how
much would it cost to add a salad?

Clerk: *Jiā shālā duō shí kuài qián. Hǎo ma?*
It would be 10 yuan extra for a salad. Is that okay?

Guest: *Hǎo, wàisòng yǒu méiyǒu jiā qián?*
That's fine, is there a delivery charge?

Clerk: *Yǒu, búguò rúguǒ ní máimǎn wǔshí kuài yǐshàng,
wàisòng miǎnfèi.*
There is, however, if your order is or exceeds 50
yuan, delivery is free.

Guest: *Hén hǎo.*
Great.

Restaurant Etiquette

At some point in your trip it's more than likely that a Chinese friend or colleague will invite you to dine with him or her at a restaurant. Though the average Chinese are not overly preoccupied with ceremony, there are some subtle rules of etiquette that are worth being aware of. In general, the Chinese will not expect you to be aware of all of their rules and customs, but knowing them and respecting them will certainly ingratiate you to your hosts.

The Bill

Going Dutch, or splitting the bill, when going out to dinner is a very American thing. When a Chinese person invites you out to dinner, he does it with the expectation that he will be paying for it. Of course, this should not stop you from politely requesting to pay yourself. But, in general, it will simply be understood that the person who invited you will pay the bill.

There are also some things you should know about paying the bill. When you first arrive at the restaurant, linger at the door for a moment or two. Or, at least wait until your host insists that you go and take a seat. The reason for this is that it is traditionally the person who is seated last who will pay for the dinner. Running to the table upon entering the restaurant may come across as an attempt to avoid having to pay for the meal.

Washing the Dinnerware

Another Chinese restaurant tradition is the act of washing the dinnerware. At most upscale restaurants this will be completely unnecessary, and at many of the mid-ranged family style restaurants it still may not be necessary, but it is a tradition nonetheless. The guests rinse their own dinnerware. When you sit down to dinner, the server will bring you two kettles and a glass bowl. The first kettle will have the tea that you will be served to drink. The second kettle will have hot water in it. The hot water is meant for you to use to rinse off your dinnerware.

A traditional Chinese restaurant dinner service will include a small bowl with a spoon, a small flat plate, a teacup, and a pair of chopsticks. You can start by pouring water into the small bowl with the spoon. Rinse them both and then wash the tea cup in the bowl by placing it on its side and turning it. To wash your chopsticks hold them at a 45-degree angle over the large plate and slowly pour the hot water over the chopsticks. When you've rinsed all your dinnerware, pour the leftover water into the glass bowl given to you along with the two kettles. The server will come by to take the bowl and the kettle of hot water and then you may pour the tea.

Dining Styles

There are two unique dining traditions in China that should not be missed. They are called dim sum and hot pot. Dim sum, which means "little snacks" in Cantonese, is a style of eating that originates in the South of China. It consists of very small portions of snack-like foods and is served with tea usually in the late morning until the early afternoon. In the past, various servers would push carts around a large dining room. The carts would hold various kinds of dim sum. The whole idea of dim sum is to sample lots of little delicacies. It's a chance to enjoy a long meal on a day of rest with good friends.

Dim sum is traditionally enjoyed on Sundays. Nowadays in China you simply order the various dim sum that you want using an order form. Give the order form to the server. The server then brings your dim sum out to you as they are prepared.

Hot pot originally came from Mongolia, but it has caught on all over Asia and become very popular. The hot pot style most popular in China these days is Sichuan style. Hot pot involves, to put it simply, a hot pot of soup or broth placed in the center of the table. Everyone sits around the table and adds various ingredients to the soup. Ingredients can range from all kinds of meats and vegetables to fish. Meats are sliced very thinly so that they may cook faster in the broth. Potatoes, carrots, and other hard vegetables are put in the broth first because they take the longest to cook.

The nature of dining hot pot style is a slow one. But because the food is cooked in the broth right before your eyes, you're meant to sit and enjoy the company of whomever you're dining with. Hot pot is very filling and nor-mally thought of as a winter eating style, though you can enjoy hot pot all year round.

Exercises

Now it's time to see what you've learned about dining in China. The follow-ing exercises include information covered in various parts of this chapter. Try to answer the questions from memory first, and then refer back to earlier pages if you need to jog your memory or perfect spelling.

1. Rearrange the following words to make a sentence: *yǐshàng miǎnfèi máimǎn kuài wàisòng wǔshí le*

   ....

   ....

2. Fill in the blanks with the most appropriate measure word:

   yì .... *kāfēi.*
   yì .... *qìxǐ.*
   yì .... *píjiǔ.*

3. Translate the sentence "I am a vegetarian."

   ....

   ....

Chapter 12

Festivities

Few Chinese social events reflect the mirth and hospitality of Chinese culture quite like the yànhuì, which you read about briefly in Chapter 9. The traditional Chinese banquet, or yànhuì, is held to celebrate a wide array of festivals, holidays, and occasions. You'll find that people host a yànhuì for everything from weddings and New Year's parties to job promotions and farewells. The banquet is exciting and represents a diversion from the norm. If you are invited to one, prepare for a night to remember.

The Commencement

Yànhuìs can be extremely elaborate and steeped in tradition and ceremony, or they can be quite simple with a minimum of cordiality, but by and large they all follow a basic format. The ceremony aspect of the banquet commences with the mere entry to the room. The most senior person or the guest of honor is supposed to enter first. This fact can cause a bit of an issue at the door as friends and coworkers will initiate a parlay of deference, each insisting that the other is either higher in rank or more deserving of the honor to enter first. Sometimes attendees get carried away and a traffic jam occurs at the door. This will soon be resolved however by the hungry people at the back of the line. Traditionally the guest of honor sits immediately opposite the host. The host usually takes the seat next to the serving door, which is considered the least honorable position.

Chinese banquets stray from the norm in terms of eating styles. Contrary to everyday eating styles where all the dishes of the meal are served at once, the courses of a *yànhuì* normally come out one or two at a time. Hot towels are distributed at the beginning of the meal for the guest's convenience. There are several courses all together, anywhere from ten to twelve. Another stray from the norm is the focus of the meal. Rice is not the focus of the banquet meal; in fact, rice is sometimes not even served at a *yànhuì*. If rice is served at all, it is served toward the end of the meal and you need only pick at it if you eat any at all. The purpose of the *yànhuì* is to celebrate prosperity, good fortune, and plenty. The dishes you will be served will likely be fairly decadent and feature a number of delicacies. The meat and vegetable dishes that are normally eaten in conjunction with the rice are eaten as the primary focus of the meal. Despite this fact, the host will apologize profoundly for the meager and poorly prepared meal you're about to partake of.

ALERT!

If you're still hungry or simply adore rice, then, of course, take some. But if you can avoid it at all try to forego any rice at a *yànhuì*. If the host sees you eat rice they may take it to mean you're still hungry and were not satisfied by the dishes that were served. As the *yànhuì* probably cost the organizers a pretty penny, try to focus on the main dishes.

The *yànhuì* can last anywhere from two to four hours depending on the occasion and the day of the week. If it is a welcome banquet it may only last an hour and a half to two hours. If it is a farewell banquet it may last the whole night, with the amount of reminiscing that might go on. At the more formal or upscale banquets the food is served to the guests by wait staff, while in less formal situations the banquet is served family style on a lazy Susan and attendees help themselves.

When all the guests have made their way into the room, the host may invite everyone to come all the way and please have a seat:

Qǐng jìnlái zuò.   **Everyone, please come in and be seated.**

Once everyone finds their seats and gets comfortable, the next part of the *yànhuì* begins. Everyone will find that their wine glass is already filled in anticipation to make a toast.

The Speech

The welcoming part of the yànhuì involves making a few short speeches and a toast. The host will likely give a lovely speech welcoming everyone called the *kāichǎngbái*. It will not be terribly long. It's simply to welcome everyone, wish everyone well, and perhaps state the purpose for the yànhuì. If this particular yànhuì is in your honor, then you will also be expected to give a *kāichǎngbái*. Now, don't panic! If you're the type of person who can easily speak in front a group, you may fare a bit better. But not everyone is a great orator. Just bear in mind that Chinese people are quite modest and somewhat shy. Your audience will sympathize and will do all they can to make sure you do not feel embarrassed or self conscious. They will listen attentively and smile. What's more, it is perfectly acceptable to prepare some notes ahead of time. The Chinese people who deliver speeches often read the speech word for word from a prepared statement.

There is no need to deliver the Gettysburg address. Be brief, to the point, polite, and humble. You should be standing for this speech, and you can begin by nodding your head in recognition to everyone. If you really want to impress, you can *bàoquán*. The *bàoquánlǐ* is a Chinese gesture that was used a great deal in the old days but is reserved today for congratulating or greeting your friends and peers on a special occasion. It is done by clenching your right fist and cupping your left hand over it as if to pray.

Now you may give your *kāichǎngbái*. Here is some common speech vocabulary that might come in handy:

Speech Vocabulary

rèliè	emphatically; warmly
dàoxiè	extend thanks
chéngméng	be indebted
yāoqǐng	invite
bèigǎn	with deep feeling
róngxìng	be honored
duì..láishuō	with respect to
bǎoguì	precious; valuable
réncái	staff member

Here's what a sample *kāichǎngbái* might sound like:

Xiānshēng xiáojiě wǎnshàng hǎo. Wǒ jiào Lynn Masi. Wǒ cóng měiguó lái. Bùhǎoyìsī, wǒde zhōngwén shuōde bútàihǎo. Wǒ xiǎng rèliè gǎnxiè nǐmen. Chéngméng yāoqǐng bèigǎn róngxìng. Wǒ xīwàng duì guìgōngsī láishuō, wǒ huì shì ge bǎoguì de réncái.

Good evening, ladies and gentleman. My name is Lynn Masi. I'm from the U.S.A. I apologize, my Chinese is not that good. I'd like to thank you from the bottom of my heart. It is a great honor to be here. I hope I can be a great asset to your company.

At this point, the host will take over again and invite everyone to *gānbēi* (cheers), which literally means "dry glass." After everyone has finished the *kāichǎngbái* toast, the host will invite everyone to begin eating by saying something like:

Dàjiā qǐng kāishǐ chī.	**Everyone please begin eating.**
Dàjiā qǐng qǐ kuài.	**Everyone please lift your chopsticks.**

Drinking Wine

Another Chinese name for the *yànhuì* is the *jiǔxí. Jiǔxí* literally means "wine feast," and there is an old Chinese saying that goes like this: *Wújiǔ bùchéng xí* (Without wine, it's not a feast). Even in Chinese poetry and prose, wine was highly romanticized, often being acquainted with being in love. Chinese don't often drink alcohol at everyday meals. Though a beer with dinner is not unheard of, most families tend to drink tea or juice with meals. As a result, for special occasions it takes on a new dimension.

In the Western tradition, the type of wine you drink depends on the food you'll be eating—red wine with red meats and white wine with fish or poultry, etc. This is not the case with the Chinese. The wine at a *yànhuì* is served according to one of two general conventions. The first convention is "the wine of the evening." In this way the host will select one form of alcohol that will be served throughout the banquet. It can be any kind of alcohol, but generally it is either a spirit, grape wine, or beer.

FACT

Arguably the most famed brand of *báijiǔ* in China is *Máotáijiǔ*. It originated in the city of *Máotái* in the Guizhou province, some two centuries ago. It is brewed using a seven-step distillation process and is considered one of the finest forms of *báijiǔ* on the market, having won an award in 1915 at the Panama Pacific exhibition. Chairman Mao served *Máotáijiǔ* to former president Richard M. Nixon on his historic visit to the PRC.

You might call the second convention the "the festival motif." There's a tradition that has grown more prevalent in China where all three types of alcohol are served at a *yànhuì*. The festival motif gets its name from colors of the alcohol served which are colors of great significance in Chinese culture. Red is a color of good luck, and happiness is represented by red grape wine. White in Chinese culture is often thought to be associated with death, though that symbolism is extrapolated from a still deeper connotation that the soul is pure energy. Thus, white, in Chinese culture, represents purity, preciousness, and clarity on a more fundamental level. White is represented by *báijiǔ*; a traditional Chinese distilled alcohol of 80 to 120 proof made from sorghum or a combination of sorghum wheat and/or glutinous rice. A few glasses of this will definitely leave you stumbling. Gold is the color of fortune, as it was also the color of the Emperor's robes, and it is represented by beer.

Toasting

Toasting is done throughout the meal. Be careful, however, as the person who lifts his or her glass to propose a toast is the person who sets the pace to drink. What this means is that if you sip, the person you're toasting with will sip. Similarly, if you *gānbēi*, then the person you're toasting will have to finish their drink as well. For your first *yànhuì*, you should probably stick to sipping. If you drink too boldly some of your peers may toast you as well and *gānbēi*. If you're drinking *báijiǔ*, this could lead to a wild evening. When toasting those sitting beside you, it's customary to clink glasses, but it is not mandatory. You should not be shy about toasting your fellow attendees, it's a truly natural part of the banquet. There are some simple toasts you can make, such as:

Wèi nǐ de jiànkāng gānbēi!	**Here's to your health!**
Wèi wǒmen de yǒuyì gānbēi	**Here's to our friendship!**

Another integral dynamic to toasting is that of making sure that everyone's glass around you is full. You should try to avoid filling your own glass. Instead, fill your neighbor's glass, they will more than likely take note if yours is empty or not and offer to do the same. When you fill someone else's glass, you should try to fill it as far as possible to the top without spilling it. You can politely ask if someone would like some more of what you are drinking by saying:

Zài lái yībēi, hǎoma? **Would you care for another glass?**

If someone asks if you'd like a refill, you may respond positively by simply saying:

Hǎode, Xièxie. **Yes, thank you.**

If you simply cannot have another sip, then you should politely decline it saying:

Bùhǎoyìsī, wǒ bù néng zài **I'm sorry, I couldn't drink another**
hē le, Xièxie. **drop, thank you.**

Alcohol Alternatives

All this talk of wine, spirits, beer, and toasting might be enough to make you a little lightheaded. But don't be too concerned; some Chinese people simply do not drink. If you don't drink, then don't feel you have to. Simply be straightforward with your host and respectfully inform him that for whatever reasons you do not drink. In addition, though alcohol is the beverage of choice for a *yànhuì*, nowadays, tea, juices, and bottled water are also commonly served. If you do not drink alcohol, the next most suitable beverage for a *yànhuì* would be *chá*, or tea. In China, you can't go wrong with *chá*. In fact, at a banquet, you're likely to be served a rather fine tea.

There are several forms of Chinese tea that are consumed frequently. The crowning four of these forms of tea are variations of what is regarded as "true tea." They are green tea, white tea, black tea and oolong tea. True tea is tea that is made from the "tea plant," known to botanists as the Camellia sinensis plant. The primary distinction between the various types of true Chinese teas is in the time at which they are harvested and their subsequent processing and level of oxidation. Distinctions between the different grades of tea are sometimes hard to gauge, but tea production has existed in China for thousands of years and as such there are some very old and famous tea producers. The price of the various teas usually accurately reflects the grade of tea.

FACT

Jasmine tea is considered in China to be a *huāchá* or "flower tea." By definition it is not technically a "true tea" because it is not cultivated from the Camellia sinensis. Originating in India, Jasmine has been cultivated in China for centuries and holds a special place in the heart of the Chinese people. Jasmine tea is very popular for its pleasant flavor and enchanting aroma. Chinese women indulge in it, as legend holds that jasmine tea enhances a person's beauty.

The most famous kind of green tea is *Lóngjǐng chá* (Dragon Well tea). *Lóngjǐng* comes from the city of *Hángzhōu* in the *Zhèjiāng* province. Green tea naturally has a pale green color. It has a light aroma and a refreshing herby cleansing taste. Green tea is loaded with antioxidants, vitamin C, and amino acids, and is reputed in China for being very good for the body. The finest variety of white tea is *Báiháoyínzhēn*, or often simply called *Yínzhēn*. *Yínzhēn* is produced in greatest quantity in the *Fújiàn* province. It is pale gold in color, often with reflective white strands in it giving it a kind of glittery appearance. It is a light refreshing tea that is slightly sweet. *Qímén* tea from the *Ānhuī* province is the premier black tea of China. This form of Chinese tea is the most widely exported to and enjoyed by the West.

Westerners who enjoy the English Breakfast blend of tea or Pekoe teas are drinking a form of Chinese black tea. However, unlike *lǜchá* and *báichá*, Chinese black tea is not *hēichá* but *hóngchá* (red tea). *Dàhóngpào* is one of the most prized of the *Wūlóng* (oolong) teas. The finest oolong teas come from *Wǔyíshān* in the *Fújiàn* province, and along with jasmine tea are the teas most often served at Chinese restaurants and banquets. You can indulge in some polite banter while enjoying some as in the dialogue below:

TRACK 47

Colleague:	*Masi tàitài, nǐ xǐhuān zhōngguó chá ma?* Mrs. Masi do you like Chinese tea?
Mrs. Masi:	*Fēicháng xǐhuān!* Yes, very much!
Colleague:	*Nǐ zuì xǐhuān názhǒng chá?* What tea do you like best?

Mrs. Masi:	*Qíshí, wǒ tèbié xǐhuān mòlìhuā chá. Hěn tián à.*
	Actually, I especially like jasmine tea. It's so sweet.
Colleague:	*Yídìng shì. Cóngqián zhōngguórén rènwéi hē*
	mòlìhuāchá huì gèng měi.
	It certainly is. In the past, Chinese believed that
	drinking jasmine tea could enhance one's beauty.
Mrs. Masi:	*Nà, yéxǔ, wǒ gāi duō mǎi yīdiǎnr.*
	Well, then, perhaps I should buy some more.
Colleague:	*Nǐ kěndìng bù xūyào, dànshì, wǒ rènwéi nǐ huì*
	hěn xǐhuān.
	You certainly don't need it, but I think you'd enjoy it.

Small Talk

chá	tea
qíshí	actually
mòlìhuā	jasmine
tián	sweet
yídìng	certainly
cóngqián	in the past
rènwéi	believed
hē	drink
yéxǔ	perhaps
kěndìng	surely

The Food

The food you eat in China will be nothing less than delectable. This could be a culinary tour of China for you featuring all of the highlights of Chinese eating styles and regional specialties and flavors. The first course is generally cold dishes served in an even number. There can be eight or ten. Afterwards there will be some sort of fine soup. Traditional soups of greatest renown are bird's nest and shark's fin, but there are hundreds of delightful Chinese soups. Unlike in the West, soup is eaten with the meal or afterwards, but not before. The rest of the dishes will come out soon after to be enjoyed with the soup which is usually poured by the host. Dishes will be varied and will include pork, fish, beef, chicken, bean curd, noodles, and if you're lucky, *kǎoyā*, or Peking duck. Peking duck is by far the crowning dish of Chinese culinary tradition and is, of course, made best in Beijing. The duck is slow roasted in brick ovens for hours, and sliced meticulously by the chef. It's eaten by being rolled into pancakes with scallions and hoisin sause. The last dinner dish is often a whole fish. The fish is generally placed such that the head is pointing at the guest of honor. Throughout the banquet you should pay a lot of compliments to the food like:

Niúròu hén hǎochī.	**The beef is very good.**
Shūcài tèbié kékǒu.	**The vegetable is particularly delicious.**
Zhūròu hén měiwèi.	**The pork is delicious.**

A good host will request dishes that reflect the diversity of China's regional cuisines. You'll likely see a curry dish, a chili pepper dish, dumplings, seafood, a sweet and sour dish, and it might be fried, boiled, or steamed. The host may pay particular attention however to the delicacies of the local regional cuisine.

Chopstick Etiquette

As most everyone knows, the Chinese do not eat with forks and knives but with chopsticks. If you don't know how to use them, this would be a good skill to learn. Restaurants rarely put forks and knives out on the table, so you would have to specially request them. What's more, it will certainly impress your hosts. But using chopsticks is not as simple as picking them up and having at it. There are certain rules to using them you should be aware of, including the following:

- If you're still undecided on what dish to try, don't brandish your chopsticks, taking special care not to wave them around too freely. They're eating utensils.

- Don't insert your chopstick into any of the food so as to keep them there. Play close attention not to stick your chopsticks into your rice. The reason for this is that in many of the temples when someone goes to make an offering they place their incense sticks in bowls of rice to hold them up in place. The Chinese are somewhat superstitious, so this uncomfortable association with death will be unsettling at a banquet.
- Try to avoid using your chopsticks to move plates around or push or pull plates away and toward you. If something is out of reach it's completely appropriate to stand up and reach for a plate, what's more you should use both hands to reach.
- You should avoid tapping or otherwise touching too much of the food. Use your chopsticks to reach for the food you want.
- After you're done eating you should rest your chopsticks on the chopstick rest that will probably be at your place setting. If there is no place setting, you can place them down flat to the left of your rice bowl.

Wrapping Things Up

You'll be clued in to the end of the evening drawing nearer by the appearance of the fresh fruit dishes. When it looks like everyone has had their fill of the fruit dishes, the guest of honor should then thank the host and attendees for a wonderful evening. You can basically repeat elements of your welcome speech:

> *Zhè bùjǐn shì yícì hén hǎo de xuéxí jīnglì, érqiě chōngmǎn le lèqù. Xièxie nǐmen shèngqíng kuǎndài.*

This has not only been a learning experience, it has also been a lot of fun. The food was delicious and the company was very charming. Thank you all for your hospitality.

After the guest of honor has said his or her thank you, the host will rise again and thank the guests for coming. It is at this point that the *yànhuì* is concluded. It's standard procedure to give a gift to the host. Gifts need not be extravagant, a simple token is very much appreciated. A gift can be anything, even a cultural token from your homeland would do nicely. Avoid jewelry, though, even if it is traditional from your homeland. Chinese urbanites generally do not wear yellow gold, favoring white gold and platinum, and Chinese women generally do not pierce their ears so earrings might be a bad idea. Gifts are generally opened in private.

Exercises

Do you remember everything you've learned about Chinese festivities? The following exercises include information covered in various parts of this chapter. Try to answer the questions from memory first, and then refer back to earlier pages if you need to jog your memory or perfect spelling.

1. Translate the phrase "*Zài lái yìbēi, hǎoma?*" to English.

   ....

2. Match the Chinese phrase with its corresponding English phrase.

rèliè	in the past
yāoqǐng	precious
bǎoguì	invitation
bèigǎn	emphatic
cóngqián	with deep feeling

3. What do you say when you can't drink another drop?

   ....

4. Arrange the following words into a sentence: *yícì xuéxí shì zhè hǎo jīnglì hén de bùjǐn.*

   ....

5. How do you say "opening speech" in Chinese?

   ....

Chapter 13

Cultural Highlights

China has an ancient and rich repertoire of artistic expression, the highlight of which is *gējù*, or Chinese opera. It is the medium where Chinese theatre, literature, and music all blend into one magnificent form of expression. Chinese opera is adored for its portrayal of China's classics of drama and folklore. To many Western ears, Chinese operatic singing will probably sound shrill and dissonant with lots of falsettos and the pounding of the *xiǎogǔ* (drums), the clacking of the *bǎn* (clappers), and the clanging of the *náobó* (cymbals). But if you're knowledgable beforehand, you'll be more equipped to understand and enjoy the experience.

Chinese Opera

As early as the Han dynasty the Chinese were combining storytelling with dance to create basic musical dramas. They were intended to communicate the lessons of friendship, morality, love, and more found in Chinese folktales. But it was not until the Tang dynasty and the court of Emperor Xuanzong that the Pear Garden opera troupe came into being. The Pear Garden's primary call was to perform the tales and pieces most beloved by the emperor. This form of theater endured through to the Song dynasty. The Mongols had begun to introduce a style of theater that would finally be realized in its stylized form in the Yuan dynasty. It was called Zájù (plays of variety). Zájù introduced several innovations, such as rhyming schemes of the dialogue and a four-act format in which songs alternate with dialogue. Singing was restricted to only one character, and the plot was minimally important when compared to the quality and poetry of the lyrics. Zájù also introduced specialized roles like the *shēng* (male), *dàn* (female), *huā* (painted-face), and *chǒu* (jester). In Modern Beijing opera, the painted face role is called the jìng.

Hailing from the *Jiāngnán* or Wu region, comprised today of Shànghǎi, the *Jiāngsū* province, and the *Zhèjiāng* province, comes *Kūnq*ǔ opera. This style is the oldest form of what is regarded as modern Chinese opera. It gets its name from the Kunshan melodies it evolved from, and as a style it is regarded as the mother of a hundred operas. Beijing opera is one of the now 368 different forms of Chinese operas that spawned from *Kūnqǔ*.

The Mechanics

If you keep some of the basic mechanics behind the *gējù* in mind, who is who and why are they doing what may make a bit more sense. Beijing opera, which has existed in its present form since the middle of the nineteenth century, is the best known of all the Chinese operatic schools. Its central features are its combination of acrobatics, acting, costumes, dance, makeup, martial arts, poetry, and singing.

Language helps to illustrate the differences between the roles, as the featured focal characters use literary Chinese and the young female characters and jesters use *kǒuyǔ*, or colloquial speech. Makeup also serves to help define the characters and their roles in the drama. Red, which is already an auspicious color in Chinese culture, represents loyalty, integrity, and courage. Black represent aloofness, changeable temperament, and silence, as well as strength and aggression. White is associated with mischief, coyness, slyness, or craftiness; the more white, the more suspicious the character. Purple is a solemn color that communicates serenity and the power of justice and righteousness. Yellow represents intelligence, guile, and bravery when it's applied to a warrior part. Blue is the color of uprightness and rigidity; blue faces are stubborn characters. Green is a follower. Green is a brave and irascible individual but still a soldier instead of a general. Gold and silver are special colors generally reserved for supernatural figures, such as immortals, demons, or monsters. The various colors help add dimension to the cast and how they interact. The *chǒu*, like the *jīng*, has a unique makeup characteristic. He has a white nose, and that is supposed to be a mark of humor. Take note of how characters are acting and being addressed by others. Also, take note of their makeup.

The Players

The *Shēng* is the primary male character in Chinese opera. He is usually some sort of male figure of importance, often a civil or military figure. Within the role of *Shēng* there are three possible sub roles. The *Lǎoshēng* (older *Shēng*) is usually bearded. He will be some sort of polished official, a dignified scholarly figure. His voice will probably be somewhat deep, ominous, and possibly thundering. The *Xiǎoshēng* (younger *Shēng*) will speak in a shrill higher voice. He is usually a young warrior, or younger man of some social stature. He will probably be dressed elaborately. Finally, the *Wūshēng* (acrobatic *Shēng*) will be an obvious acrobat, his character embodies the vitality of youth and he is physically skilled and dexterous. All the *Shēng* have relatively simple makeup. Simple makeup for Chinese opera means the three basic colors of white base, black around the eyes and red around the cheeks and eye area peaking upward between the eyebrows. Generally, there will only be slight variations between their makeup. The *Lǎoshēng* usually has no lip pigment. The *Xiǎoshēng* has lip pigment and a muted forehead streak, while the *Wūshēng* is most colorful with lip pigment and long upward forehead streak.

The *Dàn* is a female role. *Dàn* makeup is much like the *Shēng's* makeup utilizing the three basic colors. You'll be able to discern what role the actress is playing by a combination of her behaviors and outstanding features of her makeup and costume. The *Lǎodàn* is an elderly woman, she'll be distinguishable probably by a light colored wig denoting her age. *Qīngyī* is the modest virtuous young woman, often dressed elegantly. *Huādàn* is a flirtatious young woman that may have a tiny flower painted on her forehead. *Guīméndàn* is the young married woman. *Wǔdàn* is the female acrobat. She will probably be in pants allowing her to perform her feats. *Pōlàdàn* is a spiteful and unpleasant woman. Her movements are often unremarkable, resembling an average person, she speaks shrilly. *Dāomǎdàn* is a strong woman, her costume will probably be elaborate yet she will be skilled as an acrobat as well.

The *Jìng* comes in two major categories: the *Wénjìng* and the *Wǔjìng* and their face makeup and costumes are nothing less than spectacular. Hours are put into dressing the *Jìng* for their parts and as such, so it's no wonder that they portray some of the more powerful figures in the story. *Wénjìng* come in two basic categories. *Zhèngjìng* are virtuous and ethical heroes; they move about the stage with the most purpose and grace. *Fùjìng* are neither good nor evil; instead, they embody the ultimate dichotomy, representing beauty and ugliness, elegance and roughness. The audience doesn't quickly identify with this character. He may seem mysterious and unpredictable. The second category of *jìng* is the *Wǔjìng*, and they are bigger-than-life kinds of characters. They are brash yet affable and likely to make a spectacle of themselves. Finally, meet the beloved *Chǒu*. Easily identifiable by the white nose area, they are the jesters. There are three basic kinds of

Chŏu: *Wénchŏu*, the average country bumpkin townsman; *Wŭchŏu*, the animated acrobatic military jesters; and finally the *Chŏupózi*, who are female *Chŏu*. *Chŏu* provide the audience with succinct comic relief. Armed with this basic knowledge, the next stop is to find out what show you will be seeing and see if you can find out more about the story. Together, your basic knowledge of Chinese drama coupled with the background of the story will enable you to appreciate the performance far more than most any other Westerner who may also be watching it.

The Chinese Musical Tradition

In China, music appears in historical records as having developed into a culture as early as the Zhou dynasty. Emperor Han Wu Di, during the Qin dynasty, expanded the study and field of music by creating the Imperial Music Bureau. It was the duty of this organ to oversee the organization of all official court and military music as well as to evaluate folk music for recognition. Later on in China's history, her music fell under a great deal of foreign influence in part mostly due to the Silk Road. From the far reaches of Central Asia came Buddhism, Islam, and the exotic music of the nations where those religions flourished.

Confucius maintained that music exists as a medium for perpetuating tranquility and quelling unrest and lustfulness rather than for entertainment. In Confucian ideology, music is a way of achieving enlightenment and clarity.

The Chinese musical scale has five notes. The family of instruments is determined by what material the instruments are made of. China's earliest instruments were fiddle- and reed-like, but later on instrument construction evolved and became better. Instruments were composed of skin, gourd, bamboo, wood, silk, and earth. In the realm of China's cultural history, music occupies an odd dichotic role. Whereas in the past musicians and painters occupied the lower factions of Chinese society as prescribed by cultural and Confucian conventions, music was regarded as central to the national harmony and longevity.

Traditional Chinese Instruments

Chinese music history is indeed rich and comes with an entire orchestra of unique instruments. Among them one of the most beloved is the *pípá*. The *pípá* gets its name from the manner in which it's played. *Pí* means to strum from right to left with your index finger, while *pá* means to strum from left to right with your thumb. The *pípá* is a lute-like stringed instrument that is plucked and therefore it takes the playing verb tán:

Tā tán pípá tánde hénhǎo.　　　　**He plays the *pípá* very well.**

Ironically, as cherished by the Chinese as this instrument is, it is actually a fruit of the Silk Road, having originated in Persia where it was called the *barbat*. The *barbat* made it to China during Jin dynasty and its popularity flourished, becoming the most favored instrument of Tang dynasty. At that time, Persian musicians were in demand in Chángān, the Tang capital. It is at this time that some of the most strikingly designed *pípá* were constructed and some have been preserved to this day. Also considered a plucked instrument is the *gǔzhēng*. The *gǔzhēng* is a large twenty-one-stringed instrument belonging to the zither family. The *gǔzhēng* is the mother of the Japanese *koto* and the Korean *gayageum* and is easily one of China's most elegant instruments. Playing it requires not only a profound ear for the music but immense grace and poise as its play is often associated with a regulated breathing. Its strings used to be made of silk, but today most are fitted with metal strings, and players use nail attachments much the same way *pípá* players do.

Wǒyòunián de shíhòu wǒ　　　　**When I was young, I learned to play**
xuétán gǔzhēng.　　　　　　　**the guzheng.**

Often referred to by Western musicians as the Chinese violin, the *èrhú* is a two-stringed bowed musical instrument that shines as both a solo instrument and a group or orchestral instrument. Its origins date back well over 1,000 years, and it is said to have evolved from an instrument called the *xī qín*, which was described as a foreign, two-stringed lute. *Èr* is supposed to be a reference to the number of strings, while *hú* was a reference the *húqín*, another instrument that shared common characteristics with it. As a bowed instrument it takes the verb *lā*.

Tā lā èrhú lā de bǐ wǒ hǎo.	**He plays the erhu better than I.**

Among the Chinese woodwind instruments, one of the most notable is the *shēng*. The *shēng* is a free reed instrument consisting of vertical tubes reminiscent of a pan flute. The *shēng* is primarily used in the Chinese orchestra as an instrument of accompaniment, and rarely plays any melody. What is most notable about the *shēng* is that it is believed that it was brought back to Europe by Pere Amiot and Johann Wilde in the eighteenth century and that it served as the inspiration for such European instruments as the accordion, the concertina, the harmonica and the reed organ. As a woodwind instrument that is blown, the *shēng* takes the verb *chuī*.

Wǒ cónglái méi xuéguò chuī shēng.	**I never learned to play the sheng.**

Finally, another Chinese woodwind of popularity is the *dízi*. This transverse flute comes in many varieties and styles. It is beloved by Chinese musicians and patrons alike for its soft melodic tone found in folk music *gējù* and orchestral performances alike. Another primary reason for the *dízi*'s popularity in China is the fact that it is relatively easily fashioned from reasonable and accessible materials and it is lightweight and easy to carry about, thus making it accessible to the poor. *Dízi* are most commonly made from bamboo, but historically there have been *dízi* made from all manner of wood, even fragrant woods, and from marble or stone and even from jade. Jade *dízi* make fine collector's items.

Karaoke

You're probably wondering why there is a discussion of karaoke in this book. Indeed, karaoke did not originate in China but in Japan. It was invented by Daisuke Inoue, a Japanese backup drummer who was frequently asked by audience members and guests for whom he played back up if he would perform some of his back up on tape so that they could sing along when elsewhere on other engagements. When he realized he could capitalize on this by fashioning a tape recorder that would play his songs for 100-yen coins, the first Karaoke machine was born. Karaoke in Japanese means empty orchestra.

So, if karaoke is not Chinese, why discuss it in a book about the Chinese language? The reason is that the Chinese absolutely love karaoke and regard it as an important performing art.

The variation of karaoke most popular in China is KTV. KTV is a small party service intended to entertain private parties. The KTV lounge rooms come with a large TV monitor that displays the lyrics to the song while an in-theme music video plays at the same time. The videos are rarely official and are produced specifically for the KTV lounges. Most KTV lounges have ten to twenty such KTV rooms, but there is still a main lounge where the karaoke is enjoyed.

To say that KTV is a popular pastime in mainland China, Taiwan, Hong Kong, and Macau is truly an understatement of untold proportions. Successful KTV chains earn millions each year. The fascination with KTV has extended into the business world. Often business folk make use of KTV lounges to entertain potential clients. You'll often hear secretaries inquiring as to whether or not a given hotel where a client is staying has KTV facilities. If they do, it will likely be used to entertain the client.

Zhèr yǒu KTV tīng ma?	**Does this place have a KTV lounge?**
Dānjiān yǒu méiyǒu?	**Does it have single rooms?**
Dānjiān duōshǎo qián?	**How much are the single rooms?**
Àn gēqǔ háishì àn zhōngdiǎn suàn?	**Do you charge by the song or by the hour?**

Do you remember reading about how luxurious the baths in China can be? High-end KTV lounges at the fine hotels can be no less extravagant. They have their own special menus. You can order dinner, or just some snacks. There is an open bar, and you may have wait staff available to wait on the guests. You may even have your own private hostess! Here are some sample questions you might need to ask at a KTV lounge:

Nǐmen yǒu rìwéngē ma?	**Do you have Japanese songs?**
Nǐmen yǒu Yīngwéngē ma?	**Do you have English songs?**
Yǒu xiáojiě ma?	**Is there a hostess?**
Kéyǐ diǎn xiǎochī yǐnliào ma?	**Is it possible to order snacks and drinks?**
Fúwùfèi zài nèi ma?	**Is the service charge included?**

ALERT!

Take care when asking about a hostess (*Xiáojiě*; Miss), particularly if your host invites you to "Special KTV." Special KTV is deemed special due to the participation of a main hostess and other hostesses whose interaction may range anywhere from geisha-like platonic entertainment and conversation to sexual liaison. This practice is not uncommon, so if you hear the term mentioned, don't be shy to ask questions that may save you from an uncomfortable situation in the future.

KTV is popular not just in China and her territories, but throughout most of East Asia including Korea, Singapore, Malaysia, the Philippines, and Indonesia. In the West, however, it is not as popular, which highlights a very interesting irony between western and eastern cultures. The Chinese, who are ordinarily quite reserved and shy, have absolutely no fear of getting up in front of their peers, and regardless of how off-key they may sound, belting out a few songs in front of a crowd. Westerners, who are on average a bit more gregarious and open, are often quite shy about speaking, much less singing, in front of a group of friends. Karaoke first hit the United States in the 1990s, and was a bit of a flash in the pan. It never really caught on to the degree it did in Asia.

Buying Tickets

In order to enjoy all the cultural experiences China has to offer, you first need to be able to order tickets to the shows you want to see! The following vocabulary will come in handy in your conversations with people like ticket sellers and fellow audience members.

Ticket Talk

guójiādàjùyuàn	National Grand Theatre
tíqián	in advance
yǎn	act
shòu zhòngshì	beloved
shǐshī	epic
zhīyī	one of
zīliào	information
Wǎng	Net; Web
Wǎng shàng	on the Web; online
wǎngzhàn	Web site; Web page
Qiánpái zuòwèi	front row seats
zhíde	worthwhile, worth it
tóngyì	agree
kāiyǎn	begin a show
yǎnwán	end a show

Here's a sample conversation between a hopeful ticket buyer and a clerk at the opera ticket office:

Guest: *Wǒ hé wǒ lǎopó xiǎng qù kàn jīngjù, nǐ zhīdào zài nár kéyǐ mǎidào piào?*

My wife and I would like to go to the Beijing Opera,
do you know where I could buy tickets?

Clerk: *Nín kéyǐ zài guójiādàjùyuàn mǎidào piào, Dànshì
wǒ néng wèi nǐnmen mǎipiào.*
You can buy them at the Grand National Theater.
But I can buy them for you.

Guest: Zhēnde *ma?*
Really?

Clerk: Zhēnde.
Really.

Guest: *Tàihǎole. Yǒu méiyǒu jīnwǎn de piào?*
Great! Do you have tickets for this evening?

Clerk: *Yídìng yào tíqián mǎipiào, suóyǐ jīnwǎn de piào
jiù mǎibúdào. Míngwǎn kéyǐ ma?*
Tickets must be purchased in advance so we cannot
purchase tickets for tonight. Will tomorrow
night do?

Guest: *Kéyǐ. Míngwǎn yǎn shénme gējù? Nǐ zhīdào ma?*
It will do. What will tomorrow night's performance
be? Do you know?

Clerk: *Míngwǎn yǎn Xī Yóu Jì.*
Tomorrow night's performance will be "The Journey
to the West."

Guest: *Xīyóujì, hǎo bùhǎo kàn?*
Is "The Journey to the West" good?

Clerk: *Fēicháng hǎo. Xīyóujì shì zhōngguó zuì shòu
zhòngshì de shǐ shī zhīyī.*
Very good. "The Journey to the West" is one of China's
most beloved epics.

Guest: *Hǎo jí le. Nǐ zhīdào nár kéyǐ zhǎodào guānyú
Xīyóujì de zīliào?*

Excellent. Do you know where I could find information about "The Journey to the West"?

Clerk: *Wǎng shàng yǒu háojǐge yǔ Xīyóujì xiāngguān de wǎngzhàn.*

There are tons of sites on line related to "The Journey to the West."

Guest: *Qiánpái zuòwèi duóshvo qián?*

How much are front row seats?

Clerk: *Wǔbǎiwǔshí kuài yīwèi.*

550 RMB per seat.

Guest: *Hěn guì ā!*

That's pricey!

Clerk: *Guì, dànshì qù kàn Xīyóujì jiù zhíde.*

It is, but if you're going to see "The Journey to the West," it's worth it.

Guest: *Wǒ tóngyì, shénme shíhòu kāiyǎn hé yǎnwán?*

I agree, what time does the show start and finish?

Clerk: *Qī diǎn zhōng kāiyǎn, shí diǎn zhōng yǎnwán, nín jīntiān xiàwǔ kéyǐ jiē piào.*

It starts at 7:00 P.M. and ends at 10:00 P.M. You can come by and pick up your tickets this afternoon.

Exercises

Now you're all ready to take in some Chinese culture, right? Let's find out. The following exercises include information covered in various parts of this chapter. Try to answer the questions from memory first, and then refer back to earlier pages if you need to jog your memory or perfect spelling.

1. Rearrange these words to form a Chinese sentence: *shǐshī zhīyī shì zhō
   ngguó shòu zhòngshì de Xīyóujì zuì.*

   ....

   ....

2. How do you say "He plays the pipa very well" in Chinese?

   ....

   ....

3. What are the names of the four basic roles in Beijing opera?

   ....

   ....

   ....

   ....

4. What does the color red represent in Beijing opera?

   ....

   ....

Chapter 14

Health Care in China

You may be wondering why you have to worry about health care in China if you're only going to be visiting the country for a short period of time. Well, even though you may not be moving to China, it's still important to know a thing or two about how to handle different medical situations there. You never know if you'll get sick during your visit or have an unfortunate accident resulting in a sprained ankle or wrist. This chapter will fill you in on all the health care information you need.

China's Health Care History

China has one of the longest recorded histories of medicine known to humanity. And even with the introduction of the western medical tradition it still maintains its own traditional medical practices, many of which are regarded as being very effective in preventative medicine. It is this emphasis on preventive medicine that has made its way into modern Chinese medical practices.

Since the founding of the People's Republic, it has been the aspiration of Chinese health programs to maximize a health care system with limited resources and staff in order to render care to the entire population. Prevention is seen as somewhat unnecessary—if the population isn't sick there's no need to cure them. Despite this fact and the introduction of western medical practices and technology, China still suffers from a number of public health ills, not the least of which is pollution.

QUESTION?

Do a lot of people smoke in China?
Unfortunately, the answer is yes. Cigarette smoking exists in epidemic proportions, as it is perpetuated by a government-controlled monopoly on tobacco. Fortunately, though, smoking is slowly becoming "unfashionable," particularly in the major cities and among the young people.

Generally speaking, it's a good idea to stay abreast of new health-related developments. Do you remember Severe Acute Respiratory Syndrome (SARS)? In 2002, SARS struck in Guangdong province, resulting in 348 deaths. On May 18, 2004, the World Health Organization declared China free of subsequent cases of the syndrome. Avian influenza is now a major concern, not only for China but for the entire world. The Chinese government is also taking lengthy precautions to quell any spread of the H5N1 virus. These kinds of problems are good motivation for staying in the know when it comes to worldwide health issues. Get in the habit of checking out the CDC's Web site: *www.cdc.gov*.

An Ounce of Prevention

Although China's larger cities offer health care services equivalent to Western standards, it's still a good idea to take prior measures so as to minimize the need to see a doctor while you're there. In general, you should drink lots of fluids to prevent dehydration and constipation, take vitamins, and wear comfortable shoes. Much of China is very humid, so talcum powder is a useful item to bring.

Immunizations

Although the Chinese government does not require any specific vaccinations for entry except for yellow fever if you are a traveler from infected areas of tropical South America and sub-Saharan Africa, it is still a good idea in general for all of your immunizations to be current. Vaccinations for measles, tetanus, diptheria, and pertussis, for example, should be up to date. As an adult traveling to China, it would be in your best interest to consider the following vaccinations: Hepatitis B, influenza, Hepatitis A, and Japanese encephalitis. A typhoid vaccination is a good idea for travelers who will be in China during the summer, those who plan on visiting rural areas, and those who plan on being in China for more than four weeks. Vaccination regimens often require repeat administrations over a period of time. Therefore, you should contact your doctor at least three months prior to travel.

Air Quality

Allergy sufferers and asthmatics should be forewarned when traveling to China that an unsettling number of our world's most polluted cities are in China. Coal is burned for heat in the winter, and so pollution and air quality in most Chinese cities is not very good. So much so, that even the healthiest of travelers may fall ill. The situation is most dire in the north of China and China's industrial northeast, including Beijing, Shenyang, Xi'an, and Harbin. Be aware, however, that the other regions of China are not exempt from the impact of China's pursuit of energy. Cities such as Shanghai, Guangzhou, and Chongqing also suffer from poor air quality.

You should consult your private physician about the air quality in China before traveling to China. It may be useful for you to bring with you inhalers and other respiratory aids such as prescription medications.

Be Prepared for the Heat

The second biggest health concern for a traveler to China is heat exhaustion and dehydration. China is a very large country but regardless of where you go, save for a few regions of the country renowned for their excellent weather, most of China is brutally hot in the summer. Northern China borders Mongolia and Kazakhstan in the west, and is dry and arid. Heat exhaustion and salt deficiency are very common for travelers in this area. But don't be misled; even in China's more humid Southlands dehydration is still a real concern. You should drink ample amounts of fluids and take in foods rich in salt and electrolytes. You should try to avoid alcohol and caffeine.

Altitude and Sun Issues

Altitude sickness and excessive sun exposure are also big concerns for visitors to China. Some areas of China lie at very high altitudes. Tibet is known as "the roof of the world" due to its altitude and neighboring Sichuan and Yunnan province are also quite high in altitude. For this reason, travelers run a higher risk of getting sunburn and altitude sickness. UV radiation is stronger at these altitudes. In order to avoid acute mountain sickness, also known as altitude sickness, it is wise to give yourself a few days to acclimate to the altitude change if you are traveling to the Chinese highlands.

The Common Cold

Catching colds on trips, especially long trips, is not by any means unusual. In fact, it's quite common in trips of over two weeks. But a cold may not be the ill you suffer from. In reality, when traveling, you may be faced with any number of ailments. For anything really serious, you would be better off going to a western medical facility if one is nearby. For non-life threatening maladies you can seek help at one of the local hospitals. Here's some vocabulary that might come in handy:

Examination Vocabulary

Chinese	English
Dàifu	doctor
shūfú	comfortable
gǎnmào	to catch a cold
zhèngzhuàng	symptom
késòu	cough
liúbítì	runny nose
quánshēn	the whole body
xūrùo	weak
juédē	feel; think
fāshāo	have a fever
shìbiǎo	temperature
liáng	measure
tǐwēn	body temperature
dù	temperature
jiǎnchá	investigate; check out; looking to
dàgài	probably
yòngbùliǎo jǐ tiān	It'll probably still be a day

When you actually see a doctor your experience may be something like the following sample conversation. Repeat what you hear as you listen to the track on the CD.

TRACK 48

Patient:	*Dàifu, wǒ bútài shūfú.*	
	Doctor, I don't feel so good.	
Doctor:	*Nín zěnme le?*	
	What's the problem?	
Patient:	*Wǒ xiǎng wǒ gǎnmào le.*	
	I think I'm catching a cold.	
Doctor:	*Nín bìngle duōjiǔ?*	
	How long have you been sick?	
Patient:	*Dàyuē sān tiān le.*	
	About three days.	
Doctor:	*Nín yǒu xiē shénme zhèngzhuàng?*	
	What symptoms do you have?	
Patient:	*Késòu, liúbítì, quánshēn méi jìn.*	
	I have a cough, runny nose, and I feel weak.	
Doctor:	*Nín juéde fāshāo ma?*	
	Do you feel feverish?	
Patient:	*Bù, dànshì wǒ méi shìbiǎo.*	
	No, but I haven't taken my temperature.	
Doctor:	*Hǎo, wǒ shǒuxiān lái gěi nín liáng yì liáng tǐwēn ba.*	
	Okay, first how about I take your temperature.	
Patient:	*Duōshǎo dù?*	
	What's the temperature?	
Doctor:	*Sānshí bā dù sì, nín yídìng fāshāo le. Sǎngzi Hóulóng tòng ma?*	
	It's 38.4, you indeed have a fever. Does your thro throat hurt?	
Patient:	*Tòng.*	
	Yes it does.	

Doctor: *Wǒ lái jiǎnchá yīxiàr nínde hóulóng, qǐng zhāngkāi kǒu shuō "Ah."*
Let me have a look at it, open your mouth and say "ah."

Patient: *Yǒu shénme wèntí ma?*
What's wrong?

Doctor: *Suīrán nínde hóulóng zhǒngle, dànshì hǎoxiàng méi fāyán. Dàgài zhǐ búguò shì pǔtōng de gǎnmào. Zhè shì zhōngyào, zhì gǎnmào hěn yǒuxiào. Wǒ kàn yòngbùliǎo jǐtiān nín jiù huì hǎo de.*
Your throat is swollen but it doesn't appear infected. It's probably just a common cold. I'll give you Chinese traditional medicine, it's very effective for treating colds. You'll be fine in a few days.

Describing Symptoms

Though colds are common, they are not the only complaint you may have. It's not always easy to discern what is wrong with you when you're simply feeling fatigued, so you should try to be as descriptive as possible. The following list contains some symptoms you may need to mention to a caregiver.

Symptom Vocabulary

Chinese	English
kùnnán	difficult
guòmǐn	allergy
xiàng	appear
shāozhuó	burning
yīyàng	same
gǎnjué	sensation; feeling
ěxīn	nauseous
tóuténg	headache

Chinese	English
jìnlái	recently; lately
niào	urinate
liáng	amount; measurement
táng	sugar
bìng	sick
tángniàobìng	diabetes
yìzhí	continuous, straight, all the way
shīmián	insomnia
xiàntǐ	glands
zhǒng	to swell
tòng	to hurt
fālěng	the chills
chōujīn	cramps
xiè dùzi	to have diarrhea

Here are some helpful phrases including these symptoms:

I'm having trouble eating.	*Chī dōngxī kùnnán.*
I have allergies.	*Wǒ yǒu guòmǐn.*
I have a burning sensation.	*Wǒ yǒu xiàng shāozhuó yīyàng de gǎnjué.*
I'm nauseated.	*Wǒ gǎnjué ěxīn.*
I have a headache.	*Wǒ tóuténg.*
I've been experiencing frequent urination.	*Jìnlái niào liàng hěn duō.*
I'm diabetic.	*Wǒ yǒu tángniàobìng.*
I've been suffering from insomnia lately.	*Wǒ jìnlái yìzhí shīmián.*
I have swollen glands.	*Wǒ de xiàntǐ zhǒng le.*
I have a stomachache.	*Wǒ dùzi hěn tòng.*
I have the chills.	*Wǒ yǒu fā lěng.*
I have cramps.	*Wǒ chōujīn le.*
I have diarrhea.	*Wǒ xiè dùzi le.*

The following list includes some vocabulary for different parts of the body. If all else fails you can simply point at the body part and say something like *Zhèr lǐ tòng*.

Body Parts Vocabulary

English	Chinese
ankle	*jiǎohuái*
arm	*shǒubì*
back	*bèi*
breast	*rǔfáng*
chest	*xiōngqiāng*
ear	*ěrduō*
elbow	*shǒuzhǒu*
eye	*yǎnjīng*
face	*liǎn*
finger	*shóuzhǐ*
foot	*jiǎo*
groin	*fùgǔgōu*
head	*tóu*
heart	*xīnzàng*
hip	*túnbù*
knee	*xī*
leg	*tuǐ*
mouth	*zuǐbā*
neck	*bózi*
nose	*bízi*
shoulder	*jiānbǎng*
skin	*pífū*
throat	*sǎngzi (hóulóng)*
toe	*jiáozhǐ*

Dental Care

It's unlikely that during a trip to China you'd need to see a dentist. If you're planning to relocate to China, however, as many are doing these days, your best solutions for dental distress are the western medical facilities. Dentistry in China is still a bit behind the times as compared to the West. It's rare at best that expatriates go to local dentists for anything other than emergencies. For significant dental work most expats choose the western facilities or professionals outside of China. People living in the Yangtze River region and the north would go to Japan, while southerners would consider dentists in Hong Kong. The University of Hong Kong, has a reputable Faculty of Dentistry. If choosing a dentist in Hong Kong, you can rest assured they've been thoroughly trained. Still, the unforeseen may occur, in which case you should know how to express concerns such as:

My tooth really hurts.	*Wǒ de yáchǐ hěn tòng.*
I think I've broken a tooth.	*Wǒ xiǎng wǒ de yáchǐ duànle.*
My gums hurt me.	*Wǒ de yáyín tòng.*
I've lost a filling.	*Wǒ de yáchōngtián diùle.*

You should be thoroughly checked out before leaving on a vacation including a visit to the dentist for good measure.

Eye Care

Make sure that your eye care is well provided for. If you wear glasses, bring an extra pair. Likewise you should bring more than one pair of contact lenses. If you lose them or forget however, you'll be pleasantly surprised to know that optometry in China is getting much better every year. The cost of products is also affordable. So, should you misplace your contacts, for example, they're reasonably inexpensive to replace, even including an eye exam. Most Chinese seem to know what prescription their eyewear is. In case you don't, you should say something like this:

I don't know my prescription, could you examine me please.

Wǒ bù zhīdào wǒde chǔfāng, Qǐng nín géi wǒ jiǎnchá yíxiàr.

Pharmacies and Hospitals

Pharmacies abound in China. You'll be able to recognize the pharmacies throughout China as they all bear a representative green cross in a green circle. The Chinese word for pharmacy, *yàofáng*, translates roughly to "medicine parlor." You should keep that squarely in mind as unlike American pharmacies, you won't find toiletries, suntan lotion, candy, and the like. You'll find only medicinal products. You will also likely find a multitude of Chinese holistic medicines and tonics in the pharmacy.

Prescriptions and Dosages

Another huge difference between American and Chinese pharmacies is that almost all drugs for which you'd need a prescription in the United States may be bought over the counter. It's possible that one of the reasons for this is that medications in China are all packaged according to standard recipes in standard amounts. Tablets of a given antibiotic, for example, are often available in only one single particular dosage, and that dosage and regimen for administering it are printed on the box. These dosages are determined by nationwide average physical dimension standards.

ALERT!

All western medications found in China have Chinese names. What's more, often the packaging does not have the English name on it, so you will probably have to know how to say the name of your medication in Chinese in order to ask for it. Luckily, most of the large pharmacies have a catalog with English names of medications to help you out.

Communicating at a Chinese Pharmacy

Since pharmacies deal basically only in medications, communicating your needs shouldn't be at all difficult. If you've got a prescription from a doctor, all the relevant information will appear on it. So you'll need only to present it to the pharmacist and you'll be given your medication. Take it as the doctor prescribes it. If for some reason you run out of a necessary medication on your trip or your meds are misplaced, then you can likely replace them by going to any pharmacy and simply asking for the medications.

For over-the-counter remedies, you can simply approach a pharmacist and ask for a medicine that treats a given symptom by saying "*Wǒ yào zhì* [insert symptom] *de yào.*"

Going to the Hospital

In the past, travelers to China were confined to seeking health care in Chinese hospitals and clinics, but now, there are western-style medical facilities with international staffs popping up all over China. Beijing, Shanghai, and Guangzhou generally offer the best quality western-style medical care in China. In a many other cities a growing number of hospitals have so-called V.I.P. wards. These wards feature relatively modern medical technology and sound physicians who are both knowledgeable and skilled. Often these V.I.P. wards provide medical care for foreigners and expats and have English-speaking staff.

Exercises

Now let's see if you remember all you just learned about health care in China. The following exercises include information covered in various parts of this chapter. Try to answer the questions from memory first, and then refer back to earlier pages if you need to jog your memory or perfect spelling.

1. How would you tell a pharmacist that you have allergies?

   ....

2. How would you recognize a Chinese pharmacy from the outside?

   ....

Chapter 15

Mind, Body, and Spirit

At the heart of Taoist philosophy is the quest for balance, longevity, vitality, and spiritual enlightenment. This quest has manifested in many facets of Chinese culture as has the basic principle that all our experiences and actions have a causative element that influences the world around us, whether it be physical, spiritual, or intellectual. Let's take a look at some of the ways Chinese strive for a rested and relaxed mind, a nourished and healthy body, and a free-flowing spirit.

15

Mind, Body, and Spirit Are One

Close your eyes. Relax your body. Inhale deeply, hold and then exhale. Find your center; open your mind and listen to the rhythm of your body. It moves in time to the rhythm of all things. Mind, body, and spirit are regarded as all-important in Chinese culture.

Strive for oneness in mind. Apotheosis never felt so good. In your quest for oneness with the universe, find ways to relax your mind in China. One such way is by visiting Chinese baths (covered in the next section).

Strive for oneness in spirit. In ancient China it was believed that by combining various body movements with measured breathing and focused thoughts one could align their bodies with the forces of nature, merging metabolic and mental functions with the rhythmic flow of the universe. Much the same way the methodology of traditional Chinese medicine was realized after eons of trial, error, experimentation and fine-tuning, movement systems such as *qìgōng* and *tàijíquán* were similarly realized and refined. In time these systems became associated with religious expression and an important part of Taoist, Buddhist, and Confucian meditative practices.

Strive for oneness in body. As the saying goes, the body is the temple of the soul. A sound body is one that is in good physical condition inside and out. Taoist philosophy ascribes rituals, ceremonies, and disciplines to the end of cultivating, maintaining, and repairing a strong body that inevitably on occasion succumbs to illness. For several millennia, Chinese scholars and healers have observed the body's workings and tested and tried methods for repairing it when it fails. One focal conclusion drawn by the healers of old is that our bodies functions are all interrelated in a subtle order that is easily mistaken for discord. A balance exists between the composite forces of the universe yin and yang, the dark force and the light force. Our bodies are micro-universes and by maintaining balance in our bodies of these primal universal forces, we remain in good health.

Chinese Baths

In your quest for oneness with the universe, or if you simply want to pamper yourself and luxuriate for a while, don't miss out on a Chinese bath.

The high-end Chinese baths are really spas, and though they are considered high-end in China they will be remarkably less expensive than their equivalent spas in North America and Europe. Furthermore, they offer an eclectic mixture of amenities, everything from whirlpools to saunas, to steam rooms to hot and cold plunges. But that's not all. At a Chinese bath you'll also often be able to get a manicure or pedicure, a facial, eat food, watch movies, and much more. Some baths even include small movie theaters not to mention dance floors and KTV. You can even sleep at a bath.

Take a Soak

When you first enter the bath you'll likely arrive at a reception area with a desk and computer manned by several receptionists. They will probably ask if you've ever been there before and then register you as well as take your credit card information. You do not need to use a credit card, but you'll have to pay your entrance deposit. Generally there's a base admission fee and then each additional service has its own charge. You're given a medium size towel and a plastic bracelet with a number. This number will be your *zhànghù hàomǎ* (account number) and any services you'd like to enjoy after you've entered will be charged to your account. You'll then be briefed about some of the services and then invited to enjoy yourself. The encounter may go like this:

TRACK 49

Receptionist:	*Huānyíng Guānglíng, nínmen dìyīcì lái zhèr ma?* Welcome. Is this your first time joining us?
Mr. Sherbell:	*Shìde, wǒmen cónglái méi láiguò.* Yes, I've never been here before.
Receptionist:	*Hěn hǎo, wǒmen lái dēng jìkéyǐ ma?* Very well, let's register then, shall we?
Mr. Sherbell:	*Kéyǐ.* Of course.
Receptionist:	*Hǎo, nínmen zěnme chēnghū?* Okay, what are your first and last names?

Mr. Sherbell: *Wǒmen xìng Sherbell. Wǒ jiào Steven, wǒ tàitài jiào Mary.*

Our last name is Sherbell. I'm Steven, my wife is Mary.

Receptionist: *Nínde zhíyè shì shénme?*

What's your profession?

Mr. Sherbell: *Wǒ shì dàifu.*

I'm a physician.

Receptionist: *Hǎo Sherbell dàifu, Sherbell tàitài, wǒmen de rùchǎngfèi měiwèi měirì sìshí kuài qián. Rùchǎngfèi bāokuò gōnggòngyùshì, rèshuǐchí, bīngshuǐchí, zhēngqìyù, hé sāngnáyù de fèiyòng.*

Fine, Dr. and Mrs. Sherbell, our admission is 40 RMB per person per day. Admission includes use of the communal bath, hot tub, cold plunge, steam room and sauna.

Mr. Sherbell: *Nǐmen yǒu méiyǒu ànmó?*

Do you offer massages?

Receptionist: *Kěndìng yǒu. Wǒmen yǒu Hǎojǐ zhǒng ànmó, shènzhì yǒu quánshēn ànmó.*

We certainly do. We have many kinds of massage, even full body.

Mr. Sherbell: *Yǒu méiyǒu Éwài de fèiyòng?*

Is there an additional charge?

Receptionist: *Yǒu, měige éwài de fúwù dōu yǒu éwài de shōufèi. Suóyǒu éwài de shōufèi dōu huì tǐxiàn zài nínde zǒngzhàngdān.*

There is, each additional service carries an additional charge. All additional charges will appear on your final bill.

Once you're finished with registration, you're ushered off to the *gēngyīshì* (clothes changing area) to change your clothes and store them in your *guìzi* (locker). The high-end baths are usually multilevel structures, and the level in which the pools and other cleansing amenities can be found are usually segregated. Men are on one side and women on the other. Expect to be pampered and catered to the entire length of your experience. It's very common for there to be an attendant in every room ready to assist you with everything—even undressing:

Wǒ lái bāng nín tuō yīfú.   **Let me help you out of your clothes.**

Once you're undressed you'll be taken to the shower area and given a pair of plastic sandals for the shower area. Each shower stall is loaded with different body washes, soaps made from oatmeal and glycerin, all manner of shampoo and conditioner, and plain white wash cloths. Just in case you were wondering, there are attendants in the shower as well:

Wǒ lái bāng nín cā bèi   **Shall I scrub your back for you?**
hǎoma?

From the shower you may enter the communal bath area. If you hadn't noticed by now, then the communal bath will certainly impress upon you how simply beautiful the high-end baths can be. Often they are decorated in chrome, brass, marble, and glass as well as comfortable woods for reclining on. In the communal bath areas you'll find a large shallow hot tub, and a shallow cold plunge, as well as adjacent steam rooms and saunas. Often there are complimentary refreshments in the communal bath areas such as cucumber water, lemon water, and green tea. You may also find small cups of *yánshuāxǐ* (sea salt scrub) that you may take into the steam room to help exfoliate. Chinese saunas and steam rooms seem to be a fair share hotter than steam rooms and saunas in American spas and gyms. Also, Chinese steam rooms often come in pairs, scented or unscented. The scented steam room's water supply is treated with eucalyptus oil or some other astringent to cleanse the pores. Once you've experienced life from a dumpling's point of view and have been well boiled and steamed, it's time for a rinse and then a massage.

Massage

From the showers, a towel will be wrapped around you by yet another doting attendant and you may move on to the massage area. The massage areas of baths seem to vary, in some they are open areas with a few beds lined up in rows, but in many baths, massage cubicles and rooms are set up for more privacy. You can pick and choose what kind of massage you'd like, and every kind of massage is available. They cost anywhere between 20 and 45 RMB and last around twenty minutes to one hour. They use all manner of oil and skin care products to soften and tone your skin.

ALERT!

Erotic massages are also available at most baths, and this fact does not seem to phase Chinese much at all. It's quite out in the open, and though prostitution is technically illegal, it is still readily available. Prostitutes are employees of the baths, they're easily recognizable as they tend to be very elegantly dressed, often in identical dresses, and wear a lot of makeup. As employees of the baths they are afforded some legal protection and support.

After your massage, it's off for another shower then up to the lounge area. Of course, this step is not that mundane. The showers are often luxurious in and of themselves as you well know. After your shower you move to another changing area. Most of the changing rooms are warmly decorated and feel very lounge-like. There are combs, toothbrushes, toothpaste, razors, soaps, shaving cream, lotions, toners, pore cleansers, masks, cotton swabs, and an entire cosmetics drawer. It's not enough that the changing rooms are likely better stocked than your own bathrooms at home, but there's an attendant there to put the toothpaste on your toothbrush, fill your rinse cup, spray the shaving cream in your hand, comb the back of your hair, hand you a towel after doing a mask, and pass other utensils to you. The service is unbelievably decadent. Just when you thought you couldn't have anything else done for you, the attendants prepare a set of lounge clothes for you. These are the disposable clothes you may wear in the lounge areas. They include shirts, shorts, footings, and even disposable underwear. In some baths the clothes are cloth and in others they are paper compounds that are not nearly as uncomfortable as it sounds. If it weren't enough that the attendants have fetched all this for you, they then help you slip into them.

From there, you may take advantage of any number of the rest of the bath's amenities. Lounges on separate floors are carpeted and very comfortable. There are tables and chairs where you may play cards or Ma Jiang, drink tea, or order a snack. There are many lounge chairs and large plush couches with TVs attached them. These lounges are also patrolled by attendants and masseuses eager to make you feel relaxed.

Bath Banter

yùgāng	jacuzzi
zhēngqìyùshì	steam room
sāngnáyù	sauna
rèshuǐchí	hot tub
bīngshuǐchí	cold plunge
xiūzhǐjiǎ	manicure
xiūjiǎozhǐjiǎ	pedicure
jiǎnfà	haircut
ànmó	massage
yánshuāxǐ	salt scrub

The Spirituality of Food

If you've learned anything about the Chinese by now it's the importance of eating. Chinese culture is very food-centric. It's no wonder that food would take on a spiritual quality and be similarly endowed with spiritual attributes as well. If you delve deeper into Chinese cooking, traditions beyond the regional variations in schools of cooking you'll find that according to Taoist philosophy, foods are also endowed with the spiritual attributes of yin, yang, and neutrality.

Most Chinese dishes reflect this subtle balance between foods that are yin-heavy and foods that are yang-heavy. Yin foods are said to be "cold." Some example of yin foods are apples, bean curd (tofu), beer, bitter melon, winter melon, watercress, cabbage, soybeans, mung beans, water chestnuts, watermelon, cucumber, ice cream, oysters, tomatoes, duck, and most fish. Traditionally, you should avoid overdoing it with yin foods as too much yin force may cause the runs, weakness, fatigue, dizziness, and colds according to Chinese medicine. Yang foods are said to be "hot." Some examples of yang foods are: chilis, garlic, onion, curry, eggplant, mango, crab, potatoes, green peppers, chocolate, beef, chicken, turkey, smoked fish, coffee, and eggs. An excess of yang foods is said to cause skin problems, nose bleeds, gas, indigestion, heartburn, constipation, and sore throat. The third type of food is the neutral food. They are foods that have no discernible excess of yin or yang energy. Some examples of neutral foods are: carrots, cauliflower, lean chicken, milk, peaches, plums, brown rice, and steamed white rice.

A common misconception of the concepts of yin and yang is that they are opposing forces such as good and evil, but that is not at all the case. The yin force is the feminine force associated with the moon and the elements of water and metal. It is a complementary force without which the yang force would not exist. The yang force is the masculine force associated with the sun and the elements of wood and fire. The forces together represent all things and together they are associated with the element of earth as earth pervades all things.

Not only are foods themselves attributed with yin and yang properties, but cooking methods are as well. Boiling, steaming, and poaching are yin cooking methods, utilizing water. The yang cooking methods are the fire and frying methods of roasting, stir-frying, and deep-frying. It should be pointed out however that foods are not all purely yin and yang. That concept in and of itself would be unbalanced and not at all Taoist. Rather, it is believed that foods simply favor one characteristic over the other. Foods that are thought of as yin foods also possess yang force. It's just that they do not in as great a degree as the yang foods.

Traditional Chinese Medicine

Easily one of the most poorly understood aspects of Chinese culture in the western world is traditional Chinese medicine, or *Zhōng Yī Xué*. Tradition attributes the invention of medicine in China to the Yellow Emperor *Huángdì*. He is said to have authored the *Nèijīng Sùwèn*, or *The Basic Questions of Internal Medicine*, in early antiquity, but Chinese scholars maintain that it was probably compiled by a number of scholars some time between the Zhou and Han dynasties.

The ideas behind Chinese medicine are truly incredible. In an age predating the germ theory of diseases, microbiology, and organic chemistry, medical diagnosis was based largely on observation, individual practical experience, the occasional mysticism and most importantly, the knowledge of those who came before you. A physician generated remedies for ailments based on outward symptoms and observed behaviors that followed patterns deduced and recorded by physicians before them 3,000 years prior.

Chinese herbology, considered to be the most important modality employed in the practice of *Zhōng Yī Xué*, is said to have been pioneered by the mythical Yan emperor Shennong. *Shénnóng,* also regarded as the god of agriculture, is supposed to have sampled countless hundreds of herbs and recorded their medicinal and harmful properties in a tome called *Shénnóng Běncǎo Jīng*, or *Emperor Shennong's Classic of Materia Medica*. Over 365 medicines were recorded, and 252 of them are herbs. Herbal medicine prescriptions are essentially cocktails of various herbs that are catered to an individual patient and their particular problem. A good herbalist designs an herbal formula not only the primary herbs associated with the cure, but various other helping herbs which will catalyze the curatives, negate the side effects, and maintain proper balance of the individual patients yin and yang condition. This synergistic treatment of the individual patient requires great knowledge and skill and is the hallmark of Chinese traditional medicine.

Medical Vocabulary

wèizhuórè	heartburn
fāshēng	happen
Yóu ..yǐnfā	related
xiāoshī	disappear
yǐnshí	food and drink
guīlǜ	in order, with regularity
guānguāng	sightsee
piānrè	be on the hot side
Yīn	yin
Qièjì	avoid at all costs
mùlù	list
yàofāng	prescription
zhōngyào	Chinese herbal medicine
Zhǔ	boil
xū	disperse, weak

Chinese physicians of today use as their repertoire of treatment a union of both modern western medical practices and age-old tested traditional Chinese medical practices. To the Chinese physician of antiquity as well as today, the patient is regarded as a sum of a great many individual yet coalescent parts, all working in unison and treated as a whole.

The following is a sample conversation between a patient and a doctor. Listen to the track and repeat what you hear aloud. This is good practice for your own potential encounter with a Chinese doctor.

TRACK 50

Patient: *Dàifu hǎo.*
Hello doctor.

Doctor: *Nín hǎo, nín de shēntǐ yǒu shénme bùhǎo?*
Hello, what seems to be the problem?

Patient: *Wǒ měicì chīfàn yǐ hòu, jiù weishou.*
Each time after I eat, I get heartburn.

Doctor: *Yǐjīng fāshēng le duōcháng shíjiān?*
How long has it been going on?

Patient: *Sì tiān duō le.*
Over 4 days now.

Doctor: *Nín zài zhōngguó duōjiǔ le?*
How long have you been in China now?

Patient: *Zhè shì wǒmen de dìsì xīngqī.*
This is our 4th week.

Doctor: *Yóu lǚxíng yǐnfā de wèibìng tōngcháng huì zài nín*
dàodá hòu liǎng sān tiān nèi xiāoshī. Nínde
yǐnshí yǒu méiyǒu guīlǜ? Nín rújīn chīle shénme?
Travel related stomach ailments usually disappear
within two to three days of your arrival. Have you
been eating regularly? What have you been
eating?

Patient: *Qíshí, wǒmen guānguāng le hěn duō dìfāng.*
Wǒde yǐnshí méiyǒu guīlǜ.
Actually, we've been sightseeing a lot. I haven't
been eating regularly.

Doctor: *Nín hǎoxiàng piānrèle. Yīn xūle. Qièjì chī hěn là,*
hěn yóu de. Quèdìng zhǐ chī zhè mùlù shàng de
shíwù. Zhège yàofāng gěi nín. Zhè shì zhōngyào.
Yào zhǔ liǎng cì hòu cái hē.
You seem to be leaning toward hot. Your yin is weak.
Avoid eating spicy and oily foods. Make sure to
eat only the foods on this list. Here, this is a prescription. It's for Chinese herbal medicine. Boil the
medicine twice, and then you may drink it.

Qigong

Qìgōng is a meditative discipline associated with Chinese medicine and Taoist and Buddhist religious practice. It blends the synchronization of breathing patterns with various stances and body movements in an effort to channel the flow of *qì* in and through the body for physical and spiritual balance. *Qìgōng* is taught in modern China as a form of calisthenics. It is very popular among the elderly, but it is also taught in conjunction with various marital arts.

The metaphysical nature of *qì* in the various schools of Chinese philosophy is the subject of some debate. Whereas many Neo-Confucianists see *qì* as being a manifestation of matter, many Buddhists and Taoists see matter as being a manifestation of *qì*. In the martial arts, *qì* is generally thought of as your life breath, or a power generated by your very existence. *Qì* literally means breath, thus the connection between focused breathing and the manipulation of *qì*. Historically, practitioners of *qìgōng* explored the human natural range of motion and focused on motions that mimicked animal movements to understand their benefits to the body in partnership with controlled breathing. Today these movements and practices are codified and standardized, though there are several varieties or schools of *qìgōng*. It is practiced by millions of Chinese and millions more around the world regularly as a form of health maintenance and general well being. In fact, since 1989, *qìgōng* has been a recognized form of medical treatment in China and has been included in the curriculum of major universities throughout China. *Qìgōng* is also sighted as a health practice in China's national health plan.

Tai Chi

Tàijíquán, as it is called in Chinese, is regarded as an internal martial art. There are three major styles of *Tàijí* though they are all based on the Chen families system as taught to the Yang family. *Tàijí* is one of the most popular forms of calisthenics in China today, and it, like *qìgōng* also combines elements of mysticism with physical movement. You can see people performing it every morning in courtyards, gardens, parks, and temples all over

China. It is called a moving meditation and requires focus, poise, and tranquility to perform correctly.

Tàijí is heralded in China by physicians and practitioners as being very beneficial for health and stress management. In terms of exercise, the slow and purposeful repetitive movements are thought to increase and facilitate cardiovascular and other systemic body functions. The low impact stances also surprisingly burn more calories than other notably low impact aerobic exercises. Many practitioners of *Tàijí* claim to require less sleep and do not fatigue as easily as before they started. Research done even here in the West has suggested that long term practice of *Tàijí* promotes better cardiovascular fitness, improved balance, and flexibility. The benefits to the immune system are also profound.

If you are unfamiliar with *Tàijí*, you should definitely take advantage of any opportunity to learn about it while you're in China. You may be surprised to find out but many hotels, especially those with gym facilities, offer *Tàijí* classes. Here's an example conversation that might help you inquire about *Tàijí*:

Mrs. S: *Nǐ men yǒu názhǒng chénliàn kè?*
            What kind of morning exercise classes do you offer?

Clerk: *Wǒmen yǒu sān ge duànliàn kè. Zǎoshàng qī diǎn zài yī hào shì yǒu jiànshēncāo kè, zài èr hào shì yǒu yújiā kè, ér zài sān hào shì yǒu tàijíquán kè.*

            We have three exercise classes. At 7:00 A.M. in room 1 there is aerobics, in room 2 there is yoga, and in room 3 there is Tai Chi.

Mrs. S: *Wǒ tōngcháng tiào jiànshēncāo huòzhě liàn yújiā. Tàijíquán shì búshì yī zhǒng hǎo de yóuyǎng duànliàn?*

            I normally do aerobics or yoga. Is Tai Chi good aerobic exercise?

Clerk: *Tàijíquán shì yī zhǒng zhāngguó chuántǒng de duànliàn. Suīrán bú shì yóuyvng duànliàn, dànshì duì nínde shēntǐ háishì hěn jiànkāng. Wǒ zìjǐ měitiān zvoshàng dǎ.*

Tai Chi is a traditional Chinese exercise. It's not aerobic exercise, but it's still very beneficial to your health. I do it myself every morning.

Mrs. S: *Dēngjìfèi yǒu méiyǒu?*
Is there a registration fee?

Clerk: *Méiyǒu. Wèi kèrén shì miǎnfèi de.*
No, it's free for guests.

Mrs. S: *Hěn hǎo, wǒ xiǎng dēngjì.*
Great, I'd like to register then.

Exercises

Now it's time to see what you've learned about the Chinese ideas relating to mind, body, and spirit. The following exercises include information covered in various parts of this chapter. Try to answer the questions from memory first, and then refer back to earlier pages if you need to jog your memory or perfect spelling.

1. How do you say "aerobic exercise" in Chinese?

   ....

   ....

2. Rearrange these words to form a sentence: *duō le wǒmen dìfōng guānguāng hěn.*

   ....

3. What is the dark feminine force in Taoist mysticism?

   ....

Chapter 16

The Long Haul

Every financial journal from LA to London is buzzing with talk of China's economic rise. Companies with interests in every market are taking advantage of China's growing demand for foreign investment as well as western business know-how. Many global corporations are opening offices in the PRC. You could be one of those called on to act as a liaison. China's expatriate community grows exponentially each year.

Working in China

You've been asked to take a position at the Beijing or Shanghai office. You're probably a bit nervous and wondering what you've gotten yourself into. Don't worry! Your boss would not have chosen you for this assignment unless he or she thought you were cut out for it. An adventurous spirit and open mind can be the keys that open a door to a fantastic adventure for you. Sometimes, you simply have to take a chance and see what you can do.

Of course, a life change like this does require a lot of courage and adaptability. You will be experiencing a complete change of lifestyle and culture. In many cases, the Chinese company that may be working with your company will arrange for a representative who can help you to set up home and adjust to life in the PRC. This may include anything from finding an apartment and arranging transportation to guiding you around your new city and introducing you to local people in your field who might speak English. Make the most of whatever help you're given, and go forward with a sense of adventure!

Finding a Place to Live

The most important segment of your introduction to life in China is the ever-challenging and potentially frustrating apartment hunt. Housing is not as scarce in China as you might think. Since the start of the Chinese economic reform there has been a huge push to build. As a result, residential complexes are going up virtually overnight. And the Chinese are not simply expanding outward, but they are expanding inward and upward. Something of a controversy these days is the government's initiative to modernize some of the older, poorer districts of the cities. Old neighborhoods are being demolished and newer apartment complexes are going up in their stead. The residents of these older areas are being relocated to some of the outer districts in an almost overnight artificial gentrification.

Here are some new vocabulary words that will be helpful to know as you start looking for a place to hang your hat:

Real Estate Vocabulary

wòshì	bedroom
jǐ wò	how many bedrooms?
zhù	live, accommodate
huā	flower, to spend money
yuànyì	willing
yāoqiú	request, requirement
pèibèi	equip, equipment, furnishing
… zhījiān	between

Agencies

After word of mouth and the help of a native, your next best bet for finding nice lodgings would be to use a real estate agency. Real estate agencies are everywhere, but the trick is finding a reputable one. If your company hasn't provided a liaison to assist you in this, then you'll have to do it on your own. You can still rely on word of mouth by consulting some of the Chinese expat Web sites online. If you don't happen to know what they are, you can consult the embassy or consulate of your country in or nearest to the city you'll be living in. When you eventually do find an agency, your encounter with an agent may go something like this:

TRACK 51

Customer: *Wǒ jīnrì lái zhōngguó. Wǒ zài zhǎo fángzǐ.*
I have recently come to China, and am looking for an apartment.

Real Estate Agent: *Zhù jǐ ren?*
To accommodate how many?

Customer: *Zhù liǎng rén. Wǒ yǔ wǒ lǎopó.*
To accommodate two people, my wife and I.

Real Estate Agent: *Nín zhǎo jǐ wò de fángzi?*
How many bedrooms are you looking for?

Customer:	*Wó zhǎo liǎngwò de, yì jiān wòshì yào dāng bàngōngshì.* I'm looking for a two-bedroom apartment; one bedroom would be an office.
Real Estate Agent:	*Hǎo, nín yuànyì huā duōshǎo qián?* How much are you willing to spend?
Customer:	*Dàyuē měige yuè sānqiān wǔqiān kuài zhījiān.* Between around 3,000 and 5,000 RMB a month.
Real Estate Agent:	*Nín xiǎngyào yǒu pèibèi de, háishì méiyǒu pèibèi de fángzi?* Would you prefer a furnished or unfurnished apartment?
Customer:	*Wǒ xiǎng yào méiyǒu pèibèi de.* I'd prefer unfurnished.
Real Estate Agent:	*Nín yǒu qítā tèbié yāoqiú ma?* Do you have any special requirements or preferences?
Customer:	*Méiyǒu.* No, none.
Real Estate Agent:	*Nín dǎsuàn zài zhōngguó duōcháng shíjiān?* How long do you plan on being in China?
Customer:	*Wǒ huì zài zhōngguó zhìshǎo liǎng nián.* I'll be in China for at least two years.

Other Options

Aside from using the expat Web sites to find reputable real estate agencies, a great many of these Web sites have actual classified forums. You can post your intent to find an apartment and/or roommates there. Situations are easy to find, particularly if you don't mind sharing. Apart from the Web sites, the next best things are the English-language periodicals. Some of the most popular of them include the *China Daily*, *China View*, and the *Shanghai*

Daily. Check your local newsstands, as new English-language local papers are popping up all over China.

The U.S. embassy in China is located in Beijing at Xiushui Beijie 3, Beijing 100600. The phone number is [86](10) 6532-3831. There are consulates in Shanghai, Shenyang, Chengdu, and Guangzhou serving their respective regions of China. Hong Kong has its own U.S. Embassy and it serves both the Hong Kong and Macau SAR. U.S. government representation in Taiwan falls under the jurisdiction of the American Institute in Taiwan in the cities of Taipei (Táiběi) and Kaohsiung (Gāoxióng).

Furnishings and Decorations

Many apartments come furnished already. There are private owners as well as real estate agencies that offer short- to medium-term rentals and market them pointedly to expats coming to China to work. But unfurnished apartments are just as common as the furnished ones. The blank canvas of an unfurnished apartment gives you an opportunity to create a comfort zone of your own in which to retreat when you need your fix of familiarity.

Decorating Options

Get professional help! You have a few options for decorating methods and one of them is to hire an interior designer. Interior design is a fast growing field in China. There is some great talent appearing in China these days. Reputable interior designers, like Timothy Chan for example, are educated abroad and bringing their knowledge, eye and flair to your space and work with you to develop the kind of fusion between comfort and aesthetic charm that will make coming home a pleasure. Not to mention the fact that by hiring an interior designer, you relieve yourself of the time commitment and potential stress that can be accompanied by trying to decorate an apartment yourself. Decorators in China are very professional and will work with you very closely to get the most out of your space.

Do It Yourself

If you are up to the challenge or simply don't require elaborate living designs, then your second option is to go it alone. For many, fashion isn't everything and comfort counts for much more. There are dozens of *jiājù diàn* (furniture stores) throughout China, such as Jade. Chinese furniture can be either quite nice or, less than what you'd expect, but overall you'll find it to be quite reasonably priced. If you'd like furnishing options that feel a bit closer to home and more familiar, take heart, there are Ikeas in several major Chinese cities.

TRACK 52

Customer:	*Qǐng nǐ kéyǐ bǎ jiājù sòngdào wǒ fángzi lái ma?* Could you please deliver furniture to my home?
Clerk:	*Dāngrán kéyǐ Qǐng gěi wǒ kàn nínde dīngdān?* Of course, may I see your order form?
Customer:	*Géi nǐ.* Here it is.
Clerk:	*Nín xiǎng sòng shénme?* What items would you like delivered?
Customer:	*Qǐng sòng chuángdiàn, shāfā, yǔ zhuōzi.* Please deliver the mattress, sofa, and table.
Clerk:	*Wǒmen xīngqīsì sònghuò, nǐn xiǎngyào xiàwǔ háishì wǎnshàng.* We can deliver on Thursday, would you prefer afternoon or evening delivery?
Customer:	*Wǒ báitiān gōngzuò. Wǎnshàng kéyǐ ma?* I work during the day, is the evening okay?
Clerk:	*Kéyǐ.* Yes, that's fine.

Even if you don't hire a decorator, it would be best to enlist the help of natives in furnishing your apartment. This is particularly important in the major cities where space is at a premium. A great deal of Chinese furniture items are catered to saving space, thus modular furniture is very prized. Many couches and sofas are convertible. Even bed frames serve as storage units more often than not. Pay close attention when you purchase a bed, as, you may recall from our travel chapters, the Chinese prefer firm beds. By firm, I mean cement block. Well, perhaps not quite that firm, but firm indeed. Do not buy a mattress unless you've thoroughly tested it personally for comfort.

Here are a few furniture-related vocabulary words that will be helpful to know:

Delivering Furniture

jiājù	furniture
dìngdān	order form
shìxiàng	items
chuángdiàn	mattress
shāfā	sofa
zhuōzi	table

Amenities

In the West, we occasionally take our comforts for granted. In general, the items that would be considered "amenities" to Americans would be outright luxuries to the Chinese. While you may not find all of your favorite amenities during your stay in China, there are a number of substitutes you may find just as delightful. The amenities that Americans are accustomed to are more widely available in the large cities than the smaller ones.

Telecommunications

Many American travelers fear that they won't be able to be as "connected" when they go abroad. In fact, most developed countries, including China, are fairly up to speed when it comes to things like cell phones and Internet access. China's vast telecommunications network is supported by a handful of semi-private telecommunications companies. Some of the largest of these companies include China Netcom (Zhōngguó Wǎngtōng), China Unicom (Zhōngguó Liántōng), and China Telecom (Zhōngguó Diànxìn). All of these corporations provide the Chinese with all manner of services including Internet, broadband, Web hosting, and telephone service. In some of the larger cities, these corporations are divided into local subsidiaries such as Shanghai Telecom (Shànghǎi Diànxìn) serving the greater Shanghai area. This company offers local and long-distance phone service, VPN service, and IP phone cards and will also come to your home and set up your broadband for you.

Are you a mover as well as a shaker? Worry not. China Mobile or CMCC (Zhōngguó Yídòng) supports a user base of over 416 million. That's more than the number of land lines in China. Most Chinese mobile phones are unlocked so you can switch out sim cards for whatever country you travel to. Broadband services in the Hong Kong and Macau SARs are provided by PCCW and many of the newer apartment complexes in Hong Kong are already equipped with their services. Mobile phone service in Hong Kong and Macau are provided by a number of competing companies, the most popular of which are SmarTone-Vodafone, Sunday, and New World. The largest ISP serving Taiwan is Chunghwa Telecom (Zhōnghuá Diànxìn) under the brand name HINET.

Living in China you can still remain well connected by e-mail and all manner of phone service. But what does one do for a news fix? Of course, China has a wide variety of TV channels and shows to choose from. But if you're craving CNN or the BBC, your only option is satellite TV (wèixīng diànshì). Satellite TV and all satellite transmissions are illegal throughout the mainland PRC. Of course, one would never know this from looking at Beijing or Shanghai's dish-littered skyline. You won't be able to pursue satellite TV through official channels. However, quite often, the private satellite companies will pass fliers around apartment complexes. If all else fails, you can ask one of your neighbors about them:

Nǐ yǒuméiyǒu wèixīng diànshì gōngsī de diànhuà hàomǎ?

Do you have the number of a satellite TV company?

Household Amenities

In terms of household comforts, you won't see much difference in terms of luxuries in the various major Chinese cities. However, there are a few points worth being aware of. Chinese kitchens reflect the nature of Chinese cuisine. Most everything is boiled, steamed, or fried. As a result, you'll find that few if any Chinese kitchens come equipped with convection ovens. If you enjoy baking, then, you'll have to buy an electric oven. The electric ovens available look basically like large toaster-ovens.

Laundry will be another chore that will bring out a vivid difference between East and West. While almost all Chinese homes are equipped with a washing machine, few washers make use of hot water. Everyone does their laundry in cold water. The Chinese brand machines are also much smaller than western washers. You'll have to do more washes due to less space in the machine.

QUESTION?

Do the Chinese use clothes dryers?
Very few Chinese people own clothes dryers. The majority simply hang their clothes out the windows on clothes lines or in their balconies. You'll find yourself missing a clothes dryer during the spring and summer. South China is extremely humid. Clothes sometimes take a few days to dry.

Finally, you should be aware that the tap water in China is not potable. It is probably for this reason that drinking hot water as opposed to cold is so popular. For drinking water, most Chinese either buy elaborate filter systems or buy bottled water weekly. Water coolers are called *yínshuǐjī*, and bottled water may be bought from one of the local water companies. One of the biggest name brand waters is yanzhong. Here's some water-related vocabulary:

Ordering Water

zhēngliúshuǐ	distilled water
kuàngquánshuǐ	mineral water
tǒng	bottle; measure word for large tubs or vats

Here's a sample conversation about ordering water. Listen to the track and repeat what you hear aloud.

TRACK 53

Customer: *Dìngshuǐ kéyǐ ma?*
May I place an order for water?

Clerk: *Kéyǐ Nín xiǎngyào zhēngliúshuǐ háishì kuàngquánshuǐ?*
Would you like distilled water or mineral water?

Customer: Kuàngquánshuǐ jiù kéyǐ
Mineral water, please.

Clerk: *Jǐ tǒng shuǐ ne?*
How many bottles?

Customer: *Yì tǒng.*
One bottle.

Clerk: *Hǎo, nínde dìzhǐ shì shénme?*
Okay, what is your address?

Customer: *Héběi lù èrshíbā hào.*
28 Hebei Road.

Clerk: *Nín zhù zài zhèr duōjiǔ le?*
How long have you lived at this address?

Customer: *Wǒ zhùzài zhèr sānge xīngqī le.*
I've lived here for three weeks.

Clerk: *Hǎo, qī kuài qián yì tǒng, xūyào dàyuē sānshí fēn zhōng.*
Okay, that will be 7 RMB for one bottle, it will take about thirty minutes.

Grammar Lesson: Time-Measure Complements

Up until now we've dealt with time expressions in terms of adverbial phrases. Expressions such as times, days, and day referents have all been employed to add a dimension of tense to sentences. Unlike adverbial phrases, which, in Chinese, always come at the beginning of the sentences, time-measure complements are associated with the verbal predicate and follow the verb, thus showing the duration of an action or its state. An example of this use was shown earlier in this chapter in the sentence *Wǒ huì zài zhōngguó zhìshǎo liǎng nián.* The time-measure complement *liǎng nián* indicates how long the verb *zài* will last. The following are two other examples:

Wǒ xiūxīle bàntiān.	**I rested for half the day.**
Wǒ měitiān zǎoshàng duànliàn yīge xiǎoshí.	**I exercise every morning for an hour.**

Verbs that take objects may generally be repeated when forming a sentence with a time-measure complement so that they are linked. The verb is stated the first time, followed by the object then the repeated verb then the time-measure complement. See the following examples:

Tā xué zhōngwén xuéle liǎng nián.	**He studied Chinese for two years.**
Wǒ dǎ diànhuà dǎle bànge duō xiǎoshí.	**I was on the phone for over a half hour.**

If the object taken by the verb is a non-personal or inanimate pronoun, the time-measure complement maybe rendered into an adverbial phrase and be put between the verb and its object as in the sentences below:

Tā xuéle liǎng nián de zhōngwén.	**He studied Chinese for two years.**
Wǒ dǎle bànge duō xiǎoshí de diànhuà.	**I was on the phone for a half hour.**

You are not confined to always placing the subject first in the sentence. Often the object may be placed before the subject of a sentence when emphasis is desired or when the object is very structurally complex as in:

Zhège hěn dàde juédìng tā kǎolù le hǎo jǐ tiān.

He considered this very big decision for several days.

You can communicate the idea of an action still occurring by using both the aspect particle *le* after the verb, while placing the modal particle *le* at the end of the sentence. For example:

Wǒ xuéxí le hǎo jǐ nián de zhōngwén le.

I've been studying Chinese for several years.

However, if you omit the modal particle *le* at the end of the sentence and say the following, the idea that you are still currently studying it is not fully communicated.

Wǒ xuéxí le háo jǐ nián de zhōngwén.

I've been studying Chinese for several years.

Exercises

Now it's time to see what you've learned in this chapter. The following exercises include information covered in the sections you just read. Try to answer the questions from memory first, and then refer back to earlier pages if you need to jog your memory or perfect spelling.

1. Translate the following sentence to Chinese: I sat on the plane for fifteen hours.

   ....

   ....

2. Match the following words:

zhēngliúshuǐ	distilled water
kuàngquánshuǐ	willing
wòshì	equip, equipment, furnishing
huā	mineral water
yuànyì	request, requirement
yāoqiú	to spend money
pèibèi	bedroom

3. Rearrange these words to make a sentence: *měitiān duànliàn yīge Wǒxiǎoshí zǎoshàng.*

....

....

Chapter 17

Teaching in China

Why teach English in China, you might ask? Traveling to a distant land, learning a new language, learning about a new culture, and earning some money, and most of all, to enjoy teaching are but a few of the good reasons for going to China to teach English. You will not get rich from teaching English in China, but you will earn a salary that affords you a comfortable enough living such that you can accomplish your other goals there. You can work as little or as much as you want. After a time you will even have developed contacts that will allow you to get more for your work hours.

Job Opportunities

The demand for English language teachers in China is enormous. China is embarking on a new era of global economic conquest in which everyone wants a piece of the action. And, everyone recognizes that competency in English will be a huge benefit to them. Chinese schools nationwide are implementing curricula at lower and lower levels each year. Some private schools are EMI schools, standing for English Medium of Instruction, and begin English at kindergarten level. Naturally with such a great demand, there is an ample quantity of jobs for which you may apply. The type of position you will get and your pay scale will depend on your level of experience and education. But by and large there is generally something for everyone. The trick is finding a good situation.

Getting Started

You should begin your quest for employment in China by narrowing down some of your many options. Begin by choosing a region of the country you are interested in. After that list the cities you're willing to work in. It's good to start one at a time. The city or region you choose to search for work in may be arrived at by considering various factors. Start off considering what climate you like most. If you wilt in the sun, Guangzhou may not be the place for you. If the slightest chill causes you to shiver, cross Harbin and Shenyang off the list. Aside from climate, you may also want to consider average cost of living contrasted with salary potential. Do some sincere research on the schools of the region and the cost of living so you can make an educated decision.

You'd also do well to read up on the various types of ESL teacher contracts that are offered by various schools. You will no doubt find some commonalities but similarly find some huge differences A good contract offers a competitive salary based on the type of institution you are at and your education, at least return airfare (though often roundtrip is included for academic year contracts), housing and occasionally travel bonus. In the major cities a good basic salary for someone holding a bachelor's degree should be at least 3500 RMB. It could be more. If salary is a bigger factor for you then you may want to focus on work in Shanghai, Beijing, Shenzhen, or

Guangzhou. These cities also have great opportunities for extra contractual part-time work as well. But do your homework! Some of the schools in these big cities may offer impressive packages but at the expense of very long hours. Working in the large cities has its bad points too.

First Contact

Once you've decided where it is you'd like to live and work, your next step is to seek out schools in that area. There are many Web sites online that can help you with this search, such as Dave's ESL Cafe at *www.eslcafe.com*. There are also a handful of TEFL Yahoo! groups worth joining. The more you explore working in China the more clear it will become that there exists an online expatriate community that you may access for support and help.

You should have a resume at the ready with a cover letter announcing your intentions and detailing whatever other information regarding yourself that you would like a potential school to consider, including why you want to work in the city you are considering. Many job posts will specify that in addition to your resume and cover letter they require copies of your degree, passport, and a color photo of yourself.

Though they're not always requested, it's always good to have letters of recommendation from former employers or teachers to back you up. There's no need to send out this information immediately; after all, it is personal information. After you've had a few exchanges with the schools you're considering and once you've decided they are trustworthy, you can then forward some of the other information they've requested.

Be sure to explore all your routes for information. Confer with online communities, do Web searches on the school, ask as many questions as you possibly can. Some schools paint themselves to be far more than they really are, and you need to make educated decisions. Remember this important saying: *Jīn Yù Qí Wài, Bài Xù Qí Zhōng*. Literally: "Gold and jade on the outside, but rotting cotton on the inside." Figuratively: "All that glitters isn't gold."

A lot of Chinese schools and private language schools will respond to your interest in them by simply sending you a contract. Most contracts look fairly identical. Don't expect a phone interview as schools rarely perform them, but you can suggest one, as it's usually a good idea to put a voice to the resume. You'll also be able to gain more information about them, and hopefully make a more informed decision.

Be specific, where your contract talks about accommodations, ask for measurements, for the nature of the place. Often, universities will tell you that they will provide you with a furnished apartment, when in reality they provide you with a large-sized room in their international guest house or dormitory à la hotel room. Though they can be quite comfortable, a hotel room and an apartment are two different things.

ALERT!

An equitable option to signing a semester-long or year-long contract is a summer or winter program. If you have reservations about making a long-standing commitment or simply wish to visit the city or region you're considering working in, many Chinese schools offer summer or winter recess language camps. In the role of "edutainer," your function will be to deliver group activities geared toward learning English in a fun and entertaining way.

Remember what you learned in the chapter on shopping about bargaining. Don't be afraid or timid about negotiating. Chinese generally expect this. And lastly, always keep in mind that in the most populous nation on earth it is safe to say that you are in succinct demand. Don't ask for more than is fair, but don't let yourself be shortchanged either. The following are some points you may choose to negotiate:

- salary
- vacation time
- housing allowance

- travel allowance
- work hours
- contractual conditions

In addition to negotiating, also be sure to ask lots of questions. Ask about your visas, cost of medical coverage, housing, etc. You will very likely be able to reach an equitable agreement all around. Get names, numbers, and every other piece of information you can. Here are some sample questions:

Wǒ kéyǐ hé wàijiāoguān shuōhuà ma?	**May I speak to the Foreign Affairs Officer?**
Wàijiābù de chuánzhēn hàomǎ shì shénme?	**What is the fax number for the International Exchange Division?**
Xuéxiào de dìzhǐ shì shénme?	**What is the school's address?**

School Options

Now that you know how you should go about finding a school and negotiating a contract, it's time to consider what kind of school you wish to work at. You have many options. It's generally easiest to secure positions with the English Language institutes such as Hess in Taiwan and EF in China. These schools give a very heavy workload, and generally the pay does not scale to the hours worked as well as they do at public schools and universities. Benefits do, however, often include medical coverage, housing allowance, and two weeks of paid vacation a year. Furthermore they generally have an existing curriculum which would only need you to teach it.

The next most popular work option is the private kindergartens. The pluses to kindergartens are that they often pay very well and require little in the way of lesson planning and curriculum development. So if you're just interested in making some cash, this may be an option. The downside is that they often do not include other benefits such as housing allowances, medical, or airfares and they can be profoundly uninspiring intellectually. Be forewarned, if you don't care for singing, stay away.

If you have an academic background in ESL, EFL, linguistics, Chinese language, or education and are interested in a career in teaching, you can seek out a position at a Chinese university in one of the larger cities. In the past, candidates had at least as much chance securing positions at the universities as they did anywhere else. But this has changed and is still changing quite swiftly, particularly at the universities in Shanghai and Beijing. Universities offer agreeable pay and benefits and also come with the added personal bonus of the collegiate atmosphere.

Finally, the last option for full-time work is often considered the best by many foreign teachers. The *Jìsùxuéxiào,* or boarding school, is somewhat different from Western boarding schools in that they are relatively common and numerous. They are often situated throughout the suburban or rural areas of the large cities. They pay anywhere from 4,000 to 9,000 RMB a month and include housing and return airfare. These are often considered to be the best deals as the income more than meets the living expenses. Travel opportunities also abound during the *Jìsùxuéxiào* ample recesses. Generally students get a month for Spring Festival, two months for the summer, a week for Labor Day and week for National Day. Beyond this, the school also grants two weeks of paid vacation.

At universities, you are meeting and interacting with China's immediate future. You will spend a lot of time preparing lessons, grading assignments and holding exams as well as possibly holding office hours. But the prospect of meeting and interacting with China's immediate future can be extremely exciting and fulfilling.

After you've been in China for some time you can consider augmenting your income with part-time teaching and tutoring. Finding students by posting adverts and through personal connections is relatively easy. Just keep in mind that you have a lot of options. You have many choices and you should explore each and every one of them. Do not place all your hope in one option.

Lesson Planning

Nine times out of ten, as a foreign teacher, you will be asked to teach a course in conversational English. This is because China is already full of English teachers. Chinese English teachers focus their instruction on formal acquisition of the language including grammar, syntax, writing, and translation skills. Often, English classes (nonconversational English) involve lots of written exercises, recitation, and reading out loud. In the West, language education places a great deal of emphasis on conversation and listening comprehension.

Chinese students are very shy compared to western students. They require far more coaxing and coercing to speak in class. Don't expect them to raise their hands to speak or add to the discussion, just be pleased and excited when they do. Most of all, be patient! Remember: *Wù yà miáo zhù zhǎng.* Literally: "Don't help young shoots to grow by pulling them upward." Figuratively: "A watched pot never boils."

An understanding of the difference between Chinese and western students can be gained by observing how different Chinese parents are from western parents and how Chinese academia is compared to western academia. The ability to express oneself is a measurement of success for the student. Western language classrooms often place students facing each other, and instruction is geared toward eliciting and fostering student participation and interaction. This methodology is staunchly different from the more Confucian Chinese methodology of learning. In the Chinese classroom, students listen and do not speak. They do not challenge the teacher nor do they express opinions, particularly those opinions that differ from the teacher's. As a result, teaching Chinese students can be extremely challenging and occasionally frustrating for a teacher more accustomed to western student behavior.

The Western Perspective on Chinese Students

American parents generally accept that positive reinforcement yields better results than negative. Thus, American parents tend to be very affirming with their young. They encourage their children to develop in a wide range of dimensions. The American education system fosters individuality and creativity in children. Young people are encouraged to dream, be ambitious and have the confidence in themselves required to realize their goals. American academia focuses on children's abilities rather than their shortcomings and thus encourages children to expand upon their strengths. Children are encouraged to take part in extracurricular activities and team sports, aware that though the physical activity does indeed build the body, team sports build a sense of group consciousness and the ability to work as a team. Many parents believe that is it through their child's involvement in extracurricular activities that they can become well adjusted and suited to interacting with starkly different people in the future.

Though examinations do play a role in American academia, it's a common convention among teachers that tests are an imperfect measure of a student's true ability and that simply because a child performs poorly on a standardized test does not mean that the child is unsuccessful in learning, but instead that the test may have been unsuccessful in measuring a certain child's ability to perform.

Chinese education is very examination oriented. Students take many exams and their entrance to schools, major course of study, even their choice of courses is based on their scores on standardized tests. Chinese parents place an immense amount of pressure on their children and often encourage competitive and adversarial relationships between their children and their peers. Most Chinese university students who don't have a particular talent or passion for a given subject will major in what their parents suggest. Often times even if they do have a talent or skill for a certain field, parents still occasionally compel their children to major in what they recommend.

Chinese students get fewer choices and freedoms when it comes to their university life. What they major in is decided by several standardized tests. If they do not pass these exams they are relegated to major in what they qualify for. In the past, many Chinese parents considered extracurricular activities such as music, art, or sports to be wastes of time better spent in book study.

Chinese young people are often compelled by their parents to learn an instrument or other art form whether they want to or not, not because of the experience of being part of a group, but because many Chinese parents believe a knowledge of music will help their children perform better in mathematics. These approaches to parenting and academics has generated so much undo pressure on Chinese children that leaders in Chinese academia are actually advocating education reforms that will re-evaluate the importance of examinations and social interaction in endowing Chinese young people with a more rounded personal development. More and more, Chinese parents recognize the need for these sorts of education reforms as well and are eager to get their children's noses out of the books and into the world to experience life.

In the Classroom

In recent decades, the Chinese have employed new methods when it comes to education. Your presence in China as a language teacher is clear evidence of that fact. Chinese schools are embracing western teaching methodologies in an effort to foster greater communication, individuality, and creativity.

In your classroom, your lessons should focus on ways of getting your students to speak. The keys to successful lesson planning for Chinese students include topics of interest to them, open-ended questions, and topic discussion. When you choose a topic they all know about they're more apt to talk about it. Popular topics include movies, sports, music, culture, international affairs, fashion, and Chinese current events. Here is where the reality of teaching in China can be frustrating for the American teacher. Many of the truly controversial, social, economic, and political issues affecting China today are topics that you cannot discuss with students. Any criticism of the government or expression of a differing political ideology, or position on a major social issue is taboo. Chinese students do discuss these things, but they do so in private. Classrooms are considered "public forums." What's more, the major source for their news is the Xinhua News Agency, which is an organ of the Central Government and it is known to print inaccurate government-skewed articles and stories. When this is the only source of news, it's difficult to have a discussion with contradictory evidence that your students are not allowed to see. It's at this point that you can subtly point out: *Bǎi Wén Bù Rú Yí Jiàn.* Literally: "Hearing one hundred times is not like seeing once." Figuratively: "Seeing is believing."

A Day in the Life

Chinese youngsters generally start school when they are seven years old. Some start at six, and those whose parents have a little extra money will start them in private kindergartens even sooner. Primary schools consist of 6 bands and middle school consists of three bands. Unlike in the United States, most Chinese parents who cannot afford the international schools prefer to send their children to public schools. Because public schools are known to attract more of the experienced teachers and the courses are designed by the Ministry of Education with an accepted syllabus and approved textbooks, parents feel their children are getting a standard education. Public schools are also funded by the government.

Most elementary school students wear uniforms at school. Wearing uniforms is thought to foster a sense of team spirit and unity in children. Uniforms all basically look alike but do differ from school to school.

One commonality that exists throughout all the schools is the red scarf of the Young Pioneers. From second grade on, students that study hard and behave well are accepted into the Young Pioneers. Middle schools have different uniform policies. All middle schools tend to have uniforms. Many still enforce the wearing of their uniforms but some do not. Those that do not, however, reserve their uniforms for special occasions.

The Student Experience

A day in the life of a Chinese student from primary school all the way through to middle school and then even into university is a long an arduous day. It begins around 7:30 A.M. with *zǎocāo* (morning exercises). Students gather for the flag raising and national anthem, and then begin their morning calisthenics to music. *Zǎocāo* lasts about a half hour and then the students come inside to begin their day of class work. Class opens up with students standing up and bowing to the teacher with a hearty *Lǎoshīhǎo*, "Hello Teacher." From that point until around noon, students have three to four classes, each lasting about forty-five minutes.

FACT

Chinese students are responsible for keeping their own classrooms clean. Generally everyday some students are "on duty for the day," or as they know it, *Jīntiān zhírì le*. Those students are responsible for tidying up the classroom at the end of the day. Every week or every other week, the entire school gets involved in the process for one major cleaning called the *dàsǎochú*. All members of the staff take part as well.

From noon to about 2:30 P.M. there is *wǔshuì*, or the afternoon siesta. Students are allowed to sleep at school or if they live close enough they may go home for lunch and a rest. *Wǔshuì* concludes at 2:30 when classes resume until about 5 P.M. and students bid their teacher a good day with *Lǎoshī zàijiàn*, or "Goodbye Teacher." From 5:00 to 6:30 P.M. students usually take part in *kèwài huódòng* (extracurricular activities). Student then go home and generally spend the rest of the evening studying and preparing for exams.

The Teacher Experience

The Chinese say *yírìwéishī, zhōngshēnwéifù*, which means "If for but one day you are my teacher, my father will you always be." Teachers are revered and respected in China, and regarded as the Gardener of the Future. Teachers have such a special place in the Chinese heart that there is a holiday called Teacher's Day and it falls on September 10th every year. On Teacher's Day, students bring small gifts such as flowers, pens, and other tokens to show their appreciation. In terms of running the classroom the teacher has total control. Teachers not only teach knowledge they teach discipline. Students raise hands and wait to be called on before they speak or leave their seat. Maintaining discipline is paramount when the average Chinese class has forty students. Exams are very important in the children's lives. Many classes have pop quizzes weekly or biweekly. There are midterms and finals. Instead of report cards students receive score sheets. And, finally, come sixth grade, students take standardized tests for various subjects including Chinese, math, and English.

Exercises

You've learned all about teaching in China, so now it's time to take your own little quiz. The following exercises include information covered in various parts of this chapter. Try to answer the questions from memory first, and then refer back to earlier pages if you need to jog your memory or perfect spelling.

1. Give the equivalent English saying of the following Chinese saying: *Jīn Yù Qí Wài, Bài Xù Qí Zhōng.*

....

....

....

2. How do you ask for the Foreign Affair's Officer's number in Chinese?

....

....

....

3. What's the name of the principle news agency in China?

....

....

....

4. Rearrange the following words to form a Chinese saying: *Bù Wén Bǎi Rú Jiàn Yí.*

....

....

....

Chapter 18

Doing Business in China

You've been exploring various dimensions of life in China. It's been a blast seeing the sights and taking in the local flavor and learning how to successfully interact with the people. But doing business with the Chinese is another story. Think back to your *yànhuì* experience. The social interaction and behaviors you observed are invaluably helpful. Doing business in China successfully requires a lot of cultural sensitivity. Knowing how to say something is almost as important as knowing what to say. A solid understanding of Chinese culture will give you insight into some Chinese rituals and social practices.

The Business Ideology

Harmony is priceless in Confucian ideology. The idea that everyone in society plays a specific role and that each role is vital to the natural flow of society has permeated countless aspects of Chinese culture and has endured through time. In the Confucian ideology, family plays a very important role. The family is a small microcosm of society. Disharmony in an individual family has repercussions on society as a whole. The family is structured by a rigid patriarchal hierarchy in which the Father is the head of the family and therefore responsible for the behavior and conduct of all within the family. Within a family each member has a clearly defined role and relationship to the other members.

As you've read in previous chapters, family relationships can be quite complex. Filial piety, however, is universal in families as well as in society. This system of duty and obligation to superiors has translated over into the board room, as have all of these cultural conventions. The concept of *guānxì* or (relationships) is also very important to the Chinese. It's not what you know, it's who you know. And who you know can count for a lot. As a result, building relationships and bonds with people you do business with is very important. This is the reason Chinese business people make an effort to socialize with their partners or clients.

Business Cards

Everyone in China has a business card. Even people who are not involved in any type of business have business cards. They are the simplest way of keeping yourself in someone else's mind. They communicate some basic information about you as well as contain your contact information. If your company hasn't provided you with any official company business cards, you should take advantage of the cheap prices for them in China and have some made locally. You can make yours very personalized and stylized so that you're easily remembered.

Bilingual Cards

If you plan on being in China for some time, or if your company or you foresee yourself doing a lot of business in China, it would behoove you to have bilingual *míngpiàn* (business cards) printed with English on one side and Chinese on the other. It might surprise you to learn that most Chinese business people have bilingual business cards as well. This is partly due to China's increasing business dealings with the West and partly due to the fact that knowledge of English in China is associated with level education. Generally, someone's command of English is regarded as a status symbol.

FACT

Some people who do business on the mainland, Hong Kong, and Taiwan have two and sometimes three different sets of míngpiàn. This is because all three areas have some slightly different conventions for business cards. The most prominent of which is the fact that mainland China uses *jiántǐzì*, the simplified character set while Taiwan and Hong Kong use, *fántǐzì*, the traditional character set.

There is so much software available nowadays that allow you to design your own personalized business cards. With all the design possibilities it's easy to give in to a whim to be extravagant, but you should really go with simplicity and elegance. Make sure that all your information is easily recognizable and legible, in both English and Chinese.

Míngpiàn Etiquette

As with so many other facets of Chinese culture there is certain etiquette to the handling of *míngpiàn*. Firstly, the order in which business cards are distributed is very particular. They should be offered and received to the most senior ranking member of the delegation first, and then in descending order of seniority to the rest of the staff. Usually, whichever party is hosting the conference will offer their card first. If that is you, you should present your business card to the most senior member of the Chinese delegation with both hands; never with just one hand. A slight nod is encouraged. Remember, the Chinese do not bow at the waist the way the Japanese do. The Chinese generally only bow in formal situations and theirs is a muted bow from the shoulders more reminiscent of an emphatic nod. When presenting your card, the Chinese side should be upward and the text should be facing the recipient so that they may read it. If the Chinese delegation is hosting the meeting then the first business cards will be presented to the most senior member of your team. When receiving a card, in the same vein as offering one, it should be done with both hands. After receiving the card give a slight nod and follow it with a polite expression for being pleased and honored to meet them:

X xiānshēng /xiáojiě, nín hǎo. Jiúyǎng, Jiúyǎng.	**Hello Mr./Ms. X, I've been looking forward to meeting you.**
X xiānshēng /xiáojiě, xìnghuì, xìnghuì.	**Hello Mr./Ms. X, what a fortuitous meeting.**

Do not immediately put away the business cards you're given; you should scan them briefly, look at the individuals who gave them to you, and smile subtly. This achieves two goals. The first is that it is a polite acknowledgement of that individual and their information. The second is that it is an excellent mnemonic device for remembering who is who. If your delegation or the Chinese delegation happens to be somewhat sizeable, the business card exchange can take some time. It can also be quite daunting trying to remember all the faces and names. To that end you can also place the cards down on the table in front of you, it is a sign of respect and also an excellent way of remembering who is who.

The Conference

For the traveler to China who is there on business, the conference, or *huìyì*, is the pinnacle event in what has likely been a several day experience. In the western travel industry overnight flights and same day "business meeting" flights are common. The western concept of a business meeting is just that—a meeting. You need not know the party you'll be negotiating with in a personal and social context. To do business with the Chinese means having to learn a new set of customs and a new way of doing things. Understanding a bit of Chinese culture will enable you to understand why Chinese business people do the things they do. The *yànhuì* is often as much a business obligation as it is a chance to socialize and enjoy.

First Meetings

The Chinese prefer to observe a worker outside of the office before getting down to business. It is for this reason that prior to your actual meeting, your Chinese hosts almost certainly will have invited you to a *yànhuì*, a bath, or a KTV. Now that they've seen you at play, they're ready to see you at work. The *yànhuì* is as much a business obligation as it is a place to socialize and enjoy.

FACT

Most conference facilities have an anteroom just outside of the main conference room, or a reception area. This will be where you gather before entering the actual conference room. This is probably where some of your new Chinese colleagues will break the ice with you and engage in a little small talk before the seriousness of the conference.

Remember, *guānxì* is very important to the Chinese, so establishing social ties goes hand in hand with doing business. Since they entertained you before this point, you'll probably get comments or questions like the following:

Nǐ chànggē chàng de hén hǎo	**You sing very well.**
Nǐ shìyìng shíchā ma?	**Are you adjusting to the time difference?**
Nǐ zuótiān wǎnshàng wánr de hěn kāixīn ma?	**Did you have fun last night?**
Jīntiān de tiānqì tài hǎo le, duì ma?	**Today's weather is very nice, isn't it?**

You may indeed croon like Frank Sinatra, but it would be very immodest and un-Chinese of you to respond by saying *xièxiè*. You must skirt the compliment with something like *nǎlǐ, nǎlǐ* or *hái chà de yuǎn ne* (far from it). Otherwise, you may simply answer these questions truthfully:

Shìyìng shíchā xūyào hěn cháng shíjiān.

It takes me some time to adjust to the time difference.

Wǒ zuówǎn wánr de hěn yúkuài.

I had a great time last night.

Jīntiān de tiānqì tèbié liángkuài.

It's particularly cool today.

FACT

In business settings and particularly in business related writing, Chinese do not simply refer to themselves as *wǒ* or *nǐ* or *nǐ de gōngsī*. Instead, they use honorific forms of address attached to the nouns such as *běnrén* (I) and *běngōngsī* (our company). For the business they are addressing they use expressions such as *nín* (you), and *guìgōngsī* (your company).

In the West, it is normal for a subordinate, particularly a new one to the company to go and introduce themselves to their superiors. But in China this is not the case. Subordinates speak when spoken to. The senior ranking individual in the organization inquires after you. Remember this as you enter the meeting. You should always let the senior ranking officials in your delegation do the talking. This individual should also do all the introductions of their staff, paying attention to details. It can go something like this:

Nínhǎo, wǒ shì běngōngsī de zǒngjīnglǐ, Gāo Yǎjīng.

Hello, I am Company General Manager Gao Yajing.

Nínhǎo, Gāo zǒngjīnglǐ. Běnrén shì Lāluokǎ yǎuxiàn gōngsī de Gina Rose shìchǎngbù zhǔrèn. Hěn róngxìng jīntiān néng yǔ nínjiànmiàn.

Hello General Manager Gao. I am Gina Rose, Marketing Director of La Rocca Ltd. It's an honor to be able to meet you today.

It's not at all uncommon for groups of people to greet each other with applause in China. You should be prepared to return the applause in kind. From this point the two managers introduce the rest of their staffs in descending order of rank in the company. You may be offered a handshake, but if not, be prepared to nod or bow. When all the business cards have been exchanged and introductions made the hosting company escorts the visitors to their seats. Much the same way that the yànhuì begins a huìyì begins with speeches. The only difference is that the strongest drink you're likely to be served is tea. The Chinese delegation should speak first out of courtesy. They will likely say something very polite and welcoming like:

Jīntiān hěn róngxìng néng qǐng nín chūxí wǒmen de huìyì. Huānyíng gèwèi guìbīn de láilín.

We're very honored to have you attend our conference today. Warm welcome to all of our visiting guests.

Now comes the hard part: the negotiation. Unless you are fluent in Modern Standard Chinese, it is highly recommended that you enlist the assistance of a professional interpreter to take part in your negotiation. With an interpreter at the meeting, you might ask, why would you need to know any Chinese at all? The answer is quite simple: brownie points. The Chinese are immensely proud of their culture and heritage, even the most meager attempts at speaking Chinese will be taken as very flattering. It's absolutely worth the effort to try and use some Chinese if only as a gesture of respect. When the meeting draws to a close the Chinese delegation will very likely again say something exceedingly polite, such as:

Zhè cì huìyì néng yāoqǐng dào nínmen, zhēn shì wèi wǒmen de huìchǎng zēngtiān wúxiàn guāngcǎi

Literally: You were invited to come to this very meeting in order to add immeasurable brilliance to our meeting place.

Figuratively: We're immensely honored to have you here.

Much the same way the *yànhuì* concluded, this event will end with an exchange of gifts and very likely a souvenir photo to commemorate the occasion. The gift should just be a simple token, perhaps a fine company brand gift pen. You do not need to purchase gifts for all members of their delegation unless you choose, but a token for the senior manager is a necessity.

Business Discourse

When you're talking business in China you have to have your vocabulary ready. Depending on the nature of your business and the discussion at hand, some of the following terms might be useful to know:

Discourse Discussion

dǐzhì	resist
sùsòng	lawsuit
guīfàn	convention; norm
fádiǎnhuà	codification
qiángliè	vehement
ànzhào	according to
gǔpíngjiā	stock appraiser
fēnxī	analysis
tóuzī	investment
dǎoméi	bad luck
zhùfáng	housing
dàikuǎn	loan
gùdìng	fixed
lìlǜ	interest rate
hézī qǐyè	joint venture
hùlì	mutually beneficial

Sometimes, saying what needs to be said can be difficult. As you've witnessed so many times, what you say in Chinese is not always as important as how you say it. The Chinese take tact to a new level. If you find that you must decline an offer or concession offered by your colleague do so highly conditionally and offer a suggested alternative course of action. Try to always lead up to your suggestion with an ingratiating statement such as "I agree…" (*Wǒ tóngyì…*), or "I sympathize with your sentiment," (*Wǒ tóngqíng nínde gǎnjué...*), or "I understand your apprehension," (*Wǒ liáojiě nínde gùlǜ*), followed by "but, or however" (*dànshì, kěshì*), and then offer your alternative with four immensely useful words: *kénéng, yéxǔ, dàgài, and shuōbúdìng.* All of these words translate to variations of the words "maybe, and perhaps," but they mean much more, as you can see here:

> *...dànshì hézīqǐ yè kěnéng huì húlì.*
> **...but perhaps a joint venture would be mutually beneficial.**

> *...kěshì zhùfáng dàikuǎn gùdìng lìlǜ yéxǔ huì bù zhíde.*
> **...but the housing loan fixed interest rate may not be worth it.**

> *...dànshì rúguǒ dàjiā zhēn de ànzhào gǔpíngjiā de fēnxī qù tóuzī, shuōbúdìng míngtiān jiù huì dǎoméi.*
> **...however, if everyone really invests according to the stock appraiser's analysis, tomorrow our luck just might take a turn for the worse.**

> *...kěshì guòqù yīngguó dàgài shì dǐzhǐ sùsòng guīfàn fádiǎnhuà zuì qiánglliè de guójiā.*
> **...however, in the past, England probably vehemently resisted the codification of lawsuit conventions.**

Body Language and Unspoken Communication

At some point in your life you may have been taught that what you do not say is almost as important as what you do say. Nonverbal communication is profoundly complex and informative, and every nation on Earth has its own unspoken language of gestures and postures. For example, the Chinese gesture for "come here," the outstretched arm with palm facing downward making a waving motion, could almost certainly be mistaken in the United States for a "goodbye" gesture. Two Americans of the same gender over the age of ten would almost never be found holding hands, while women of all ages in China who are friends hold hands or walk arm in arm. It's not even unheard for two Chinese men who are good friends to walk with their arms around each others shoulder or waist. These staunch differences are illustrations of the drastic differences between Chinese and western concepts of personal space, privacy, and contact. Take this into consideration as you meet and interact with Chinese.

Many Americans find the Chinese personal space of comfort to be much closer than their own. This is something that living in the most populous nation on Earth prepares you for. When standing in a group of Chinese, you may feel the need to take a step back to preserve your personal space. Don't let it shock you too much when the Chinese simply move closer. Western visitors to China are often taught that although the Chinese area of personal space is quite small the Chinese do not like to be touched. There are few human beings that do not have an instinctive need for touch. The Chinese are no different. In fact, young Chinese men and women tend to be far more demonstrative of affection with their respective genders than Americans. But this sort of intimate touch is reserved for close friends and familiar situations. When in formal situations with strangers, touching is to be kept to a minimum.

Try to avoid hugging, back patting, or too much other physical contact with people you don't really know. What may seem a simple gesture of pointing something out using your index finger will seem rude in China. Avoid using your index finger to call or motion to others. When seated, try to avoid showing the soles of your shoes.

Office Dynamics

Possibly a hold over from the days of the Red Guard, information in China is generally all on a need-to-know basis. Gossip may spread in an office like wildfire simply due to the fact that nobody talks to anyone else about what is going on. Memos, or procedures changed in one department may not be announced because they do not effect your department. This general lack of overall information sharing can damage a company, but much of it arises from an inherent "us versus them" way of thinking that has existed in China for centuries. If something occurs in your office and you wish to know about it, often the coworkers you ask will say something like:

Zhè bú shì wǒmen de shìqíng.	**This isn't our affair.**
Zhè bú shì guānyú wǒmen de.	**This isn't related to us.**

This "us versus them" attitude is not something reserved for non-Chinese. It is applied to the Chinese from all different regions, different cities, different companies, etc., on down the line. It can be difficult moving to a new area of China for this reason. A good deal of this ideology is no doubt influenced by Confucian notions of propriety, association, and duty to one's community. Chinese people care a lot about what other people think of them. Peer pressure in China is a very powerful tool for keeping society in line. As a result, the Chinese pay very close attention to whomever they associate with and their reflection on themselves. As the Chinese saying goes: *Rǎn yú cāng zé cāng, rǎn yú huáng zé huáng.* Literally: "Dye with black to yield black, dye with yellow to yield yellow." Figuratively: "You are who your friends are."

During the afternoon of the warmer months you start to notice people taking much longer breaks. This is because of *wǔshuì,* the afternoon break. Often meetings will not be schedule later than 11:00 A.M. due to fear that it might run over into the *wǔshuì.* If for some reason a meeting does tend to run late, everyone will likely agree to the senior bosses recommendation to reconvene after *wǔshuì*:

Wǒmen wǔshuì zhī hòu, zài jìxù zhàokāi ba?	**Shall we continue this after** *wǔshuì?*

Exercises

Now it's time to see what you've learned about doing business in China. The following exercises include information covered in various parts of this chapter. Try to answer the questions from memory first, and then refer back to earlier pages if you need to jog your memory or perfect spelling.

1. Rearrange these words to form a Chinese sentence: *hùlì kěnéng tóngyì dànshìqǐyè Wǒ huì hézī.*

   ....

   ....

2. Describe how you should present a business card.

   ....

   ....

   ....

3. What is the name of the Chinese concept of social networking?

   ....

   ....

4. Change the following pronomials into their respective honorific forms.

   Wǒ ....

   Nǐ ....

   Nǐ de gōngsī ....

5. How would you introduce yourself formally using your own company's job and title?

   ....

   ....

   ....

Chapter 19

Hosting a Chinese Exchange Student

Travel can be an expensive proposition, so it may not be entirely practical for you to visit China yourself. But that fact need not in any way curb your natural appetite for experience and knowledge. If visiting China is not feasible, bring the mountain to Mohammed, as they say. Consider hosting a Chinese exchange student, and discover China and yourself in your own home.

Getting to Know You

The cultural barriers between a young Chinese person and his American counterpart may seem as awesome as the Great Wall itself. But you're embarking on an exciting adventure that will give the tools to scale that Great Wall. You will come away with a deeper understanding of another person, another culture, your own culture, and yourself.

What's in a Name?

For you, the student of Chinese, pronouncing a Chinese name may come a little easier. Be patient and work with your family in pronouncing it. Remember that most Chinese names are three syllables. Chinese always say their surname first and their given name second. Surnames are usually one syllable, but there are exceptions such as the two syllable surname *ōu yáng*. Still, it doesn't hurt to clarify. Thus far we've learned three phrases for asking someone his or her name:

Nǐ guì xìng?	**What is your surname?**
Nǐ jiào shénme míngzi?	**What's your given name?**
Nǐ zěnme chēnghū?	**What's your first and last name?**

In any of the appropriate answers for these questions you'll always find the same words. *Xìng* means surname, and *míng* and *míngzi* mean name.

ALERT!

You'll find the word *zǐ* as the second sound component in many Chinese nouns. The character itself is added mostly just to add syllabic harmony to nouns. Modern Standard Chinese likes dual syllable words.

For further clarification you may ask the student to write out his name for you so you can read it.

Nǐ zěnme xiě nǐ de míngzi?	**How do you write your name?**

Something to consider when writing Chinese names in the Roman alphabet is where your exchange student comes from. A mainland Chinese exchange student will write his or her name in Hanyu Pinyin, which you've read throughout this book. But a student from Taiwan, for example, may use another system of romanization. Once you've established where your student comes from, if he does not know Hanyu Pinyin, you may have to improvise with your own phonetics. Another point of information to keep in mind is the trend among Chinese people today to choose English names. Many choose English names to facilitate interactions with foreigners who may have trouble pronouncing their Chinese names. Other Chinese people simply consider having an English name as being chic. Be forewarned some Chinese students pick English names that might sound a little odd to you. Some Chinese pick words from the dictionary that they like and simply use the English words for them like galaxy, ocean, etc.

Breaking the Ice

Like most East Asian peoples, the Chinese are not big on demonstrative acts of affection. So when you first receive your student, leave the greeting to a hearty handshake and just smile a lot. You'll find at first that your student will also be smiling a lot. He or she may even giggle a bit at seemingly odd and almost inappropriate times. The reason for this is that in Chinese culture laughter is often a response indicative of endearment as well as anxiety. When a young man is trying to woo a young lady in China with some modest demonstration of his affection she may laugh. An American man might be heartbroken thinking she is laughing at him in ridicule. But a Chinese man knows she is laughing at him in amusement and appreciation. Another occasion for laughter in Chinese culture is when one is embarrassed or nervous. You can try to convince your student to relax:

Búyào hàixiū.	**Don't be shy.**
Wŏmen dōu shì yī jiā rén.	**We're all family here.**

But it will probably just take some time and patience. Students and young people in general tend to speak a little extra on the soft side when addressing elders simply out of respect. Quite often, they will gaze downward as well trying to avoid eye contact out of respect. It may be necessary to ask them to speak up a bit.

Nǐ kéyǐ dàshēng yēdiǎnr shuō?   **Could you speak a little louder?**

Chatting

Sometimes a good way to further break the ice is to get your student to talk about himself and his life. Try to be very inquisitive and interested. Remember that sometimes getting to know a person requires a bit of investigative reporting. Ask open-ended questions that do not allow for a yes or no answer. When an opinion is made, ask why.

Here is some basic vocabulary that might help you communicate with your student:

Chatting Vocabulary

hàixiū	shy
dàshēng	in a loud voice
pànwàng	look forward to
juéde	feel; think
zàotái	kitchen range
zàolútóu	range burner
wàimiàn	outside
dùn	simmer
xísú	custom
wénhùa	culture

Getting the 411

A sure-fire line of questioning that will get your student to open up and which will provide you with potentially very useful information is that of the student's likes and dislikes. Keep a dictionary handy in case he mentions words you're completely lost on.

Nǐ xǐhuān shénme cài?	**What foods do you like?**
Nǐ zuì xǐhuān de cài shì shénme?	**What are your favorite foods?**
Nǐ yǒu méiyǒu bú tài xǐhuān de cài?	**Are there any foods you don't like so much?**
Nǐ yǒu méiyǒu tèbié bù xǐhuān de cài?	**Are there any foods you particularly dislike?**

ALERT!

It would be best to include rice in at least one meal a day that your student will be eating, as most Chinese people eat rice with each meal. Sugar would be something to try to exclude as much as possible. Most Chinese foods including sweets do not use as much sugar as western foods. One of the biggest strains that your young person may experience is the drastic change in diet.

Your student has most likely been selected by his school for demonstrating keen intellect, an open mind, and fine moral character, as well as being in good mental and physical health. Outstanding moral character in Chinese terms means that they are exceedingly polite and displaying the utmost respect for their peers and elders alike. This will probably mean that they'd be willing to try almost anything, and far too modest and polite to admit to not liking anything. You may likely get answers such as those below:

Wǒ pànwàng xīn de jīngyàn.	**I look forward to new experiences.**
Wǒ shénme dōu chī.	**I can eat everything.**
Yīqiè hái kéyǐ a.	**Everything is okay.**
Méiyǒu rènhé wǒ bù xǐhuān de	**There isn't anything I don't like.**

If there is indeed something they particularly don't like, their idea of being bold is to suggest that they like something more than something else. Instead of outright saying that they really love tea or bean curd, they will probably say that they prefer those items over other things. For example:

Wǒ juéde chá bǐ kāfēi hǎo hē.	**I like tea better than coffee.**
Wǒ juéde dòufu bǐ niúròu hǎochī.	**I find bean curd tastier than beef.**

Turning the Tables

As your guest begins to warm up to you and your family you will hopefully see a change in the tide of the inquisition as well. You'd be surprised how many facets of everyday American life may seem quite curious to an average Chinese. Basic home rituals and practices differ between the two nations. This will be no doubt one of the more enriching parts of the hosting experience; seeing your life through the eyes of another.

Zài zhèr de zàotái wèishénme yǒu sìge zàolútóu?	**Why do stoves here have four burners?**
Jìn fángzi de shíhòu, nǐmen wèishénme bù tuōxié?	**Why don't you take off your shoes when you enter the house?**
Nǐmen wèishénme bú zài wàimiàn gān yīfu?	**Why don't you dry your clothes outside?**
Měiguórén wèishénme xǐhuān hē bīngshuǐ?	**Why do Americans like to drink cold water?**

These questions just scratch the surface. There will no doubt be questions you never thought of and that you never really considered before. When you simply do not know the answer, just say so:

Yīnwéi yǒude xīcài yào dùn hén jiǔ, suóyǐ xūyào duōyìxiē de zàolútóu lái zuò bié de cài.	**Because some Western food needs to simmer a long time, and we need more burners in order to make other food.**

Zhège xísú bú shì wǒmen wénhùa de yī bù fèn.	**This custom isn't a part of our culture.**
Qíshíhěn duō měiguórén zài wàimiàn gān yīfú. Dànshì, wǒmen yǒu yìtái gānyījī.	**Actually, many Americans dry their clothes outside. But we have a clothes dryer.**
Wǒ zhēn bù zhīdào.	**I really don't know.**

Grammar Lesson: The Comparative Preposition

The Chinese preposition *bǐ* allows you to express comparison between two nouns or objects. In sentences with an adjectival predicate such as a stative verb, *bǐ* falls between the two noun phrases being compared such, as in:

Wǒ bǐ Ryan gāo.	**I am taller than Ryan.**
Mike de fángzi bǐ wǒde fángzi dà.	**Mike's house is bigger than mine.**
Yīngwén bǐ Fǎwén nánxué.	**English is harder to learn than French.**

Bǐ can also express comparison in some sentences with a verbal predicate. In such sentences, it's understood that the main subject manifests the result of the verb to a greater extent than the contrasted subject such that:

John bǐ wǒ liǎojiv yúfǎ.	**John understands grammar better than I.**
Kelvin bǐ Richie xǐhuān tī zúqiú.	**Kelvin likes to play soccer more than Richie.**

When used in conjunction with verbs in the complement of degree format, *bǐ* may be placed between the two contrasted subjects or following the verb:

Jason bǐ wǒ zǒu de kuài. OR *Jason zǒu de bǐ wǒ kuài*	**Jason walks faster than I.**

Barb bǐ Eva huā de qián duō.
OR
Barb huā de qián bǐ Eva duō.   **Barb spent more money than Eva.**

In the verb + object complement of degree format where the verb is repeated, *bǐ* may be placed either before the reiterated verb or before the complement, as in:

Kaaren shuō yīngwén bǐ tā lǎogōng shuō de liúlì.
OR
Kaaren shuō yīngwén shuō   **Kaaren speaks English better**
de bǐ tā lǎogōng liúlì.   **than her husband.**

In order to negate the comparison simply place the negator *bù* before *bǐ* as below:

Renee měitiān qǐchuáng bù bǐ Ray qǐ de zǎo.
OR
Renee měitiān qǐchuáng   **I wake up every morning later**
qǐ de bù bǐ Ray zǎo.   **than him.**

It is ungrammatical to use adverbs such as *hěn*, *fēicháng*, *tèbié*, or *zhēn* before adjectival predicate sentences like static verbs. You can, however, use adverbs such as *gēng* or *hái*.

Finally, there is one more way of making comparisons, and that is by using the verbs *yǒu* and *méiyǒu*. You should note however that comparisons using these two expressions are made primarily in negative or interrogative contexts. *Yǒu* may be used in sentences with an adjectival predicate or in some sentences with a verbal predicate in order to express comparison. In such sentences, *yǒu* occupies the same position as *bǐ*. For example:

David méiyǒu Kurt xǐhuān gúdiǎn yīnyuè.	**David doesn't like classical music as much as Kurt.**
Nǐ tiàowǔ tiào de méiyǒu tā hǎo.	**You don't dance as well as he does.**

It should be pointed out that *méiyǒu. . .* and *bù bǐ. . .* do not have the exact same meaning. Take these two sentences:

Jenny méiyǒu Caroline lái de zǎo.	**Jenny didn't arrive as early as Caroline.**
Tammy bù bǐ Laurie lái de zǎo.	**Tammy didn't arrive as early as Laurie.**

What is communicated using *méiyǒu* is that Jenny absolutely did not arrive as early as Caroline. Caroline was there at noon, and Jenny arrived an hour later. However, in the second sentence, *bù bǎ* communicates that Laurie arrived earlier than Tammy, but perhaps not by much. They may have arrived at the same time and one simply walked in before the other.

Chinese Families

The notion of family is important in all cultures. For most of human history family units have played important roles in societies on many levels. In China, the family is the backbone unit of society. A basic understanding of it may give you invaluable insight into your exchange student and his behaviors and attitudes. To truly grasp some of the underlying themes of Chinese society we must look backwards in time to Imperial China. The notion of family was defined for thousands of years in China by the teachings of Confucius. Confucius rendered the social patriarchal hierarchy into canon and in turn this hierarchy was extended to include many other layers of Chinese society. The father or patriarch was the leader of the family unit, zunder him was the eldest son and under the eldest son, everyone else. This system was called filial piety and social rituals at the time existed to perpetuate it. It is from this system that we get the Chinese expression *zhòngnán qīngnǚ*, which means "Heavy on men and light on women."

A son was a treasure to be prized above all things for a son could carry on the family name in his father's stead. The son was the only one able to properly venerate his parents and pay homage to them and his ancestors. Obligation to one's family was paramount above all things. In modern times the family in China has undergone some incredible changes not the least of which was Mao instituting *nànnǚ píngděng* or gender equality and marriage laws like the 1950 laws outlawing traditional practices that were detrimental to women. Since the advent of the economic reforms of the 1970s and 1980s, the Chinese family has once again had to adapt. Populations have adapted to a new economy and migration has occurred. That affects all facets of life. Men and women alike are considering employment that sometimes takes them away from home, while a great deal of China's poor flock to the major cities in search of a better life. This of course has resulted in one parent being away from the family for extended periods of time. Then, looming in the background of the evolving Chinese family is the question of China's massive population and how the One Child Policy has shaped things for Chinese citizens. Although efforts had been made to bring about change in Chinese cultural concepts regarding children's gender, some Chinese still favor having sons over daughters. As a result, China faces an impending gender gap that has never been seen before. The Chinese family has indeed evolved with the times. The modern urban Chinese family is an amalgam of traditional Chinese values, Maoist values of state and government, capitalism, and western cultural influence.

In Case of Emergency

Emergencies arise out of their own nature. Accidents simply happen, and there's little we can do to undo them. But what we can, indeed, do is either prevent them or prepare for them. The best weapon in your defensive arsenal in this case is knowledge. Your student will most likely have passed a battery of tests assuring that he or she is physically fit for the journey and not at risk for any adverse environmental effects. If the school does not provide you with materials concerning your student to this effect, you should by all means request them. In the mean time, ask a lot of questions.

Allergies

The Chinese word for allergy is *guòmǐn*. Allergens are many and awareness is often few. Knowing if your student has any particular allergies may help you immensely in preventing allergic reactions and in treating your guest if a problem arises. Allergies to dust and allergy-associated asthma is quite common in China due to pollution. It might be useful to keep a spare albuterol inhaler pump on hand just in case.

Nǐ yǒu méiyǒu rènhé guòmǐn?	**Do you have any allergies?**
Nǐ yǒu méiyǒu bù néng chī de?	**Is there anything you cannot eat?**
Rúguǒ nǐ gǎndào bù shūfú, qǐng gàosù wǒ.	**If you start to feel sick, please tell me.**

By and large your student should be well aware of any environmental allergies they may have, often they are nothing more than annoyances. But some can be more serious, and those are the kind the student will probably make a point of communicating:

TRACK 54

Wǒ bù néng chī xiārén.	**I can't eat shrimp**
Wǒ duì gǒu yǒu guòmǐn.	**I'm allergic to dogs.**
Wǒ bù néng chī jīdàn hé huángyóu.	**I can't eat eggs or butter.**

Stomach Ailments

Remind your guest that western cuisine is significantly different from Chinese *jiācháng* food. Your guest will be trying all manner of foods they probably do not otherwise eat at home. The probability that there will be something that does not agree with them is very good. Not every reaction will be an allergic one, some may simply be from not being accustomed to the cuisine. If your student is just in some moderate discomfort and what ever ails him seems relatively harmless, you may still want to see what's going on. Treat your student the way you'd treat your own family member in this situation. Bear in mind that this student is someone's son or daughter and is very far from home. Care for your student the way you'd hope someone would care for your child or relative.

Exercises

Now it's time to see what you've learned about hosting a Chinese student. The following exercises include information covered in various parts of this chapter. Try to answer the questions from memory first, and then refer back to earlier pages if you need to jog your memory or perfect spelling.

1. How do you ask someone to speak a little more loudly in Chinese?

   ....

   ....

2. Create a sentence from the following words: *yīfú měiguórén gān hvn zài duō wàimiàn*

   ....

   ....

3. Translate this sentence to Chinese using the comparative preposition bǐ: I arrived earlier than my elder brother.

   ....

   ....

   ....

4. Translate this sentence to Chinese using *méiyǒu* as the comparative element: "I don't speak Chinese as well as my wife."

   ....

   ....

   ....

Chapter 20

Put Your New Knowledge to Use

You've nearly reached the end of your education about China and her language. An integral part of this education is exercise. You need to practice what you've learned or you'll lose it quickly. The Chinese say *shú néng shēng qiǎo* (practice can yield skill). There are far more Chinese cultural resources around you than you would imagine. It's not enough to simply read about a language; you must live it to really improve in it. This final chapter will set you on the path to completing your goals in China!

Chinese Cultural Resources

Living in a country like the United States with a significant Chinese American and Chinese expatriate community, the opportunity to find outlets for experiencing a bit of Chinese culture are higher than elsewhere. Many major cities have "Chinatowns" in which you can experience a superficial degree of Chinese culture. But more importantly, often where there are Chinatowns there are Chinese cultural organizations.

The Chinese Embassy

The Chinese Embassy is located in Washington D.C. There are Chinese consulates located in the cities of Chicago, Houston, Los Angeles, New York City, and San Francisco. These institutions all have ties to several national organizations that host cultural events and workshops relating to Chinese culture, politics, and social issues. Many of their Web sites also have links to online sources of information at your disposal such as *www.hanyu.com.cn*. This site is hosted by the Office of Chinese Language Council International of the People's Republic of China and maintained by East China Normal University. It is intended to be an Online Chinese Language resource. Many challenges face Chinese living in the United States and Americans living in China. Some of these organizations may even be able to help you prepare for relocating to China if that is your plan. One such organization, for example, is The China Institute in New York City. The Institute's School of Chinese Studies was founded in 1933 and is the oldest Chinese cultural education center of the kind in the United States. It offers seminars and classes in everything from the language to calligraphy, to painting, to travel workshop classes. They often feature lectures, literary, musical, and other performance-related events by renowned lecturers, writers, and artists.

Chinese Communities

The best resource for practicing your listening and hopefully speaking skills are Chinese speaking communities. There are approximately 4 million Chinese Americans and most populate the urban and suburban areas of

New York City, San Francisco, Honolulu, Los Angeles, Seattle, Philadelphia, and Boston. Chinatowns in these cities are among the most famous and most of these cities have multiple Chinese American enclaves which are distinguished mostly by the time period associated with their wave of immigration. Chinese have been calling the United States home for a long time. The most famous wave of Chinese immigration was to San Francisco during the gold rush. Of course, Chinese Americans do not only inhabit the urban areas, many make homes in rural regions of the country as well as the secondary cities and college towns.

QUESTION?

Where is the largest Chinese American population found in the U.S.?
The largest concentration of Chinese Americans is in California, the northeast and Hawaii, where they constitute 3 percent, 2 percent, and 10 percent of the state populations respectively. If you live in any of these areas, finding Chinese speakers to listen to and interact with will be considerably easier.

Overall, Chinese American populations are growing in the United States due to immigration, but the American born Chinese birthrate is lower than European Americans. Another interesting phenomenon is the recent trend of American families adopting children, especially girls, from China.

Practice Techniques

Learning a language is more than just translation. A language is a living thing. It is dynamic and changing and reflects the broad range of feelings and thoughts that a human being has. Thus, truly speaking a language requires you to think in that language. That can sound like a truly staggering challenge to meet. In fact, it is. Truly acquiring a language requires a commitment from you. That being said, it does not mean you must walk the length of the Great Wall in a day. Be patient with yourself, and be open to the idea of learning a new way of thinking.

At Home

The first way to begin cultivating a new way of thinking for yourself is by re-examining the landscape of your everyday surroundings. To begin thinking of your environment in a different way, in a Chinese way, you can start by thinking of the names of the objects in your environment in Chinese. You can start just with the nouns. When you look at a chair, instead think *yǐzi*. When you look at a lamp, instead think *dēng*. Sit down on your *shāfā* (sofa) and watch *diànshì* (TV). Perhaps you can pick up the *diànhuà* (phone) and call your (*péngyǒu*) friend. Look at your *biǎo* (watch); what time is it? Have you eaten *wǎnfàn* (dinner)?

An old method for improving your pronunciation is by speaking in front a mirror. Take your list of the sounds of Chinese and take note of your expression and mouth and tongue position as you enunciate. Listen to the CD track with the sounds of Chinese and compare and contrast. Don't focus too hard as you may over do it on some of the enunciations and sound unnatural. Just practice in a relaxed state of mind and do your best to imitate the speaker.

To supplement this mode of thinking and to also give you a hand in case you're not the best at remembering vocabulary, try an old tested tried and true trick of the trade. Name labels are the way to go. Put Post-its or sticky labels (the kind that do not damage the walls) with the Chinese words for everything around your house. You can use the larger sized ones to include short sentences and phrases.

Chinese Media

An excellent vehicle for improving your listening skills is by taking advantage of the spectrum of Chinese media that you may have never realized is available on the Internet. Though some digital TV markets carry Chinese language service, they are often not free. They should, however, be quite reasonable, and if you're going to be going to spending an extended period of time in China, the expense for a month or two might be worth it. Otherwise, many major urban area PBS stations broadcast an hour or two hour newscast in Chinese. You may have never noticed it before, but rest assured where there are Chinese speakers, there is Chinese media.

Your best bet is still the Internet. There are many Chinese language Web casts accessible to you with Windows Media Player, Real Player, and iTunes. A nice comprehensive list of Internet radio stations from all over mainland China, Hong Kong, Singapore, and Taiwan can be found at *www.multilingualbooks.com/online-radio-chinese.html*. Make sure you have the most recent versions of the media players and then tune in and listen.

If you'd like some visual stimulation while listening to Chinese, another viable option is visiting the foreign films section at your local video chain. The large chains carry many movies in stock, and if they do not have a label you're looking for you can request to special order it. If you've never seen a Chinese movie, then now is the time to be initiated into a worldwide fan base of Chinese film enthusiasts. Chinese film has not had the brightest of histories, but in the last twenty years it has made untold strides. If you're not sure what movie to choose, you can safely and likely thankfully take a stab in the dark with most any movie by *Chén Kǎigē* whose film *Farewell My Concubine* (1993) was not only nominated for two Academy Awards, but won the coveted Palme d'Or at the Cannes Film Festival. Another great, is *Zhāng Yīmóu*, whose film *Hero* in 2002 became one of the few non-English language films to top the U.S. box office.

Preparation

Before your journey, take some time to really sit down and think about what you've learned here and how you can apply it to possible future situations. You should also take some time to put some of yourself into the lessons you've had. Think about some of the situations you've encountered as you've moved through the book. How would you answer some of the questions you've asked? How would you introduce yourself? Who are your relatives? To help you along, in addition to spreading the Post-its around the house to help you with your vocabulary retention, begin compiling a personal profile of yourself with information about yourself that you can now express in Chinese. A useful format for that is a *rìjì* (journal). Use as much Chinese as you can, use English when you don't know the Chinese words. Observe your progress as time goes by and you'll see that the Chinese increases and the English decreases. Start it off with your basic information. Introduce yourself:

> *Qīnài de rìjì,*
> *Wǒde míngzì shì Roseanne. Wǒ yǒu yīge mèimèi, tāde míngzì shì Lucille. Wǒ yǒu liǎngge háizi. Wǒ érzi de míngzì shì Jeffery. Wǒ nǚér de míngzì shì Alyssa. Wǒmen zhùzài Niǔyuēzhōu. Wǒ měitiān zǎoshàng liùdiǎn zhōng qǐchuáng.*

> Dear Diary,
> My name is Roseanne. I have a younger sister, her name is Lucille. I have two children. My son's name is Jeffrey. My daughter's name is Alyssa.
> We live in the state of New York. Every morning I get up at 6:00.

Keep this journal everyday and try to add more and more about yourself to it. Invest in a good English-Chinese Chinese-English dictionary and you'll be able to increase your own vocabulary at your leisure. Take note of your progress.

Reach Out

Be proactive. Don't sit back and wait for opportunities to improve your Chinese to come to you. If you live in an area where there simply is not a substantive Chinese American community, then finding Chinese-speakers is going to be a bit more of a challenge. But there are ways if there is the will. Practice your *guānxì* skills by seeking out language partners and building yourself a social network. You'd be surprised how many resources there are around you.

Chinese Culture Around You

Let's think for a moment. What aspects of Chinese culture are very popular in the United States? That answer should be easily answered with the martial arts! The Chinese martial arts, both internal and external are extremely popular in the United States; why not take one up? Sign up for a Tai Chi course, or perhaps a form of Kung Fu. If the instructors are not Chinese themselves, they can more than likely point you in the direction of a local or regional Chinese community. If that seems a bit too high impact for you, try your local college or university. Many four year colleges nowadays offer Chinese. If you don't have the time or resources to register for one yourself, contact the foreign languages department and ask about language exchange partners or tutors. Perhaps there is a Chinese foreign exchange student attending the school who would welcome the opportunity to improve their English while teaching you about Chinese culture and helping you with your Chinese. You could even go to the campus itself and post a flier on a student bulletin board looking for language partner. Ask around, you certainly have options.

The way the Chinese answer the phone is a little mystery. Whenever a phone dialogue is written out, the character wèi, in the fourth tone is written. However, years of living in China will demonstrate that nobody answers the phone this way. It's also wéi, in the second tone. Why a suitable wei character in the second tone was not selected remains a puzzle for the ages.

Literature

Where else but in the classics of Chinese literature and philosophy could you gain some insight into Chinese culture and society? The big name book chains often have a sizeable collection of East Asian philosophy titles. Almost all the great Chinese literary classics have been translated into English, though, truth be told, reading them in the original is far more rewarding.

Consider that a lofty goal for the future. For the present, think back on your studies and recall the many references we've made to Taoism, Buddhism, and Confucius. These belief systems play as fundamental a role in shaping Chinese culture as Greco-Roman religion, Judaism, Islam, and Christianity play in shaping the cultures of Europe. Pick up the *Tao Te Ching*, or the *Amitabha Sutra*, or the Confucian Analects and it might open your eyes to a whole new way of thinking for yourself.

If you're less interested in enlightenment and more interested in a good story, China is certainly rich in those. The famed Four Great Classics form the cornerstone of Chinese literature. Ask your bookseller for *Outlaws of the Marsh* by Shi Naian and Luo Guanzhong, *Dream of the Red Mansion* by Cao Xueqin, *Journey to the West* by Wu Chengen, or *Romance of Three Kingdoms* by Luo Guanzhong.

When in China...

Please don't do as the Chinese do. Don't be shy. Timidity is the bane of every English teacher in China. Chinese language pedagogy up to now has focused a great deal on competency in grammar and syntax. While these elements are of course vital, they are no more or less key to language acquisition than creative expression and initiative. Most Chinese English students, by the time they've reached university, have a fair command of English grammar and an agreeable vocabulary. Their listening comprehension is superior, but their oral expression is often abysmal. This is due to lack of practice and to the fact that Chinese education conventions do not generally encourage expression. Western English teachers in China spend a great deal of time pulling teeth trying to get their polite but shy Chinese students to open up and say what's on their mind.

Lead by example. Show everyone you are not afraid to make mistakes. Take risks, take constructive criticism, but also, be prepared to take compliments. It is really no great exaggeration when it is said that the Chinese are extremely pleased and touched when they see a *Lǎowài* (foreigner) trying to speak Chinese. You'll receive so much encouragement that you'll sincerely want to improve.

A Word to the Wise

Hanyu Pinyin is an indispensable tool to the English-speaking Chinese student, as it instantaneously makes Chinese vocabulary accessible to you. If you do choose to continue your Chinese studies, you would do wise to learn to read Chinese characters. As daunting a task as that may seem it actually tends to make learning to speak the language far easier. Many Chinese words are homophonic, meaning they sound alike but have different meanings which you can only discern by reading them or from context. Take for example the case of the two de particles. They are represented by two different characters in the written language but sound identical when spoken. A great deal of poetic meaning lies in the characters as well, they are both communicative and artistic and a pleasure to read and write.

Exercises

This is your final opportunity to quiz yourself on what you've learned. The following exercises include information covered in various parts of this chapter. Try to answer the questions from memory first, and then refer back to earlier pages if you need to jog your memory or perfect spelling.

1. How do the Chinese answer the phone? ....

2. What is a polite Chinese word for a foreigner? ....

3. Translate the Chinese idiom *shú néng shēng qiǎo* to English.

   ....

   ....

Appendix A

Chinese-to-English Glossary

Chinese	English
A	
ànmó	massage
ānpái	arrange
ànzhào	according to
Aòmén	Macau
B	
bā	eight
bàba	father
bái	white
bǎiwàn	one million
bàn	half
bàn(shì)	take care of..
bàozhǐ	newspaper
bāshì	bus
běi	north
biān	side
biāozhì	sign
bīngshuǐchí	cold plunge
bù	department
bú, bù	negator, no
búyòng	there's no need
C	
cān	meal
cāng	cabin/compartment
wǔcānròu	lunchmeat
céng	floor
chá	tea
chákàn	look into

Chinese	English
chē	vehicle; cart
chēcì	train number
chéngshì	city
chènshān	shirt
chù	area
chuángdiàn	mattress
chūjìng	to exit a country
chūzū qìchē	taxi
cífú lièchē	maglev train
cóng	from
cóngláibù/ cóngláiméiyǒu	never
cóngqián	in the past

D

Chinese	English
dàchúshī	chef
dāi	stay
dàikuǎn	loan
dàizǒu	to take something with you; carry something
dān	list; slip
dānchéng	one-way
dāngrán	of course
dàodá	arrive
dǎoméi	bad luck
dàshēng	in a loud voice
dǎsuàn	plan
dàtīng	hall
dàxué	university
dàyī	coat
dàyuē	about; approximate
děng	wait
děng	wait; class/type
dēngjì	to register
diǎncài	to order food
dìdi	younger brother
dìng	reserve
dìngdān	order form
dìtiězhàn	subway station

Chinese	English
dìxiàlièchē	subway train
dǐzhì	resist
dōng	east
dōngbù	eastern area
duì	correct, yes
duìhuàn	exchange
duìmiàn	opposite; opposite side
dùjià	vacation
dùn	simmer
duōdà	how big
duōjiǔ	how long (time)
duōshǎo	how many/much
duōzhòng	how heavy

E

èr	two
érxí	daughter-in-law
érzi	son

F

fā	set off, launch
fāchē	to depart
fádiǎnhuà	codification
fángjiān	room
fāpiào	receipt
fāshēng	happen
fēi	prohibit, no, not
fēijī	airplane
fēixīyānchù	non-smoking area
fěnhóng	pink
fēnxī	analysis
fùqián	pay

G

gēge	elder brother
gēn	with; and
gèng	more

Chinese	English
gēngyīshì	changing room
gēnsuí	follow
gēnzhe	follow
gònghéguó	people's republic
gōngyuán	park
guǎi	to turn
guānguāng	sightsee
gùdìng	fixed
guì	expensive
guīfàn	convention; norm
guīlǜ	in order, with regularity
guòlái	come by
Guóyǔ	Chinese (Taiwan)
gǔpíngjiā	stock appraiser

H

Chinese	English
hǎiguān	customs
hàixiū	shy
háiyǒu	and; furthermore;
Hàn	Nationality of Chinese
Hànyǔ	Chinese (PRC)
hào	number
hǎochī	delicious, tasty; good
hē	drink
hēi	black
hěn	very
héziqǐyè	joint venture
hóng	red
hòutiān	the day after tomorrow
huā	flower, to spend money
huànchéng	exchange
huànchéng	transfer
huáng	yellow
Huáyǔ	Chinese (SG)
huī	grey
huì	be able to, would
hùlì	mutually beneficial

Chinese	English
hūn	meat foods
huǒchē	train
huǒchēzhàn	train station
huótuǐ	ham
hùzhào	passport

J

Chinese	English
jǐ	which
jiā	add
jiājù	furniture
jiàn	see
jiǎnfà	haircut
jiànkāng	health
jiāotōng	transportation, communication
jībĕn	basic
jídiǎn	at what time
jiĕjie	elder sister
jìn	close
jīntiān	today
jiǔ	nine
jǐwò	how many bedrooms?
juéde	feel; think
júhóng	orange
jūliú	residence
jūliúzhèng	residence permit

K

Chinese	English
kǎ	card; pass
kāfēi	brown
kāiyǎn	begin a show
kè	visitor
kèfáng	guest's room
kèfáng yòngcān fúwùbù	room service
kĕndìng	surely
kèrén	guest
kĕxīyānchù	smoking area
kéyǐ	possible, able, may, can

Chinese	English
kuài	fast
kuàngquánshuǐ	mineral water
kùzi	pants

L

là	spicy; hot
lái	come
láihuí	round trip
lán	blue
láojià	excuse me
lǎogōng	husband
lǎopó	wife
lèi	tired
lìlǜ	interest rate
lǐngdài	tie
liù	six
lǜ	green
lù	street
lùkǒu	corner

M

máimǎn	purchase up to/at least
māma	mother
màozi	hat
mǎshàng	immediately; right away
mèimei	younger sister
měiyuán	U.S. dollars
miǎnfèi	free
miàntiáo	noodle
mílù	get lost, lose one's way
míngbái	understand
míngtiān	tomorrow
mínguó	republic
míngzi	name
mòlìhuā	jasmine
mùlù	list

Chinese	English
N	
nán	south
năr	where
nàr	there
náshŏucài	specialty dish
néizhŏng	what kind
nĭ	you (colloquial)
nín	you (formal)
niúròu	beef
nǚchènshān	blouse
nvér	daughter
nǚxù	son-in-law
P	
pángbiānr	side
pànwàng	look forward to
páozi	robe
pèibèi	equip, equipment, furnishing
pèicài	sidedish
piānrè	be on the hot side
piào	ticket
pídài	belt
píng	bottle
pù	berth
pǔtōng	common
Pǔtōnghuà	Chinese (PRC)
Q	
qī	seven
qián	straight
qiáng	wall
qiángliè	vehement
qiánpái zuòwèi	front row seats
qiānshǔ	sign
qiántiān	the day before yesterday
qiānwàn	ten million

Chinese	English
qiánwǎng	bound for, toward
qiānzhèng	visa
qièjì	avoid at all costs
qǐng	please
qīngjiéjì	detergent
qíshí	actually
qítā	other, cursory
qúnzi	skirt

R

ránhòu	then, afterwards
rén	person
rènhé	any
rénmín	the people
rènwéi	believed
rèshuǐchí	hot tub
ruǎn	soft
rùjìng	enter a country

S

sān	three
sāngnáyù	sauna
sānmíngzhì	sandwich
shāfā	sofa
shéi	who
shēnbào	declaration
shénme shíhòu	when
shénme	what
shēnmíng	declaration
shí	ten
shì	be; is; are
shì	style
shǐshī	epic
shíwàn	one hundred thousand
shìxiàng	items
shōu	receive
shòu zhòngshì	beloved
shòuhuòjī	vending machine

Chinese	English
shǒuxiān	firstly
shǔ	potato
shuāng	double, pair
sì	four
sìchuānrén	Sichuanese
sòngcān	delivery (food)
sònghuò	delivery (general items)
suíbiàn	at your convenience
suíshí	whatever time is convenient
sùsòng	lawsuit

T

Chinese	English
tāng	broth
tángzhuāng	Tang Zhuang
tànqīn	visit relatives
tàocān	set meal
tè	special; especially
tèkuài	express
tèxuǎn	preference
tiān	day
tián	fill out
tián	sweet
tiáo	sticks
tíqián	in advance
tǒng	bottle; measure word for large tubs or vats.
tóngyì	agree
tōngzhī	notify, inform
tóuzī	investment
tuìfáng	checkout
tuījiàn	suggest

W

Chinese	English
wàihuìquàn	foreign exchange certificate
wàimài	take away
wàimiàn	outside
wàitào	jacket
wǎng shàng	on the Web; online

Chinese	English
wǎng	toward
wǎng	Net; Web
wǎng	to; toward
wǎngzhàn	Web site; Web page
wǎnshàng	evening
wèi	for
wèi	measure word for people
wéijīn	scarf
wèikǒu	appetite
wèishénme	why
wèizhuórè	heartburn
wénhùa	culture
wénjiàn	documentation
wǒ	I
wò	recline; sleep
wòshì	bedroom
wǔ	five
wǔqiān	five thousand

X

xǐ	wash
xī	to smoke
xī	west
xiǎng	think
Xiānggǎng	Hong Kong
xiǎngyào	would like
xiànjīn	cash
xiāoshī	disappear
xiàwǔ	afternoon
xīcān	western food
xìng	surname
xínglǐ	luggage
xīngqī	week
Xīnjiāpō	Singapore
xísú	custom
xiūjiǎozhíjiǎ	pedicure
xiūzhíjiǎ	manicure
xīwàng	hope, wish, expect

Chinese	English
xǐyījiān	laundry room
xū	disperse, weak

Y

Chinese	English
yǎn	act
yángròu	lamb
yānròu	bacon
yánshuāxǐ	salt scrub
yǎnwán	end a show
yào	want; will
yàofāng	prescription
yāoqiú	request, requirement
yèxiāo	late night snack
yéxǔ	perhaps
yí tào yīfú	dress
yī	one
yìbǎi	one hundred
yìbān	general; in general
Yìdàlì	Italy
yídìng	certainly
yīfú	clothes
yígòng	all together
yǐjīng	already
Yīn	Yin
yìng	hard
yīnggāi	should, ought to, must
Yīngguórén	Briton
yǐnshí	food and drink
yìqiān	one thousand
yǐshàng	upwards of; and above
yíwàn	ten thousand
yíyì	one hundred million
yòng	use
yòngwán	use up
Yóu ..yǐnfā	...related
yǒu	to have, exist, there is
yòu	right

Chinese	English
yòubiān	right side
yǔ	language
yú	fish
yuǎn	far
yuànyì	willing
yùdìng	reserve
yùgāng	jacuzzi

Z

Chinese	English
zài	be; at; in; on
zàolútóu	range burner
zàotái	kitchen range
Zěnme	How
zhá	deep fry
zhàn	stand
zhǎodào	have found
zháshǔtiáo	french fries
zhèng	pass
zhēngliúshuǐ	distilled water
zhēngqìyùshì	steam room
zhèr	here
zhídé	worth while, worth it
zhijiān	between
zhīyī	one of
zhōng	middle
Zhōngguóhuà	Chinese (PRC)
Zhōnghuá	China
Zhōngwén	Chinese (PRC)
zhōngyào	Chinese herbal medicine
zhù	live, stay, reside
zhù	live; stay
zhǔ	boil
zhù	live, accommodate
zhù	wish, blessing
zhùfáng	housing
zhuōzi	table
zhūròu	pork

Chinese	English
zǐ	purple
zīliào	information
zuì	most
zuò	do, make
zuò	to sit
zuò	sit; seat
zuǒ	left
zuǒbiān	left side
zuótiān	yesterday

Appendix B

English-to-Chinese Glossary

English	Chinese
A	
about; approximate	*dàyuē*
according to	*ànzhào*
act	*yǎn*
actually	*qíshí*
add	*jiā*
afternoon	*xiàwǔ*
agree	*tóngyì*
airplane	*fēijī*
all together	*yígòng*
already	*yǐjīng*
analysis	*fēnxī*
and; furthermore	*háiyǒu*
any	*rènhé*
appetite	*wèikǒu*
area	*chù*
arrange	*ānpái*
arrive	*dàodá*
at what time	*jídiǎn*
at your convenience	*suíbiàn*
avoid at all costs	*qièjì*
B	
bacon	*yānròu*
bad luck	*dǎoméi*
basic	*jīběn*
be able to, would	*huì*
be on the hot side	*piānrè*
be; at; in; on	*zài*
be; is; are	*shì*

English	Chinese
bedroom	wòshì
beef	niúròu
begin a show	kāiyǎn
believed	rènwéi
beloved	shòu zhòngshì
belt	pídài
berth	pù
between	zhījiān
black	hēi
blouse	nǚchènshān
blue	lán
boil	zhǔ
bottle	píng
bottle; measure word for large tubs or vats	tǒng
bound for, toward	qiánwǎng
Briton	Yīngguórén
broth	tāng
brown	kāfēi
bus	bāshì

C

English	Chinese
cabin/compartment	cāng
card; pass	kǎ
cash	xiànjīn
certainly	yídìng
changing room	gēngyīshì
checkout	tuìfáng
chef	dàchúshī
China	Zhōnghuá
Chinese (PRC)	Hànyǔ, Pǔtōnghuà; Zhōngguóhuà; Zhōngwén
Chinese (SG)	Huáyǔ
Chinese (Taiwan)	Guóyǔ
Chinese herbal medicine	zhōngyào
city	chéngshì
close	jìn
clothes	yīfú
coat	dàyī

English	Chinese
codification	*fádiǎnhuà*
cold plunge	*bīngshuǐchí*
come by	*guòlái*
come	*lái*
common	*pǔtōng*
convention; norm	*guīfàn*
corner	*lùkǒu*
correct, yes	*duì*
culture	*wénhùa*
custom	*xísú*
customs	*hǎiguān*

D

daughter	*nǔér*
daughter-in-law	*érxí*
day	*tiān*
declaration	*shēnbào*
declaration	*shēnmíng*
deep fry	*zhá*
delicious, tasty; good	*hǎochī*
delivery (food)	*sòngcān*
delivery (general items)	*sònghuò*
department	*bù*
detergent	*qīngjiéjì*
disappear	*xiāoshī*
disperse, weak	*xū*
distilled water	*zhēngliúshuǐ*
do, make	*zuò*
documentation	*wénjiàn*
double, pair	*shuāng*
dress	*yí tào yīfú*
drink	*hē*

E

east	*dōng*
eastern area	*dōngbù*
eight	*bā*

English	Chinese
elder brother	*gēge*
elder sister	*jiějie*
end a show	*yǎnwán*
enter a country	*rùjìng*
epic	*shǐshī*
equip, equipment, furnishing	*pèibèi*
evening	*wǎnshàng*
exchange	*duìhuàn*
exchange	*huànchéng*
excuse me	*láojià*
expensive	*guì*
express	*tèkuài*

F

far	*yuǎn*
fast	*kuài*
father	*bàba*
feel; think	*juéde*
fill out	*tián*
firstly	*shǒuxiān*
fish	*yú*
five thousand	*wǔqiān*
five	*wǔ*
fixed	*gùdìng*
floor	*céng*
flower, to spend money	*huā*
follow	*gēnsuí*
follow	*gēnzhe*
food and drink	*yǐnshí*
for	*wèi*
foreign exchange certificate	*wàihuìquàn*
four	*sì*
free	*miǎnfèi*
french fries	*zháshǔtiáo*
from	*cóng*
front row seats	*qiánpái zuòwèi*
furniture	*jiājù*

English	Chinese
G	
general; in general	*yībān*
get lost, lose one's way	*mílù*
green	*lǜ*
grey	huī
guest	kèrén
guest's room	kèfáng
H	
haircut	jiǎnfà
half	bàn
hall	dàtīng
ham	huótuǐ
happen	fāshēng
hard	yìng
hat	màozi
have found	zhǎodào
health	jiànkāng
heartburn	wèizhuórè
here	zhèr
Hong Kong	Xiānggǎng
hope, wish, expect	xīwàng
hot tub	rèshuǐchí
housing	zhùfáng
how	zěnme
how big	duōdà
how heavy	duōzhòng
how long (time)	duōjiǔ
how many bedrooms	jǐwò
how many/much	duōshǎo
husband	lǎogōng
I	
I	wǒ
immediately; right away	mǎshàng
in a loud voice	dàshēng
in advance	tíqián

English	Chinese
in order, with regularity	guīlù
in the past	cóngqián
information	zīliào
Interest rate	lìlù
investment	tóuzī
Italy	Yìdàlì
items	shìxiàng

J

jacket	wàitào
jacuzzi	yùgāng
jasmine	mòlìhuā
joint venture	hézīqǐyè

K

kitchen range	zàotái

L

lamb	yángròu
language	yǔ
late night snack	yèxiāo
laundry room	xǐyījiān
lawsuit	sùsòng
left	zuǒ
leftside	zuǒbiān
list	mùlù
list; slip	dān
live, accommodate	zhù
live, stay, reside	zhù
live; stay	zhù
loan	dàikuǎn
look forward to	pànwàng
look into	chákàn
luggage	xínglǐ
lunchmeat	wǔcānròu

English	Chinese
M	
Macau	*Aòmén*
maglev train	*cífú lièchē*
manicure	*xiūzhíjiǎ*
massage	*ànmó*
mattress	*chuángdiàn*
meal	*cān*
meat foods	*hūn*
middle	*zhōng*
mineral water	*kuàngquánshuǐ*
more	*gèng*
most	*zuì*
mother	*māma*
mutually beneficial	*hùlì*
N	
name	*míngzi*
negator, no	*bú, bù*
net; web	*wǎng*
never	*cóngláibù/ cóngláiméiyǒu*
newspaper	*bàozhǐ*
nine	*jiǔ*
non-smoking area	*fēixīyānchù*
noodle	*miàntiáo*
north	*běi*
notify, inform	*tōngzhī*
number	*hào*
O	
of course	*dāngrán*
on the Web; online	*wǎng shàng*
one hundred million	*yíyì*
one hundred thousand	*shíwàn*
one hundred	*yìbǎi*
one million	*bǎiwàn*
one of	*zhīyī*
one thousand	*yìqiān*

English	Chinese
one	yī
one-way	dānchéng
opposite; opposite side	duìmiàn
orange	júhóng
order form	dìngdān
other, cursory	qítā
outside	wàimiàn

P

English	Chinese
pants	kùzi
park	gōngyuán
pass	zhèng
passport	hùzhào
pay	fùqián
pedicure	xiūjiǎozhǐjiǎ
people's republic	gònghéguó
perhaps	yéxǔ
person	rén
pink	fěnhóng
plan	dǎsuàn
please	qǐng
pork	zhūròu
possible, able, may, can	kéyǐ
potato	shǔ
preference	tèxuǎn
prescription	yàofāng
prohibit, no, not	fei
purchase up to/at least	máimǎn
purple	zǐ

R

English	Chinese
range burner	zàolútóu
receipt	fāpiào
receive	shōu
recline; sleep	wò
red	hóng
related	yóu..yǐnfā

English	Chinese
republic	*mínguó*
request, requirement	*yāoqiú*
reserve	*yùdìng*
reserve	*dìng*
residence	*jūliú*
residence permit	*jūliúzhèng*
resist	*dǐzhì*
right	*yòu*
right side	*yòubiān*
robe	*páozi*
room	*fángjiān*
room service	*kèfáng yòngcān fúwùbù*
round trip	*láihuí*

S

English	Chinese
salt scrub	*yánshuǎxǐ*
sandwich	*sānmíngzhì*
sauna	*sāngnáyù*
scarf	*wéijīn*
see	*jiàn*
set meal	*tàocān*
set off, launch	*fā*
seven	*qī*
shirt	*chènshān*
should, ought to, must	*yīnggāi*
shy	*hàixiū*
Sichuanese	*Sìchuānrén*
side	biān
side	*pángbiānr*
side dish	*pèicài*
sightsee	*guānguāng*
sign	*biāozhì*
sign	*qiānshǔ*
simmer	*dùn*
Singapore	*Xīnjiāpō*
sit; seat	*zuò*
six	*liù*

English	Chinese
skirt	*qúnzi*
smoke	*xī*
smoking area	*kěxīyānchù*
sofa	*shāfā*
soft	*ruǎn*
son	*érzi*
son-in-law	*nǚxù*
south	*nán*
special; especially	*tè*
specialty dish	*náshǒucài*
spicy; hot	*là*
stand	*zhàn*
stay	*dāi*
steam room	*zhēngqìyùshì*
sticks	*tiáo*
stock appraiser	*gǔpíngjiā*
straight	*qián*
street	*lù*
style	*shì*
subway station	*dìtiězhàn*
subway train	*dìxiàlièchē*
suggest	*tuījiàn*
surely	*kěndìng*
surname	*xìng*
sweet	*tián*

T

English	Chinese
table	*zhuōzi*
take away	*wàimài*
take care of..	*bàn(shì)*
Tang Zhuang	*tángzhuāng*
taxi	*chūzū qìchē*
tea	*chá*
ten million	*qiānwàn*
ten thousand	*yíwàn*
ten	*shí*
the day after tomorrow	*hòutiān*
the day before yesterday	*qiántiān*

English	Chinese
the people	*rénmín*
then, afterwards	*ránhòu*
there	*nàr*
there's no need	*búyòng*
think	*xiǎng*
three	*sān*
ticket	*piào*
tie	*lǐngdài*
tired	*lèi*
to depart	*fāchē*
to exit a country	*chūjìng*
to have, exist, there is	*yǒu*
to order food	*diǎncài*
to register	*dēngjì*
to take something with you; carry something	*dàizǒu*
to turn	*guǎi*
to; toward	*wǎng*
today	*jīntiān*
tomorrow	*míngtiān*
toward	*wǎng*
train	*huǒchē*
train number	*chēcì*
train station	*huǒchēzhàn*
transfer	*huànchéng*
transportation, communication	*jiāotōng*
two	*èr*

U

understand	*míngbái*
university	*dàxué*
upwards of; and above	*yǐshàng*
U.S. dollars	*měiyuán*
use up	*yòngwán*
use	*yòng*

English	Chinese
V	
vacation	*dùjià*
vehement	*qiángliè*
vehicle; cart	*chē*
vending machine	*shòuhuòjī*
very	*hěn*
visa	*qiānzhèng*
visit relatives	*tànqīn*
visitor	*kèrén*
W	
wait	*děng*
wait; class/type	*děng*
wall	*qiáng*
want; will	*yào*
wash	*xǐ*
Web site; Web page	*wǎngzhàn*
west	*xī*
western food	*xīcān*
what kind	*něizhǒng*
what	*shénme*
whatever time is convenient	*suíshí*
when	*shénme shíhòu*
where	*nár*
which	*jǐ*
white	*bái*
who	*shéi*
why	*wèishénme*
wife	*lǎopó*
willing	*yuànyì*
wish, blessing	*zhù*
with; and	*gēn*
week	*xīngqī*
worth while, worth it	*zhídé*
would like	*xiǎngyào*

English	Chinese
Y	
yellow	*huáng*
yesterday	*zuótiān*
Yin	*Yīn*
you (colloquial)	*nǐ*
you (formal)	*nín*
younger brother	*dìdi*
younger sister	*mèimei*

Appendix C

Answer Key

Chapter 4

1. *Wǒ lái zuò shēngyì.*
   Wǒ yào zhù Jǐge xīngqī
2. *Bùxiè, bù kèqì, búyòng xiè, or búyòng kèqì*
3. *Tāmen chīfàn ma.*
4. *Zhè shì wǒde bàozhǐ.*
5. *Tā bú shì Zhōngguó rén.*
   Wǒ méi yǒu qiānzhèng.Wǒmen bù xǐhuān tiàowǔ.

Chapter 5

1. *Wǒ xiǎng zhù dàjiǔdiàn huòzhě bīngguǎn.*
   Wǒ bù zhīdào zhètái diànshì shì zhōngguóde háishì měiguóde.
2. 7:30—*Qīdiǎn sānshí fēn or Qīdiǎnbàn*
   9:45—*Jiúdiǎn sìshíwǔfēn*
   10:28—*Shídiǎn èrshíbāfēn*
3. *Wǒ zhùzài sì lóu.*

Chapter 6

1. Jiangsu lu subway station is on the #2 line; go three streets east from there.
   Go straight ahead down this road and then turn left at the street corner.
2. *Zhè shì wǒ de qìchē*
   Wǒ mǎi de qìchē hěn guì.
   Hóngsè de qìchē shì wǒ de.
3. *hěn*
   hěn
   shì
4. *Wǒ xiáng mǎi liǎngzhāng dàoBeǐjīng de dānchéng piào.*
5. *Zhōnguó Shànghǎi shì Xúhùi qū Guìlín lù yāolínglíng hào.*

Chapter 7
1. so-so
2. *xiàwǔ hǎo*—good afternoon.
   zěnmeyàng a—how are you?
   jiǔyǎng dàmíng—I've heard so much about you.
   chīle ma—have you eaten?
   wǎnān—good night.
   wǎnshàng hǎo—good evening.
3. *Bùhǎoyìsī*
4. *Xīwàng wǒmen xiàcì zài yǒu jīhuì chīfàn.*

Chapter 8
1. *kāidechē*
2. *Bùkāichē*
3. *wǒ yǒu liǎngge jiějie.*
4. *Wǒ zhēn xǐhuān zhōngguó cài.*

Chapter 9
1. *Wǒ chībǎo le.*
2. *Zhèr shì tuōxié, bǎ zhè dāng zìjǐ de jiā yíyàng.*
3. *Guì*

Chapter 10
1. *xiōngwéi* (bust), *yāowéi* (waist), *túnwéi* (hips), *nèicháng* (inseam), and *shēngāo* (height)
2. domestic textiles = *zhōngguó fúzhuāng*
   export textiles = *wàimào fúzhuāng*
3. blue or green

Chapter 11
1. *máimǎn wǔshí kuài yǐshàng wàisòng miǎnfèi le*
2. *yì bēi kāfēi.*
   yì píng qìxǐ
   yì píng píjiǔ.
3. *Wǒ bù chī hūn*

Chapter 12

1. Would you like another glass?
2. *rèliè*—emphatic
   yāoqǐng—invite
   bǎoguì—precious
   cóngqián—in the past
   bèigǎn—with deep feeling
3. *Bùhǎoyìsī, wǒ bù néng zài hē le, Xièxie.*
4. *Zhè bùjǐn shì yícì hén hǎo de xuéxí jīnglì.*
5. *Kāichǎngbái*

Chapter 13

1. *Xīyóujì shì zhōngguó zuì shòu zhòngshì de shǐshī zhīyī.*
2. *Tā tán pípá tánde hénhǎo*
3. *Shēng, Dàn, Jìng, Chǒu*
4. Loyalty, integrity, and courage.

Chapter 14

1. *Wǒ yǒu guòmǐn.*
2. green crosses

Chapter 15

1. *yóuyǎng duànliàn*
2. *wǒmen guānguāng le hěn duō dìfāng*
3. Yin

Chapter 16

1. *Wǒ fēijī zuòle shíwǔ ge xiǎoshí*
2. *zhēngliúshuǐ*—distilled water
   kuàngquánshuǐ—mineral water
   wòshì—bedroom
   huā—flower, to spend money
   yuànyì—willing
   yāoqiú—request, requirement
   pèibèi—equip, equipment, furnishing
3. *Wǒ měitiān zǎoshàng duànliàn yíge xiǎoshí.*

Chapter 17

1. All that glitters isn't gold
2. *Wŏ kéyĭ hé wàijiāoguān shuōhuà ma?*
3. Xinhua News Agency
4. *Bvi Wén Bù Rú Yí Jiàn*

Chapter 18

1. *Wŏ tóngyì dànshì hézīqĭyè kĕnéng huì hùlì*
2. With both hands, present it Chinese side up and with the text facing the recipient.
3. *Guānxì*
4. *bĕnrén*
   Nín
   guìgōngsī
5. *Nínhăo, wŏ shì bĕngōngsī de* [insert name and title].

Chapter 19

1. *Nĭ kéyĭ dàshēng yīdiănr shuō*
2. *hĕn duō mĕiguórén zài wàimiàn gān yīfú*
3. *Wŏ bĭ wŏ gēgē lái de zăo* or
   Wŏ láide bĭ wŏ gēgē zăo
4. *Wŏ shuō zhōngwén méiyŏu wŏ lăopó shuō de hăo* or
   Wŏ shuō zhōngwén shuō de méiyŏu wŏ lăopó hăo

Chapter 20

1. Wéi
2. Lăowài
3. Practice makes perfect.

Index

The Everything® Language Series

Your tour guide to an exciting language journey!

The Everything® Speaking Mandarin
Chinese Book with CD
$19.95, 1-59337-723-1

The Everything® Conversational
Japanese Book with CD
$19.95, 1-59337-147-0

The Everything® German
Practice Book with CD
$19.95, 1-59337-618-9

PASSPORT

Adams Media

The Everything® Russian
Practice Book with CD
$19.95, 1-59337-724-X

The Everything® Spanish
Practice Book with CD
$19.95, 1-59337-434-8

Software License Agreement

YOU SHOULD CAREFULLY READ THE FOLLOWING TERMS AND CONDITIONS BEFORE USING THIS SOFTWARE PRODUCT. INSTALL-ING AND USING THIS PRODUCT INDICATES YOUR ACCEPTANCE OF THESE CONDITIONS. IF YOU DO NOT AGREE WITH THESE TERMS AND CONDITIONS, DO NOT INSTALL THE SOFTWARE AND RETURN THIS PACKAGE PROMPTLY FOR A FULL REFUND.

1. Grant of License
This software package is protected under United States copyright law and international treaty. You are hereby entitled to one copy of the enclosed software and are allowed by law to make one backup copy or to copy the contents of the disks onto a single hard disk and keep the originals as your backup or archival copy. United States copyright law prohibits you from making a copy of this software for use on any computer other than your own computer. United States copyright law also prohibits you from copying any written material included in this software package without first obtaining the permission of F+W Publications, Inc.

2. Restrictions
You, the end-user, are hereby prohibited from the following:
You may not rent or lease the Software or make copies to rent or lease for profit or for any other purpose.
You may not disassemble or reverse compile for the purposes of reverse engineering the Software.
You may not modify or adapt the Software or documentation in whole or in part, including, but not limited to, translating or creating deriva-tive works.

3. Transfer
You may transfer the Software to another person, provided that (a) you transfer all of the Software and documentation to the same transferee; (b) you do not retain any copies; and (c) the transferee is informed of and agrees to the terms and conditions of this Agreement.

4. Termination
This Agreement and your license to use the Software can be terminated without notice if you fail to comply with any of the provisions set forth in this Agreement. Upon termination of this Agreement, you promise to destroy all copies of the software including backup or archi-val copies as well as any documentation associated with the Software. All disclaimers of warranties and limitation of liability set forth in this Agreement shall survive any termination of this Agreement.

5. Limited Warranty
F+W Publications, Inc. warrants that the Software will perform according to the manual and other written materials accompanying the Software for a period of 30 days from the date of receipt. F+W Publications, Inc. does not accept responsibility for any malfunctioning computer hardware or any incompatibilities with existing or new computer hardware technology.

6. Customer Remedies
F+W Publications, Inc.'s entire liability and your exclusive remedy shall be, at the option of F+W Publications, Inc., either refund of your purchase price or repair and/or replacement of Software that does not meet this Limited Warranty. Proof of purchase shall be required. This Limited Warranty will be voided if Software failure was caused by abuse, neglect, accident or misapplication. All replacement Soft-ware will be warranted based on the remainder of the warranty or the full 30 days, whichever is shorter and will be subject to the terms of the Agreement.

7. No Other Warranties
F+W PUBLICATIONS, INC., TO THE FULLEST EXTENT OF THE LAW, DISCLAIMS ALL OTHER WARRANTIES, OTHER THAN THE LIMITED WARRANTY IN PARAGRAPH 5, EITHER EXPRESS OR IMPLIED, ASSOCIATED WITH ITS SOFTWARE, INCLUDING BUT NOT LIMITED TO IMPLIED WARRANTIES OF MERCHANTABILITY AND FITNESS FOR A PARTICULAR PURPOSE, WITH REGARD TO THE SOFTWARE AND ITS ACCOMPANYING WRITTEN MATERIALS. THIS LIMITED WARRANTY GIVES YOU SPECIFIC LEGAL RIGHTS. DEPENDING UPON WHERE THIS SOFTWARE WAS PURCHASED, YOU MAY HAVE OTHER RIGHTS.

8. Limitations on Remedies
TO THE MAXIMUM EXTENT PERMITTED BY LAW, F+W PUBLICATIONS, INC. SHALL NOT BE HELD LIABLE FOR ANY DAMAGES WHAT-SOEVER, INCLUDING WITHOUT LIMITATION, ANY LOSS FROM PERSONAL INJURY, LOSS OF BUSINESS PROFITS, BUSINESS INTER-RUPTION, BUSINESS INFORMATION OR ANY OTHER PECUNIARY LOSS ARISING OUT OF THE USE OF THIS SOFTWARE.
This applies even if F+W Publications, Inc. has been advised of the possibility of such damages. F+W Publications, Inc.'s entire liability under any provision of this agreement shall be limited to the amount actually paid by you for the Software. Because some states may not allow for this type of limitation of liability, the above limitation may not apply to you.
THE WARRANTY AND REMEDIES SET FORTH ABOVE ARE EXCLUSIVE AND IN LIEU OF ALL OTHERS, ORAL OR WRITTEN, EXPRESS OR IMPLIED. No F+W Publications, Inc. dealer, distributor, agent, or employee is authorized to make any modification or addition to the warranty.

9. General
This Agreement shall be governed by the laws of the United States of America and the Commonwealth of Massachusetts. If you have any questions concerning this Agreement, contact F+W Publications, Inc., via Adams Media at 508-427-7100. Or write to us at: Adams Media, an F+W Publications Company, 57 Littlefield Street, Avon, MA 02322.